SIGNAL DETECTION: MECHANISMS, MODELS, AND APPLICATIONS

A Volume in the
Quantitative Analyses
of Behavior series

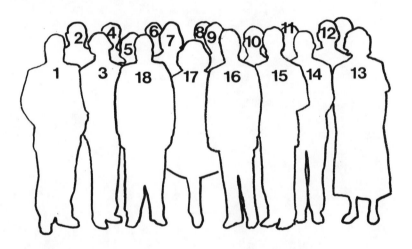

1) Michael L. Commons
2) Charles E. Metz
3) Richard G. Swensson
4) R. Duncan Luce
5) Marie F. Kijewski
6) John Donahoe
7) Philip F. Judy
8) J. Gregor Fetterman
9) Michael C. Davison

10) Brent Alsop
11) Werner K. Honig
12) Anthony Wright
13) Alexandra Logue
14) Geoffrey White
15) John A. Nevin
16) Eric Heinemann
17) Sheila Chase
18) Malvin C. Teich

SIGNAL DETECTION: MECHANISMS, MODELS, AND APPLICATIONS

A Volume in the
Quantitative Analyses
of Behavior series

Edited by

MICHAEL L. COMMONS
Harvard Medical School

JOHN A. NEVIN
University of New Hampshire

MICHAEL C. DAVISON
University of Auckland

Managing Editor

SHEILA M. McDONALD
Harvard University

LEA LAWRENCE ERLBAUM ASSOCIATES, PUBLISHERS
1991   Hillsdale, New Jersey   Hove and London

Lawrence Erlbaum Associates, Inc., Publishers
365 Broadway
Hillsdale, New Jersey 07642

Library of Congress Cataloging-in-Publication Data
LC card number: 86-640678
ISBN 0-8058-0823X

Printed in the United States of America
10 9 8 7 6 5 4 3 2 1

Volumes in the QUANTITATIVE ANALYSES OF BEHAVIOR series:
Sheila M. McDonald, Managing Editor

- DISCRIMINATIVE PROPERTIES OF REINFORCEMENT SCHEDULES. Edited by
  Michael L. Commons, *Harvard University* and John A. Nevin, *University of New
  Hampshire*

- MATCHING AND MAXIMIZING ACCOUNTS. Edited by Michael L. Commons,
  Harvard University, Richard L. Herrnstein, *Harvard University,* and Howard
  Rachlin, *State University of New York, Stony Brook*

- ACQUISITION. Edited by Michael L. Commons, *Harvard University,* Richard L.
  Herrnstein, *Harvard University,* and Allan R. Wagner, *Yale University*

- DISCRIMINATIVE PROCESSES. Edited by Michael L. Commons, *Harvard University,* Richard J. Herrnstein, *Harvard University,* and Allan R. Wagner, *Yale
  University*

- THE EFFECT OF DELAY AND OF INTERVENING EVENTS ON REINFORCEMENT
  VALUE. Edited by Michael L. Commons, *Harvard University,* James E. Mazur,
  Harvard University, John A. Nevin, *University of New Hampshire,* and Howard
  Rachlin, *State University of New York, Stony Brook*

- FORAGING. Edited by Michael L. Commons, *Harvard University,* Alejandro
  Kacelnik, *Oxford University,* and Sara J. Shettleworth, *University of Toronto*

- BIOLOGICAL DETERMINANTS OF REINFORCEMENT. Edited by Michael L.
  Commons, *Harvard University,* Russell M. Church, *Brown University,* James R.
  Stellar, *Northeastern University,* and Allan R. Wagner, *Yale University*

- BEHAVIORAL APPROACHES TO PATTERN RECOGNITION AND CONCEPT
  FORMATION. Edited by Michael L. Commons, *Harvard Medical School,* Richard
  J. Herrnstein, *Harvard University,* Stephen M. Kosslyn, *Harvard University,* and
  David B. Mumford, *Harvard University*

- COMPUTATIONAL AND CLINICAL APPROACHES TO PATTERN RECOGNI-
  TION AND CONCEPT FORMATION. Edited by Michael L. Commons, *Harvard
  Medical School,* Richard J. Herrnstein, *Harvard University,* Stephen M. Kosslyn,
  Harvard University, and David B. Mumford, *Harvard University*

- SIGNAL DETECTION: MECHANISMS, MODELS, AND APPLICATIONS. Edited by
  Michael L. Commons, *Harvard Medical School,* John A. Nevin, *University of New
  Hampshire,* and Michael C. Davison, *University of Auckland*

All volumes available from
LAWRENCE ERLBAUM ASSOCIATES, PUBLISHERS

Contents

About the Editors

Michael L. Commons is Lecturer and Research Associate in the Department of Psychiatry at Harvard Medical School, Massachusetts Mental Health Center, and he is also Director of the Dare Institute. He did his undergraduate work at the University of California at Berkeley, and then at Los Angeles, where in 1965 he obtained a BA in mathematics and in psychology. In 1967, he received his MA, and in 1973, his PhD in psychology from Columbia University. Before coming to Harvard University in 1977 as a Postdoctoral Fellow, and then becoming Research Associate in psychology, he was an Assistant Professor at Northern Michigan University. He has co-edited *Quantitative Analyses of Behavior,* Vols. 1–10, and *Beyond Formal Operations: Late Adolescent and Adult Cognitive Development.* His area of research interest is the quantitative analysis of the construction and understanding of reality as it develops across the life span, especially as these elements affect decision processes, life-span attachment and alliance formation, and ethical, social, cross-cultural, educational, legal, and private sectors.

John A. Nevin, Professor of Psychology at the University of New Hampshire since 1972, received his PhD from Columbia University in 1963 and served on the faculty at Swarthmore College and Columbia University. He has served as Editor of the *Journal of the Experimental Analysis of Behavior* and co-editor of previous volumes in this series. His research interests include schedules of reinforcement, choice behavior, stimulus control, and psychophysics.

Michael C. Davison gained a BS (Honors) from Bristol University, a PhD from Otago University, New Zealand, and a DS from Auckland University. He is a Fellow of the Royal Society of New Zealand and of the New Zealand Psychological Society. He currently holds a Personal Chair at the University of Auckland.

About the Contributors

Brent Alsop received his PhD from the University of Auckland, New Zealand, and is currently Killam Postdoctoral Fellow at Dalhousie University. His research interests are quantitative analysis of behavior in concurrent schedules, concurrent chain schedules, and signal-detection procedures, and control of behavior by successively presented stimuli.

Sheila Chase obtained her BA and MA degrees from City College of New York and her PhD from the City University of New York. She has been a Visiting Scientist at the Massachusetts Institute of Technology, a Visiting Professor at Kyoto University, Japan, and is currently Professor of Psychology at Hunter College of the City University of New York. Her research interests include learning processes, decision processes, and comparative cognition.

J. Gregor Fetterman received his PhD from the University of Maine in 1982 under the direction of Alan Stubbs. He received a postdoctoral fellowship in 1985 to study with Peter Killeen, and spent four years enjoying the Arizona desert and doing research. His research interests include time perception, relational learning, and foraging behavior. He is presently an Associate Professor of Psychology at Indiana University-Purdue University at Indianapolis.

Eric G. Heinemann has been Professor of Psychology at Brooklyn College of the City University of New York since 1963. He obtained his BA from Swarthmore College in 1949, his MA in 1951, and his PhD in 1952 from

Cornell University. Before joining the faculty at Brooklyn College, he was an instructor and lecturer at Harvard University, Assistant and Associate Professor at Vassar College, and Associate Professor at the New School for Social Research. His research interests include visual perception, learning processes, and decision processes.

W. K. Honig studied psychology at Swarthmore College and took his PhD under the direction of Norman Guttman at Duke University in 1958. He then taught at Denison University in Ohio for six years before moving to Dalhousie University, Halifax, Nova Scotia in 1963. He has published numerous articles on stimulus control and animal memory, as well as several review chapters. He edited or co-edited five books, including two editions of *Operant Behavior,* and *Cognitive Processes in Animal Behavior.* Dr. Honig held a Guggenheim Fellowship in 1970–1971, and a National Research Service Award in 1979-1980. He is currently working on cognitive aspects of stimulus control.

Alexandra W. Logue is Professor of Psychology at the State University of New York at Stony Brook. She received her AB and PhD degrees from Harvard University in 1974 and 1978, respectively. She is a Fellow of the American Psychological Association, and the American Association for the Advancement of Science. Her research concerns learning and motivation, particularly mathematical models of choice behavior and food preferences.

Dianne McCarthy is a Senior Lecturer in the Department of Psychology, and Deputy Dean of the Faculty of Science, at the University of Auckland, New Zealand. She is an Associate Editor of the *Journal of the Experimental Analysis of Behavior* and co-author (with Michael Davison) of *The Matching Law: A Research Review.*

William J. McGill was the 16th President of Columbia University, 1970–1980. He is currently President Emeritus and President Emeritus of Psychology. Dr. McGill holds the Revelle Medal, University of California, San Diego, 1981; the Alexander Hamilton Medal, Columbia College, 1979; Berkeley Campus Honors, 1973; plus 23 honorary degrees. Since 1980, he has been in residence at the University of California, San Diego, where he once served as Chancellor, 1968-1970.

Monica L. Rodriguez received her PhD from the State University of New York at Stony Brook in 1985, when she was awarded an NIH Postdoctoral Research Fellowship to work with Dr. Walter Mischel at Columbia University. She is currently an Associate Research Scientist at Columbia.

Her recent research has focused on the development of self-regulatory and cognitive competencies in at-risk children.

Malvin C. Teich was born in New York City. Since 1967, he has been a member of the faculty in the Department of Electrical Engineering, Columbia University. In 1969, he was the recipient of the IEEE (Institute of Electrical and Electronics Engineers) Browder J. Thompson Memorial Prize Award for his paper "Infrared Heterodyne Detection," and in 1981 he received a Citation Classic Award of the Institute for Scientific Information for this work. He was awarded a Guggenheim Fellowship in 1973. Dr. Teich is a Fellow of the American Association for the Advancement of Science, the American Physical Scoiety, the Institute of Electrical and Electronics Engineers, and the Optical Society of America. He is a member of the New York Academy of Science, Sigma Xi, the Acoustical Society of America, and the Association for Research in Otolaryngology. He served as a member of the Editorial Advisory Panel for the journal *Optics Letters* from 1977–1979, and is currently a member of the Board of Editors of the journal *Quantum Optics.*

K. Geoffrey White is Professor of Psychology and Head of Department at the University of Otago, New Zealand. He has been President of the New Zealand Psychological Society and Editor of the *New Zealand Journal of Psychology.* His research covers different aspects of discrimination processes, and he co-edited a special issue of the *Journal of the Experimental Analysis of Behavior,* on the experimental analysis of cognition.

Michael Woodford is Associate Professor of Economics at the University of Chicago. He received his BA in philosophy from the University of Chicago in 1977, his JD from Yale University Law School in 1980, and his PhD in economics in 1983 from the Massachusetts Institute of Technology. He was the recipient of a MacArthur Foundation Award while a graduate student at MIT, and from 1984–1986 he taught at Columbia University.

Anthony A. Wright was born in Los Angeles, California. He earned his BA at Stanford University in 1965, his MA in 1971, and his PhD at Columbia University in 1971. He was Assistant Professor at the University of Texas at Austin, 1971-1972; he has been at the University of Texas Health Science Center at Houston, from 1972 to the present, and Professor of Neural Sciences in Sensory Sciences Center since 1982. In 1983-84, he was a Fogarty Senior International Fellow at University of Auckland, New Zealand, and from 1989–1992 is a Humboldt Senior Fellow at Konstanz University, Germany. His current research interests are concept learning, memory, and decision processes.

Preface

The present volume is the 11th in the *Quantitative Analyses of Behavior* series. We continue to seek topics in the analysis of individual behavior that yield theoretical formulations at a level of rigor and generality beyond the narrowly descriptive.

The contents of the present volume were first prepared for and presented at the Tenth Symposium on Quantitative Analyses of Behavior held at Harvard: Signal Detection, on June 12–13, 1987. Subsequent revision and expansion of the papers resulted in a text relating to issues of signal detection.

The symposium was organized by the editors and supported in part by the Society for the Quantitative Analyses of Behavior, the Dare Association, Inc., and the Department of Psychology at Harvard University.

We owe thanks for the local arrangements to Rebecca M. Young, Patrice M. Miller, and Dean Gallant, with assistance from Maria Agnes Broderick, Jan Ellis, Dorothy Emerson, Tina A. Grotzer, Patricia McCallum, Jennifer Parker, Joseph A. Rodriguez, and Sharon Anne Stein. For help in reviewing the chapters for stylistic and organizational improvements, we thank the staff of the Dare Institute.

Michael L. Commons
Harvard Medical School

Introduction

John A. Nevin, Michael C. Davison,
and Michael L. Commons

This volume is based on the 10th annual Harvard Symposium for the Quantitative Analyses of Behavior. The first Harvard Symposium, in 1977, was devoted to signal-detection analyses of reinforcement and choice behavior. Contributions based on the symposium presentations were published in 1981 as the first volume of the *Quantitative Analyses of Behavior* series. Subsequent symposia and volumes have addressed topics ranging from theories of operant choice behavior to models of neural mechanisms. In this volume we return to the signal-detection theme, with added insights based on 10 years of experimental and theoretical analyses.

The fundamental signal-detection problem requires the subject to detect a signal embedded in a background of noise by responding Yes if the signal is present, and No if it is absent. The probability of presenting a signal may be varied, and explicit consequences — payoffs, costs, or feedback for humans; food, water, or shock for nonhuman animals — may be arranged for correct or incorrect choices. In signal-detection experiments of this sort, signal intensity can be varied independently of stimulus presentation probability or the consequences of choice to separate the discriminability of the stimuli from the biasing effects of nonstimulus factors. Related problems require the subject to differentiate between two stimuli that differ in location along some physical continuum such as duration. Again, stimulus values may be varied independently of feedback or reinforcement.

When signal-detection theory was introduced into psychology by Tanner and Swets (1954), its principal impact was in sensory psychology, especially on theories of the threshold. Unlike traditional theories that emphasized a discontinuity between observable (supraliminal) and unobservable (subliminal) stimuli, detection theory proposed that the effects of stimuli were continuous. On this view, the "threshold" was better construed as an adjustable criterion for reporting a signal than as a barrier to be crossed by the signal. Immediately, it became clear that the behavior of an observer in a psychophysical experiment was determined not only by the value of the signal relative to its background, but also by nonstimulus variables that affected the response criterion, including instructions, signal presentation probability, and payoffs or costs. A vigorous research program ensued, emphasizing the detailed quantitative analysis of individual performance in psychophysical situations.

At the same time, the experimental analysis of behavior was developing methods for the quantitative study of individual behavior by antecedent stimuli and reinforcing or punishing consequences. However, research on these two classes of variables proceeded separately for the most part. Stimulus-control analyses generally pursued methods introduced by Guttman and Kalish (1956), using reinforcement schedules as tools rather than as fundamental variables, whereas the study of reinforcement schedules followed the work of Ferster and Skinner (1957) and generally neglected stimulus variables.

The signal-detection paradigm provides a method for the integrative study of both classes of variables. For example, Nevin (1970) used the paradigm to demonstrate that variations in antecedent stimuli and consequences could have functionally similar effects on behavior, and Davison and Tustin (1978) proposed a quantitative model for evaluating the joint effects of stimuli and reinforcers in the detection paradigm. The integrative analysis of stimulus and reinforcer effects suggests the possibility of a truly comprehensive theory of behavior within which the traditional concerns of discrimination, generalization, and psychophysics can come together with more recent quantitative accounts of control by the consequences of behavior.

In the most general terms, signal-detection paradigms involve confusable environmental situations, differing frequencies with which those situations are encountered, and differing consequences for responses to those situations. Thus, the paradigms provide close models for well-nigh universal problems involving choice between alternatives when only partial or ambiguous information is available. Some of these problems have general significance for human well-being. For example, in a talk presented at the symposium, Swensson (1987) presented data on the detection of lesions in chest X-rays, a problem that is much like detecting a weak signal in noise. He showed that information about a patient's prior medical history biased the radiologist's judgments of whether a given shadow on the X-ray film was a lesion, but did not affect the discriminability of lesions. Information about prior history altered response biases in the same way as variations of signal probability or payoffs in laboratory experiments with carefully controlled physical stimuli. This biasing effect can be taken into account if its determiners are understood.

Still more critical examples often arise in military combat. The *Vincennes* episode provides a recent example. On July 3, 1988, while operating in the Persian Gulf, the ship engaged in combat with several Iranian patrol boats. At the same time, her commanding officer was informed that an unidentified aircraft appeared to be in position to attack. Despite a number of uncertainties, he and his subordinates decided that the aircraft was hostile, and surface-to-air missiles were fired at the target, which proved to be an Iranian airliner with 290 civilians on board. The consequence was their death, with major national and international repercussions (Friedman, 1989). Given incomplete information about the target, it seems likely that the commanding officer's decision was biased by the context of ongoing hostilities and the potential costs of withholding fire. Again, understanding of the biasing effects of contexts and consequences may help to prevent future tragedies of this sort.

Although these examples have stressed biasing effects, the analysis of signal variables is equally important. For example, knowledge of the sensory mechanisms involved in detecting visual stimuli, such as shadows in an X-ray film or displays on radar monitors, could be used to enhance the discriminability of the signals on which responding is based. Because discriminability and bias are represented as independent parameters within signal-detection theory, the theory provides a framework within which experimental and applied analyses of both sorts of factors may be effectively pursued.

Studies of behavior in relation to confusable stimuli have employed a wide variety of approaches. Some researchers have emphasized detailed quantitative analysis of the stimuli to isolate their critical dimensions, and have proposed models for the internal mechanisms intervening between stimulus presentation and occurrence of the overt response. Others have concentrated on the interrelations between stimuli, overt responses, and their consequences, with little regard for internal mechanisms. Still others have taken the signal-detection approach for granted and have used it to analyze a variety of situations that are quite remote from the fundamental detection problem. This volume represents this diversity in full. It is divided into three sections. The first emphasizes stimulus processing or behavioral mechanisms; the second exemplifies the use of signal-detection models to interpret behavior in a variety of discrimination situations; and the third applies detection analyses to problems that have typically been treated in other ways.

MECHANISMS

The origins of signal-detection theory are described by McGill and Teich (Chap. 1). Its tradition of quantitative analysis of signal properties and mathematical modeling of the mechanisms that intervene between reception of a signal and an overt response is ably represented in their work. They argue that variations in behavior cannot be understood adequately by reference to variations in the stimulus alone, and show how a neural amplifying mechanism can account for a wide variety of experimental data on auditory detection. They also point out areas in which their model does not perform well, and thus pose challenges for future theory and research. They do not, however, consider biasing factors that may affect choice independently of the physical signal.

An alternative approach is presented by Alsop in Chap. 2. He bypasses consideration of internal stimulus-processing mechanisms and, following Davison and Jenkins (1985), proposes that the relations between two responses and their consequences may be confusable in the same sense that two stimuli may be confusable. His model treats the effects of confusable signals and confusable response–consequence relations equivalently, and thus raises the possibility of a single account of two sources of control over choice. His experimental data support the need for this sort of analysis but indicate some limitations on the generality of his model.

In Chap. 3, Davison employs a closely related model to give a comprehensive account of behavior in situations involving multiple stimuli that vary in their discriminability. He demonstrates that behavior in situations involving multiple temporal or visual stimuli can be described well by a simple two-dimensional model involving the sensory distance between pairs of stimuli and a conceptually equivalent behavioral distance between pairs of choices and their respective consequences. He tests various metric rules for their combination, and thus makes systematic contact with the problem of multidimensional scaling.

In Chap. 5, Honig analyzes some behavioral processes that affect stimulus discriminability. He argues that the effects of physical differences between stimulus elements in a complex display are subservient to their distinctiveness, which depends on the extent to which the elements are differentially associated with the consequences of responding. His argument is based on data from a free-operant discrimination paradigm that involves mixtures of elements correlated with reinforcement or nonreinforcement, a paradigm that differs in many ways from the fundamental signal-detection problem. However, it is directly relevant to Alsop's and Davison's models of the role of the discriminability of choice–consequence relations, except that Honig's dimension of distinctiveness involves stimulus–reinforcer rather than response–reinforcer relations.

MODELS

Chap. 4, by Fetterman, applies a signal-detection model to choice discrimination performance where the stimuli are two successive temporal intervals that may be the same or different. His use of duration pairs contrasts to Davison's (Chap. 3) use of single durations to signal the correct response, but is similar in that the critical second duration (which signals whether the "different" or "same" response is correct) may be either shorter or longer than the first. To interpret his findings, he expands the classical signal-detection model for two-stimulus procedures to represent three kinds of stimulus presentations: second duration shorter than, same as, or longer than the first, with two independent response criteria. This generalization not only provides a framework for summarizing many aspects of his data, but also offers an alternative to Davison's account of cases more complex than the basic two-stimulus detection problem.

In Chap. 6, Chase and Heinemann treat still more complex cases involving identification of multiple stimuli. After reviewing earlier work showing how a signal-detection approach can address the traditional problems of stimulus generalization and selective attention, they describe a model that incorporates memory for previous stimulus–response–consequence events and show how the model explains the decrease in accuracy with increasing numbers of stimuli in the multiple-stimulus identification problem. To the extent that limitations on memory for stimulus–response–consequence relations are equivalent to reduced discriminability of these relations, their model is related to Alsop's (Chap. 2). In addition, their analysis is related to those of Davison (Chap. 3) and Fetterman (Chap. 5), who also consider multiple-stimulus discriminations.

Chap. 7, by Commons, Woodford, and Trudeau, takes up the special case of stimuli that consist of elements (food pellets) presented at irregular intervals, where the subject is required to discriminate their rate. Because such stimuli are necessarily extended in time, food presented early in a stimulus period may contribute less to overall signal effectiveness than later presentations. Commons and his associates demonstrate that the signaling effectiveness of food decays hyperbolically with time before a choice, a result that relates nicely to Mazur's (1987) finding that the effectiveness of food as a reinforcer decays hyperbolically with time after a choice. The parallel treatment of signaling and reinforcing functions is consistent with Alsop's and Davison's approaches (Chaps. 2, 3).

In Chap. 8, Logue and Rodriguez contrast two approaches to the control of behavior by antecedent stimuli and consequent reinforcers: signal detection and the matching law. They describe two experiments in which correct responses and errors are defined with respect to antecedent temporal stimuli according to the conventional signal-detection matrix, and rates of food reinforcement for these response classes are arranged by concurrent variable-interval or variable-ratio schedules. They suggest that differences in the effects of interval and ratio schedules may result from memory limitations arising from the time between temporal cues and reinforcers, and conclude that signal-detection and matching-law approaches are complementary. Their approach is related to those of Alsop and Davison (Chaps. 2, 3), which assume matching of choice allocation to reinforcer allocation as it is discriminated by the subject, and to that of Commons et al. (Chap. 7), which explicitly models the decay of the effects of reinforcing stimuli in time.

Wright's Chap. 9 extends his earlier work (Wright & Sands, 1981) on signal-detection analyses of performance in the widely studied matching-to-sample paradigm. Here, he considers a subject's overt choice behavior on each trial as a consequence of a series of observations, each of which involves acceptance or rejection of a comparison stimulus as a correct match to the sample on that trial. His approach makes the process of attending explicit, and thus provides a potential empirical base for the attentional component of the model proposed by Chase and Heinemann (Chap. 6). His approach also permits analysis of behavior during acquisition in a way that complements the treatment of presolution behavior by Chase and Heinemann (Chap. 6). In addition, Wright's detection model incorporates the effects of the discriminability of the samples to be matched, and the delay between sample offset and choice, in a way that complements that of White (Chap. 10). Moreover, it is entirely compatible with recent analyses of performance in the radial-arm maze by Brown, Wheeler, and Riley (1989), who propose a signal-detection analysis of choice in this equally widely studied paradigm.

APPLICATIONS

In Chap. 10, White takes a psychophysical approach to the study of remembering in conditional discrimination procedures related to signal detection and matching to sample. He employs a bias-free measure of discriminabilitiy derived by Davison and Tustin (1978; see also McCarthy & Davison, 1981, and Nevin, 1981, in Vol. 1 of this series), and shows that the initial level of discriminability at zero delay, and the rate of decay of discrimination as delays increase (forgetting), are independent aspects of delayed discrimination performance. His analysis separates variables, such as the physical difference between samples or the observing response to the sample, which alter initial discriminability, from retroactive interference by stimuli during the delay interval or proactive interference from previous trial stimuli, which alter the rate of decay of discrimination in time.

In Chap. 11, McCarthy applies the Davison-Tustin (1978) approach to signal detection to analyze the nature of performance deficits resulting from head injury, sleep deprivation, hypoxia, drugs, and aging. Her interest centers on the extent to which deficits are evident in the subjects' sensitivity to stimulus probability or differential consequences, as measured by their effects on response bias, which, in signal-detection analyses, are readily distinguished from deficits in stimulus discriminability. She concludes that in many cases performance deficits involve reduced effects on response bias. Her analyses should serve to guide therapeutic programs into more effective directions.

Finally, in Chap. 12, Nevin applies the signal-detection approach to perceptual judgments in experimental settings that cannot, by their nature, arrange differential outcomes, such as the thoroughly studied Muller-Lyer illusion. He concludes that illusions may be understood as shifts in response bias rather than changes in stimulus discriminability. He also applies a detection analysis to the effects of stereotypical verbal descriptions on judgments of occupation, and concludes that the representativeness of a description — a "heuristic" in the terms of Kahneman and Tversky (1974) — can be construed as an effect on response bias. Thus, his chapter joins McCarthy's (Chap. 11) in stressing the importance of separating bias effects from discriminability. More generally, it joins Wright's (Chap. 9) and White's (Chap. 10) in showing that signal-detection analyses can provide effective alternatives to cognitive interpretations of behavior involving inferred processes such as attention, perception, memory, and judgment.

SUMMARY

The chapters collected in this volume illustrate how signal-detection theory, first advanced to account for performance in threshold-level sensory discriminations, has broadened to encompass a variety of psychological problems involving discriminations between confusable stimuli. The approach is quantitative in its emphasis on estimation of independent parameters of the discrimination process, and analytical in its efforts to separate the determiners of discriminability and bias and to identify the mechanisms of their operation. Above all, it is broadly integrative in its approach to diverse problems, as exemplified here. Perhaps, 10 years from now, a third volume of contributions will encompass still more psychological processes within the general framework of signal detection.

REFERENCES

Brown, M. F., Wheeler, E. A., & Riley, D. A. (1989). Evidence for a shift in the choice criterion of rats in a 12-arm radial maze. *Animal Learning and Behavior, 17,* 12-20.

Davison, M., & Jenkins, P. E. (1985). Stimulus discriminability, contingency discriminability, and schedule performance. *Animal Learning and Behavior, 13,* 77-84.

Davison, M., & Tustin, R. D. (1978). On the relation between the generalized matching law and signal detection theory. *Journal of the Experimental Analysis of Behavior, 29,* 331-336.

Ferster, C. B., & Skinner, B. F. (1957). *Schedules of reinforcement.* New York: Appleton--Century-Crofts.

Friedman, N. (1989). The *Vincennes* incident. *U.S. Naval Institute Proceedings, 115,* 72-80.

Guttman, N., & Kalish, H. I. (1956). Discriminability and stimulus generalization. *Journal of Experimental Psychology, 51,* 79-88.

Kahneman, D., & Tversky, A. (1974). Judgment under uncertainty: Heuristics and biases. *Science, 185,* 1124-1131.

Mazur, J. E. (1987). An adjusting procedure for studying delayed reinforcement. In M. L. Commons, J. E. Mazur, H. Rachlin, & J. A. Nevin (Eds.), *Quantitative analyses of behavior: Vol. 5. The effects of delay and intervening events on reinforcement value.* Hillsdale, NJ: Lawrence Erlbaum Associates.

McCarthy, D., & Davison, M. (1981). Matching and signal detection. In M. L. Commons & J. A. Nevin (Eds.), *Quantitative analyses of behavior: Vol. 1. Discriminative properties of reinforcement schedules.* Cambridge, MA: Ballinger.

Nevin, J. A. (1970). On differential stimulation and differential reinforcement. In W. C. Stebbins (Ed.), *Animal psychophysics.* New York: Appleton–Century–Crofts.

Nevin, J. A. (1981). Psychophysics and reinforcement schedules: An integration. In M. L. Commons & J. A. Nevin (Eds.) *Quantitative analyses of behavior: Vol. 1. Discriminative properties of reinforcement schedules.* Cambridge, MA: Ballinger.

Swensson, R. G. (1987). *ROC applications to chest-film interpretation.* Paper presented at the 10th Symposium on Quantitative Analyses of Behavior, Harvard University, Cambridge, MA.

Tanner, W. P., & Swets, J. A. (1954). A decision-making theory of visual detection. *Psychological Review, 61,* 401-409.

Wright, A. A., & Sands, S. F. (1981). A model of detection and decision processes during matching to sample by pigeons: Performance with 88 different wavelengths in delayed and simultaneous matching tasks. *Journal of Experimental Psychology: Animal Behavior Processes, 7,* 191-216.

1 Auditory Signal Detection and Amplification in a Neural Transmission Network

William J. McGill
Malvin C. Teich
Columbia University

A topic as large and as intricate as signal detection poses inevitable frustrations for both reader and writer. The general reader is entitled to clear, unambiguous prose. What he or she gets is an argument sometimes requiring word-by-word translation as though it were written in some long-lost, hieroglyphic script. The reader is often as baffled by what is omitted as by what is said.

The writer, conscious of all the limitations of research, tries to say what is true, but ends up with sentences that are either clear, yet subtly wrong, or so carefully hedged as to be barely decipherable. Such dilemmas, we say, are practically unavoidable. They ensure that the communication of knowledge in complex areas will always be painful. Each of us must do the utmost to minimize that pain. Accordingly, at the very beginning, we owe our readers a simple account of what we attempted, what we omitted, and why we chose as we did.

Detection theory has become a fixture of modern psychology because it provides useful quantitative tools and an easily understood vocabulary for describing relations that typically occur when a stimulus emerges in some distinctive way from a background. The ROC curve portrays expected tradeoffs between false alarms and missed signals when outcomes, stimulus probabilities, or decision criteria are varied. The detectability measure d', obtained from the ROC curve, adds quantitative precision to the meaning of discriminability.

The idea that there are tradeoffs rather than fixed thresholds lies at the heart of signal detection theory. Moreover, the tradeoffs are not limited to detection errors. Similar relations exist between d' and decision latencies where speed can be traded off against accuracy.

We cite these familiar landmarks because the reader will search this chapter from beginning to end without finding even one ROC curve. Discriminability measures are developed but they are not labeled d'. The time variable is central to our arguments but it appears as a *sensory integration time*, and we omit all mention of decision latencies. The reader might well ask whether anything can be left of signal detection theory if we admit to having cut its heart out from the very beginning.

The answer is that detection theory has more than one heart. It does not take precisely the same form in all its manifold applications. In this chapter we consider a particular form of the theory dealing with flows of information between the ear and the brain. When the scope of detection theory is narrowed in that way, the theory grows both more powerful and more intricate. ROC curves and the d' measure might not ever be mentioned (although they are always there ready to be computed). This is because other questions are more likely to preoccupy us at first. Such other questions involve attempts to characterize the machinery that processes signals passing through the auditory network.

If you know the energy or amplitude distribution of a signal as it enters the ear, and you also know the detectability of the signal from psychophysical experiments, can you find a consistent mechanism that will transform the one into the other? The configuration of that mechanism, the distortions it introduces, the expected changes from one class of stimuli to another: These are the first questions to which our version of detection theory addresses itself. Over the past 50 years great progress has been made toward answering a number of deep questions about the two major senses: vision and audition. We have written our chapter to give an account of the work in audition, to indicate what we now know about detection, the puzzles that remain unresolved, and finally to suggest new forms for the sought-after processing mechanism.

Ever since Green's (1960) study of intensity discrimination in white noise, together with two closely related papers by Pfafflin and Mathews (1962), and Jeffress (1964), each dealing with sinusoids masked by white gaussian noise, we have been tantalized by the knowledge that a wide range of auditory masking phenomena can be predicted in remarkable detail from the statistics of the stimulus. The discovery suggested that if auditory stimuli could be specified in just the right way, the entire detection problem might be handled without ever leaving the stimulus domain. There would then be no absolute requirement to confront any of the complexities of mechanisms processing information in the ear, the auditory pathways, or the brain itself; or so we once thought. These complexities would instead become details of a well-organized network whose functional characteristics might be better understood from the information passing through it than from meticulous study of its interconnections.

This chapter can also be described as a reluctant but necessary step back from the elusive simplicity of this pure stimulus-oriented approach to auditory detection. Stimuli provide the driving force, but there is no escaping an equivalent need to analyze or at least characterize the transmission network carrying messages away from the ear. We continue to struggle with this sought-after characterization. It has proved to be a formidable challenge although the outline of an acceptable solution is easy to state and ordinarily that is half the battle.

We seek to devise a process that extracts certain critical information from the stimulus and then operates on it in a clearly prescribed way. All inputs must be dealt with in exactly the same way, but outcomes can vary from one class of stimuli to another as dictated by the functional properties of the processing network. The problem is considered solved when the system generates outputs consistent with experimental data on signal detection, and especially when it forecasts results of experiments not yet attempted.

At least three, perhaps four, significant ideas have been suggested for characterizing the auditory detection system. They do not quite represent increasing levels of complexity, although without question recent efforts embody mechanisms not considered in earlier approaches.

Ideal Observers

The first of these major ideas involves some form of *ideal observer*. The principle is simple. The auditory system is said to extract a particular signal from a particular noise in the best possible way. It is assumed that the processing network must be structured so as to perform the extraction but the essence of the problem is mathematical, not structural. The probability distribution of signal/noise amplitudes is compared with the analogous distribution of noise alone, and a way is found to make decisions leading to the best possible separation.

The apparent simplicity of an ideal observer is illusory because the auditory system must be able to do whatever is demanded. Simplification shows itself only when a limit is imposed on the system, in other words, when the information to which the system can respond is somehow constrained.

The concept of an ideal observer traces back at least to Lawson and Uhlenbeck (1950). Their book summarized the scientific work of the wartime MIT Radiation Laboratory seeking clever ways to extract radar signals from noise clutter. The ideal observer was a mathematical construct embodying the best possible compromise between missed signals and false alarms. It prescribed an operation on received signals and a decision mechanism that would minimize detection errors. Subsequently Peterson, Birdsall and Fox (1954) improved the idea by altering the test of optimality from minimum error to maximum likelihood ratio. In this form gains and losses from various outcomes become part of the decision calculation. They also calculated optima for a wide variety of signal and noise combinations, including many typically used in auditory experiments. For example, they showed that the optimal process for detecting sine wave signals in gaussian noise involves cross-correlating the received and transmitted wave forms, whereas the optimum for detecting intensity changes in bursts of noise would be an energy detector.

Ideal observers experienced a brief blush of popularity in audition during the 1960s, but the vogue soon passed with the realization that the nature of the ideal changes along with the information available to the processing system. Marill (1956) developed a formula for the probability of a correct decision in two-alternative, forced-choice detection of a sine wave signal in gaussian noise. His calculation was based on an ideal observer lacking information on signal phase. It was evident that Marill's formula conformed more closely with auditory data than the Peterson, Birdsall and Fox optimum (although hardly perfect; Marill's psychometric function was some 5–10 db better than the typical experimental data). The shape, slope, and signal-to-noise ratio properties of Marill's equation were superior to anything proposed earlier as a model for the detection system. And so for a time Marill's ideal observer (lacking signal phase information) suggested itself as the preferred solution to the detection system puzzle.

Then it was discovered (McGill, 1968a) that Marill's ideal observer is in fact a narrow-band energy detector. As soon as it became clear that an energy detector, which smears its input together without any elaborate analysis, can perform almost as well as much more complex analytical devices, the ideal observer approach to auditory signal detection was deemed expendable. Moreover, there was an even deeper problem. Any ideal device should experience no difficulty in detecting minute differences in phase-locked pure tones since they have no variance at all. But human listeners find it almost as difficult to separate small intensity differences among pure tones as among comparable bursts of noise. What manner of ideal would classify pure tones, lacking statistics altogether, with random noise?

The difficulty is fundamental. For a time, advocates of the ideal observer tried to argue that pure-tone generators must also contain a hidden, unmeasured gaussian noise. But Green's calculation showed that this background noise is too weak to affect detectability, and eventually the argument was abandoned (see Tanner, 1961; Green, 1967).

Neural Counting

A second major idea for system characterization has had a long and distinguished history. It was pioneered by Hecht, Shlaer and Pirenne (1942) who sought to outline the steps transforming the energy in a flash of blue-green light into psychometric functions describing detectability of the flash by the visual system. This approach applied to audition would generate a neural counting process somewhere in the network leading back from the ear, presumably following an energy exchange in the receptor organ.

Hecht et al. originally defined their system so as to require only the tracing of lost light energy in the ocular media and in the retina itself. Transformations of the light signal other than losses incurred in its passage through the receptor were disregarded. Some years later Barlow (1956) modified the counting process to include additional events not set off by the absorption of light. These additional events were thought to be generated spontaneously in the visual system. They form a background noise level that mixes with stimulus events creating occasional confusions and false alarms. Noise of this kind, independent of the stimulus, is called *additive noise*.

Another type of noise is sometimes found in chains of events such as those occurring when information passes from the periphery to the brain via successive stages. This second type of noise arises when an event at a prior stage of the chain generates a cluster of events at a subsequent stage. Information as it passes from stage to stage increases in volume but not always in the same amount or in the same way. Hence it is said to be perturbed by a noisy process.

In many such cases the noise is traceable directly to the stimulus. It is not additive but multiplicative in nature. The easiest and most reliable way to detect *multiplicative noise* is to observe the proportionality between means and variances of events as they pass from stage to stage. Additive noise displays no such linkages. Both types of noise are currently thought to be important in sensory analysis. Hecht et al. (1942) made no provision for either, limiting consideration entirely to losses in transit.

Radiant light energy is conveniently treated as a Poisson counting process. Losses in transit can then be represented as random deletions from the flow of energy, leaving the Poisson distribution intact and changing only its mean level. Evidently Hecht et al. had in mind that absorption of a critical (small) number of light quanta within a circumscribed region of the retina would set off a secondary event of some kind, signaling detection provided the critical number is reached or exceeded. This implies that the huge transmission network between the eye and visual cortex can be taken to be essentially inert for detection purposes. Details of the assumed secondary event are evidently important, but not crucial to system characterization in a preliminary treatment of visual detection. Hecht et al. did not speculate on such details.

In this simple form the model has managed to withstand the assaults of time, even without sanctification of several of its key points. The possible critical numbers generate successive cumulative gamma distributions establishing a template for judging visual psychometric functions on a log-energy plot. Barlow (1956, 1957) and Nachmias and Steinman (1963), showed that the experimental data are compatible with an unmeasured additive internal noise ("dark light"), as well as with critical numbers set by instructions, that is, flexible high-level decision criteria rather than fixed neural summation rules. Subsequently, Barlow, Levick, and Yoon (1971) found evidence of a multiplicative noise—noise associated with neural cascade effects in the retina. This suggested to Teich, Prucnal, Vannucci, Breton, and McGill (1982a) that weak neural signals following registration of light quanta in the eye might be multiplied (i.e., amplified) as they pass to higher centers. Such stochastic multiplication generates variance or spread in the counting distribution. It is not the big bang assumed by Hecht et al. because it also multiplies spontaneous firing not directly linked to light energy absorption. The Teich et al. result is best described as a noise typically found in amplifier devices.

These alterations do little to diminish the power of the Hecht et al. principle that analyzing visual detection requires us to begin with the energy distribution of the stimulus, and then step by step to distill out of it the detection curve of the eye. Emphasis on light *energy* as the key information variable passed to the detection network reflects a host of energy relations involving both area and time found to obtain near absolute threshold. Furthermore, the Hecht et al. counting model leads immediately to a square root law of intensity discrimination which characterizes all simple Poisson processes (McGill, 1971). This square root law, the deVries–Rose law, is in fact found in visual brightness discrimination under suitable conditions in the intensity region just above absolute threshold (see, for example, Bouman, 1961).

The unique attraction of the Hecht et al. system network is its testability, or so one might think. The psychometric function of the visual system is said to be fully determined by the statistics of the stimulus. To test the model, you simply change the probability distribution of the stimulus and see whether the psychometric function conforms with the change. Unfortunately tests are easier to conjecture than to carry out. No readily available light source has yet to yield anything other than Poisson energy statistics at low output levels near the visual threshold. When lasers first came into common use as laboratory instruments their energy output was investigated and found to have a noncentral negative binomial form (see, for example, Magill & Soni, 1966; Teich & McGill, 1976). It was conjectured at first that varying a laser's intensity during the flash period might permit manipulation of the energy statistics of low-intensity flashes. Teich et al. (1982a) performed just such manipulations and showed alterations in the resulting psychometric function, but the statistics of the source proved to be superpositions of Poisson counting processes with different mean values.

Similar conjectures have been voiced recently for sub-Poisson (photon-number squeezed) light sources (Teich et al., 1982b; Teich & Saleh, 1988), which cannot be represented as Poisson superpositions. But the development of reliable nonclassical light stimuli as practical visual instrumentation is still a distant prospect. We shall have to see.

As with ideal observers there is also a deeper problem affecting all versions of the Hecht et al. system network. The problem in this case has to do with the ubiquity of the Poisson distribution. Hecht et al. argue that absolute visual threshold data resemble cumulative gamma distributions. Consequently there must be an underlying Poisson counting process and the statistics of the light source must be heavily implicated. But the causal chain is not nearly as solid as Hecht et al. claimed it to be. Many additive combinations of signal and noise yield nearly the same psychometric function when plotted against signal energy. It was this phenomenon that caused Barlow (1956) to conjecture the existence of "dark light."

Moreover, several important theorems were developed after the 1950s dealing with superposition of point processes (see, for example, Cox & Smith, 1954; Drenick, 1960). These findings suggest that under suitable conditions repetitive, point-like events flowing down independent channels will approach a Poisson limit when the number of channels increases and the events are smeared together, that is, superposed. Comprehensive study of such superposition effects was undertaken shortly thereafter and summarized in a well-known chapter by Çinlar (1972). This treatment shows that fully Poisson behavior is an abstraction not easily achieved, but quasi-Poisson processes are commonplace. The most familiar examples are the flow of traffic on a superhighway or the arrival of telephone calls at a switchboard. Each of these is a completely deterministic sequence yet each exhibits Poisson behavior when the nitty gritty details of the sequence are either unknown or ignored.

The important point here is the close resemblance of such superposition effects and the smearing operations characteristic of energy detection. Both imply that information on crucial details of the sequence is ignored or lost. Accordingly, virtually any stimulus, including many that are nonstatistical, can give rise to quasi-Poisson counting processes in the sensory nervous system. The chief requirement is that information be lost or subtracted. A primitive observer located somewhere in the network would see a deterministic flow of data passing to higher centers as though it were a random process. This means that Poisson-like behavior might be found nearly everywhere in sensory tracts if the observing mechanism were sufficiently ignorant of details of the information flow.

By a feat of legerdemain we have passed quickly from ideal decision-making to an extremely limited observing system lacking the ability to analyze information passing through it. Yet even this primitive mode of operation does no serious violence to the data on visual or auditory signal detection. The latter seem to require a mass flow of information instead of the structured signals that generate typical percepts. Indeed, it may be the same information looked at in two different ways. The first 10,000 digits of *pi* make an excellent random number table if we start with, say, the 10th digit. But inserting the first 9 provides a clue enabling us to calculate each and every digit in turn. The sequence is deterministic, yet to a primitive observer it appears random (Wolfram, 1985). Everything turns on the discriminations available to the observer.

The fact that visual threshold data point to an underlying Poisson counting process does not tell us where the Poisson behavior is located or what its nature might be. This is the distinction that Barlow (1957) exploited in taking the system a step beyond Hecht et al.'s original prescription into neural counting only partly driven by the statistics of the stimulus flash.

Differential Analyzer

A third major idea on system characterization comes from Laming (1986), whose work revived serious interest in sensory networks. Laming notes remarkable functional differences when signal and noise are delivered in separate stimulus "packages" separated by a blank interval, from cases in which the signal is added to one of two or more observation intervals marked out on a continuous noisy background. These differences eventually led Laming to consider jettisoning energy exchanges and counting models, turning instead to a cleverly constructed system that forms a running derivative of incoming stimulation.

A steady background stimulus in a sensory tract will then fade out leaving a residual zero-mean gaussian noise. This background internal noise is continuously monitored for transients marking the beginning and end of any brief stimulus. Moreover, Laming's network responds to stimulus amplitude rather than energy. When a transient appears following the onset of a stimulus, it is detected as a sudden change in the variance of the residual noise amplitude distribution. This may, and perhaps does, involve some form of counting, but omitted from Laming's formulation is any one-to-one linkage between stimulus energy (or amplitude) and a proportional counting process in sensory neurons behind the receptor.

Laming's network successfully predicts a hitherto unexplained finding thought to be critically important in auditory detection. Green's study of noise intensity discrimination (1960) displays psychometric functions having roughly double the slope generated by an equivalent energy detector. Since in all other respects Green's data on noise bandwidth and duration reflect the expected behavior of an energy detector, these slopes were regarded as an anomaly until Laming showed that they might point to the nature of the detection process, and that in fact his mechanism generated slopes consistent with the data whereas simple energy detection does not.

Amplifier Networks

The work to be reported here is a less fundamental departure from conventional detection theory than is Laming's differential analyzer. Our primary effort is aimed at the auditory system because of the latter's diversity of potential signals with widely varying statistical properties, mostly all now fairly well understood. But it is evident that we remain strongly influenced by the Hecht–Barlow visual system formulation: An energy exchange in the receptor triggering off and driving a counting process in the transmission network. Basic departures from earlier ideas will be evident in new properties assigned to the network, making the latter less of a passive transmitter, and more of an active detector.

Our transmission network is asked to amplify weak signals and at the same time to curb or diminish strong ones. Amplification is readily achieved by structuring the transmission as some form of birth–death–immigration process. The latter is a class of well-known stochastic processes in which each stage of the process may see a net increase in the number of events over prior stages. Events tend to multiply as they pass up the system. Active processes of this kind are a bit more complicated than Poisson counting, but far less sophisticated than the neural networks typically invoked to explain advanced forms of cognition (see, for example, Hopfield, 1982; Rumelhart, Smolensky, McClelland, & Hinton, 1986).

Intense inputs must somehow be curbed by such a network. Otherwise they would grow exponentially in the multiplicative cascade defining a birth process, leading to explosive chain reactions that could saturate and ultimately paralyze all transmission. A stochastic birth process will undergo exponential growth with any input. This outcome is delightful when inputs are small, but disastrous when they are large. Some kind of limiting action is a virtual necessity. This means that simple energy exchanges in the receptor must be ruled out. We look instead for an energy transformation, either a log or a fractional power function, or perhaps some combination of both, either at the input or perhaps at many stages of the process. Counterbalancing a transformed input signal against the exponential growth of neural activity expected from a birth–death process can generally be achieved so as to guarantee that information passes up the network essentially in linear form, but with weak signals amplified and strong ones constrained.

Testing or verifying these conceptions requires studying the output of typical birth–death–immigration networks in order to measure agreement with the psychophysical data that we are trying to understand. Such conformity has been the goal of system characterization efforts from the very beginning. But ultimately we must also judge each proposed characterization by considering anatomical and neurophysiological evidence as well. Any such review would be premature until the principles governing the transmission network are reliably known. For now we observe only that the lower levels of both the auditory and visual systems seem designed to amplify weak signals, and that the envelope of activity set off by any given input signal appears to expand as messages pass to successively higher centers (see, for example, Ryan, Braverman, Woolf, & Axelsson, 1989; Saleh & Teich, 1985). Finally, studies of firing rates in auditory transmission generally show linearity with log intensity. This is what attracts attention to birth processes.

The proposed network, once designed, must be able to process pure tones, sine waves in noise, pure noise, so-called "frozen" noise, and a host of other inputs, operating on each in exactly the same way, and generating outcomes that correspond closely to the rich vein of experimental data guiding all current efforts to build an auditory detection theory. Such powerful constraints practically guarantee that even the cleverest characterizations will eventually fail. Our object is not to avoid failure, but rather to achieve interesting and significant failures pointing the way to new knowledge.

DETECTION THEORY IN THE STIMULUS DOMAIN

Signal Energy Distributions

We begin with a brief review of what is currently known about the energy statistics of typical auditory stimuli. Energy distributions are required as the first step of our analysis since we start with the idea that some kind of energy transformation occurs in the ear, triggering and driving an active counting process in the transmission network leading to higher centers. Such distributions, or their close relatives, also form the heart of all stimulus-oriented detection theories.

It is startling but true that despite extensive knowledge of the statistical properties of gaussian noise developed in early studies of Brownian motion, and elaborated subsequently by S. O. Rice (1944, 1945) in his classical papers on mathematical analysis of random noise, very little information had been codified prior to 1960 on the energy distribution of acoustic sine waves in noise. All the necessary information existed, but physicists and engineers displayed little interest in the relatively wide bandwidths and long durations typical of auditory stimuli. Hence, signal detection theorists were forced to work out the answers for themselves. The principal results can be found in Green (1960), Jeffress (1964), McGill (1967), Green and McGill (1970), and Teich and McGill (1976). Important details of the proofs mentioned in this section, as well as on the theory of a passive Poisson network, can also be found in the papers cited.

The energy level of a pure tone is found by integrating the squared displacement of a sine or cosine wave form over its duration. If the duration is taken as T this works out to be:

$$Energy = \tfrac{1}{2} Amplitude^2 \cdot T, \tag{1}$$

where amplitude is the distance from zero displacement to the peak of the wave form. Basic measurements of this sort are usually difficult to perform. We generally measure energy or power (energy/time) relative to some convenient standard. Of course, a pure tone of center frequency ω_0 and fixed duration is no longer pure. The energy spectrum of a short duration sinusoid has the form

$$sinc^2 (\omega - \omega_0) T = \frac{\sin^2 (\omega - \omega_0) T}{[(\omega - \omega_0) T]^2} ,$$

where ω is the frequency variable. This spectrum consists of a main lobe erected over the center frequency and side lobes falling away symmetrically above and below it. Each side lobe is $1/T$ wide and is bounded by a pair of zero points. The spread of energy across frequency is infinite but falls off very rapidly when the duration of the signal is sufficiently long. Hence, the spread may be conveniently represented by its *equivalent rectangular band width,* a rectangular spectrum having the same peak energy as the $sinc^2$ spectrum and a bandwidth of $1/T$. About 77% of the total energy in the $sinc^2$ spectrum is found within these limits, but the equivalent rectangular band has an energy content identical to that of the entire sinusoid. The reasoning that leads us to define things this way becomes clearer when we consider gaussian noise. It will turn out to be the case that equivalent rectangular bands are mutually orthogonal and thus completely additive. Hence it is a simple matter to construct a wide-band noise out of such narrow-band units. Notice that pure tones having the same amplitude and duration will always have exactly the same energy content. There is no probability distribution.

In the case of a pure tone embedded in a narrow-band gaussian noise, that is, noise having the rectangular bandwidth just defined, there will be a probability distribution of the signal/noise combination. The energy distribution is given by its density function:

$$f_s(x) = \frac{1}{N_0} \exp\left[-\frac{E+x}{N_0}\right] \cdot I_0\left[2(Ex)^{1/2}/N_0\right], \quad 0 \leq x \leq \infty. \quad (2)$$

In this somewhat forbidding expression x is the energy in the signal/noise combination, E is the energy of the added sine wave signal, and N_0 is the average noise energy in the unit rectangular band. The symbol $I_0[\cdot]$ represents a zero-order Bessel function with purely imaginary argument. This notation was originally devised by Rice (1944) and is found in many engineering textbooks on signal detection. We reproduce it here out of deference to such history, but it is cumbersome. As we shall show in the argument leading to equation (8), equation (2) is purely real. In fact, it turns out to be a linear transform of noncentral chi-square. Rice derived the signal/noise process as an amplitude distribution. We change the variable to energy according to the rule in equation (1).

The analogous narrow-band energy distribution of pure noise is obtained by setting $E = 0$ in equation (2) and noting that $I_0(0) = 1$:

$$f_0(x) = \frac{1}{N_0} \exp\left[-\frac{x}{N_0}\right]. \quad (3)$$

This is the famous Rayleigh energy distribution of narrow-band (pure) noise. Strictly speaking, equation (3) is not a Rayleigh distribution (which describes amplitude fluctuations in a narrow-band noise) but rather an exponential distribution. It is the distribution of the square of a Rayleigh variable. They are close relatives, each one determining the other. Suitably standardized, equation (3) is a central chi-square distribution with two degrees of freedom. The gaussian distribution of noise perturbations produces a chi-square distribution of noise energies. The latter has two degrees of freedom because samples of noise extending over several cycles of the wave form are constructed out of two independent sinusoidal components (two quadratures).

Forced-choice Psychometric Functions

The pair of energy distributions, signal in noise and pure noise, can now be used to define a psychometric function in two-alternative forced-choice (2AFC) procedure. To do it we need only calculate the probability that the energy in the signal/noise combination exceeds the energy of the pure noise.

An energy detector will always choose the larger sample as the signal. Hence the probability of a correct judgment must be:

$$P(S > N) = \int_0^\infty f_0(x) \left[1 - F_s(x)\right] dx. \tag{4a}$$

Equation (4a) states a simple probability argument. First, choose a noise and compute the probability that the signal/noise energy combination is greater. Then integrate over all possible noise samples. The outcome is a remarkably simple formula that proves to be Marill's (1956) ideal observer for the case in which signal phase information is missing:

$$P(S > N) = 1 - \frac{1}{2} \exp(-E/2N_0). \tag{4}$$

Our argument, of course, establishes Marill's observer to be an energy detector. The results are useful for displaying our methods in simple form. They also have considerable theoretical interest, but as a practical matter not much has been done with narrow-band noise. Ronken (1969) constructed narrow-band noise stimuli by computer techniques and studied the listener's 2AFC psychometric function. His data are interesting chiefly because they suggest a consistent internal noise of undetermined origin shifting the psychometric function above the energy detector. But the data do not permit any critical test of the energy detection hypothesis.

Wide-band Noise

To accomplish the latter we need to go to wide-band noise. We have already noted that it is easy to construct such noise from narrow-band components since equivalent rectangular bands are mutually orthogonal and additive. First compute the moment generating function of equation (2):

$$M_x(\theta) = \int_0^\infty e^{\theta x} f_s(x) \, dx, \tag{5}$$

$$= \frac{\exp(E\theta/1 - N_0\theta)}{(1 - N_0\theta)}.$$

Then go to the convolution of ν such contiguous narrow-band signal noise processes:

$$M_x(\theta) = \frac{\exp[(E_1 + E_2 + E_3 + \ldots E_\nu)\,\theta\,/\,1 - N_0\,\theta]}{(1 - N_0\,\theta)\,(1 - N_0\,\theta)\,(1 - N_0\,\theta)\,\ldots\,(1 - N_0\,\theta)},\tag{6}$$

$$= \frac{\exp(E\,\theta/1 - N_0\theta)}{(1 - N_0\theta)^\nu}.$$

The term E now represents the sum of the signal energies in each of the narrow-band components, a result that clearly establishes the smearing or superposition action of an energy detector. In theory, the placement of the signal within the noise band should be irrelevant. In practice it is usually added to a single component at the center of the noise band. This is because the mathematical model is only a rough approximation of the actual spectrum. We get our best approximation when the signal is at the center of the noise band. The width of the latter is now constructed as an equivalent rectangular band W in which each component unit is $1/T$ Hz wide. Hence:

$$W = v \cdot 1/T,$$

$$v = W\,T, \quad where \; v = 1,2,3 \ldots \tag{7}$$

We have in fact constructed an orthogonal partition of the energy spectrum of a band-limited noise. Inverting the generating function in equation (6) produces the density function of the noise mixture:

$$f_s(x) = \sum_{i=0}^{i=\infty}\left[w_{E/N_0(i)}\right] \cdot \left[\frac{\dfrac{1}{N_0}\left[\dfrac{x}{N_0}\right]^{i+\nu-1}\exp\left[-\dfrac{x}{N_0}\right]}{\Gamma(i+\nu)}\right].\tag{8}$$

In equation (8), Bessel function notation has been abandoned and we introduce instead Poisson weights operating on classical gamma distributions:

$$w_{E/N_0}(i) = \frac{(E/N_0)^i \exp(-E/N_0)}{i!}.$$

Equation (2) can be expressed in this form by setting $\nu = 1$ in equation (8). The representation in equation (2) is typical of the engineering literature. Equation (8) is found in the statistical literature. We show the identity because it is sometimes necessary to translate results in one notation into the counterpart form in order to follow a complicated argument.

The probability density of wide-band pure noise energy is found by setting $E = 0$ in equation (8):

$$f_0(x) = \frac{\dfrac{1}{N_0}\left[\dfrac{x}{N_0}\right]^{\nu-1} \exp\left[-\dfrac{x}{N_0}\right]}{\Gamma(\nu)}. \tag{9}$$

This is the equivalent of the Rayleigh noise energy distribution but for a wide-band process with 2ν degrees of freedom. Using equations (8) and (9) we can then construct the 2AFC psychometric function for the wide-band signal/noise combination against pure noise of the same bandwidth. It proves to be:

$$P(S > N) = 1 - \sum_{i=0}^{i=\nu-1}\left[w_{E/2N_0}(i)\right]\left[\sum_{j=0}^{j=\nu-i-1}\binom{2\nu-1}{j}(1/2)^{2\nu-1}\right]. \tag{10}$$

Again, when $\nu = 1$, equation (10) reduces to Marill's formula. Notice that the infinite sum in equation (8) has disappeared. The summation trick by which this is done is explained in McGill (1968b, p. 373).

With wide-band pure noise, equation (9) leads to a similar 2AFC comparison of a noise level N_s containing a slight energy increment, against a background level N_0 in which the increment is omitted. The psychometric function based on the prescription established in equation (4a) is a partial binomial sum:

$$P(N_S > N_0) = \sum_{j=0}^{j=\nu-1}\binom{2\nu-1}{j}\left[\frac{N_0}{N_0 + N_S}\right]^j\left[\frac{N_S}{N_0 + N_S}\right]^{2\nu-1-j}. \tag{11}$$

In principle, equations (10) and (11) are exact psychometric functions. They make it easy to construct templates determined by successive values of ν. The calculations are programmed on a desktop computer or a handheld programmable calculator. Our computations for the energy distributions involving sine waves in band-limited noise and wide-band noise intensity discrimination, are given in Figs 1.1 and 1.2. These are templates, similar to those provided by Hecht et al. (1942) for noiseless visual detection, enabling the researcher to estimate key parameters from data. On the basis of such comparisons typical psychometric functions for 1000-Hz signals in noise lie near $\nu = 10$ whereas for noise intensity discrimination ν is estimated to be

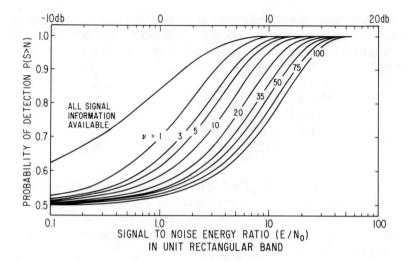

FIG.1.1 Two-alternative forced-choice psychometric functions governing detection of a pure tone in bandlimited gaussian noise. These stimulus-based psychometric functions are computed from the probability that the energy in the signal/noise condition exceeds the energy in the noise condition. They are computed from equation (10) in the text and are exact. The parameter ν is one-half the degrees of freedom of the noise band. It is based upon the ear's critical bandwidth and integration time. Psychometric functions such as these serve as templates for estimating bandwidth and integration time from typical experimental data. The curve labeled *All Signal Information Available* is the Peterson, Birdsall, and Fox (1954) optimum for the case of the signal known exactly. Similarly, the function at $\nu = 1$ is Marill's (1956) equation in which the signal is known except for phase. Neither of these ideal observers comes close to the data.

roughly 100. Original versions of these templates were developed by Green and McGill (1970), using a variety of approximations. Modern computing methods encourage precise calculations, and these are embodied in the updated figures.

Estimated Bandwidth

Equations (10) and (11) both obey Weber's law. If the degrees of freedom parameter remains constant, fixing the signal to noise ratio also fixes detectability—Weber's law. We rarely know much about the degrees of freedom parameter. Ordinarily it is determined by the ear's internal band width and integration time, and is generally estimated from threshold detectability at the 75th percentile point of the 2AFC psychometric function. Thus for sine wave signals in wide-band noise:

$$\hat{\nu} \cong 1.099 \, [E_{75/N_o}]^2 - [E_{75/N_o}] \,, \tag{12}$$

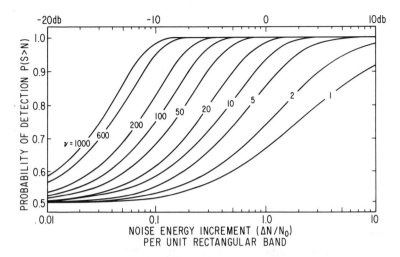

FIG.1.2 Two-alternative, forced-choice psychometric functions governing detection of a small increment ΔN in the average power level N_o per unit of bandwidth of a band-limited gaussian noise. The functions between ν $= 1 - 100$ are computed from equation (11) in the text and are exact. For $\nu \geq 100$, our psychometric functions are based on a simple normal approximation. At $\nu = 100$, the two computations differ in the third decimal place over the operative range of the curve. For practical purposes, they too are exact. These are stimulus-based psychometric functions. The parameter ν is one-half the degrees of freedom in the effective noise band. Again the functions serve as templates for estimating bandwidth and (noise) integration time from typical experimental data on noise-intensity discrimination. Note that the curves become more sensitive as the product of bandwidth and integration time increases, and that with increasing sensitivity the functions grow steeper on a log energy plot. The steepening is slight, however, not enough to account for Laming's (1986) observations on the slope of the psychometric function in noise intensity discrimination.

where E_{75}/N_0 is the threshold signal-to-noise energy ratio and $\hat{\nu}$ is the estimated degrees of freedom parameter. Jeffress (1968) obtained values for ν ranging from 5 to 10 by working in this way.

The small size of the parameter indicates a relatively narrow bandwidth (see equation [7]). This takes us directly into calculation of the ear's critical bandwidth. It is not a simple problem because signal durations with which listeners feel most comfortable (500–1000 ms) are somewhat longer than the effective stimulus determined by the ear's tonal integration time. We can (and often do) estimate it (using values of the order of 100 to 200 ms), but the threshold variable we typically measure, stimulus power, and the parameter we typically estimate, ν, are insufficient to pin down the ear's critical bandwidth. Estimates of the latter based on the best fit of the experimental data to the template in Fig. 1.1 typically run from 50 Hz–150 Hz at a center frequency of 1000 Hz. Bandwidth estimates will increase systematically with assumed integration time for a fixed value of threshold power. Their product determines ν and so the entire system is seen to be heavily constrained.

The fact that the energy statistics of signals in noise turn out to have so much explanatory impact in good agreement with the experimental data is simply remarkable. Clearly we are onto something, and the reader can now appreciate the excitement among auditory researchers when these relations were first discovered.

Similarly, in pure-noise intensity discrimination:

$$\hat{\nu} \cong \left[\frac{N_{75}}{N_0} - 1 \right]^{-2}. \tag{13}$$

The typical measurement of N_{75}/N_0 at threshold in studies of noise masking proves to be approximately 1.10 (see Miller, 1947; Green, 1960). This number inserted into equation (13) generates an estimate of ν of the order of 100. The bandwidth is much wider, as might have been expected, but perhaps not wide enough to make us really comfortable. The masking band for noise should be wide in order to produce sharp discriminations. The wider the band, the more acute is the discrimination if the stimulus model is accepted at face value. The empirical slope of the psychometric function in noise-intensity discrimination is steep, roughly double that of the template at $\nu = 100$ in Fig. 1.2. Green's (1960) measurements found this slope anomaly, and Laming's (1986) theoretical work successfully explained it. The ear's processing of pure noise behaves in many ways as we might expect if we are dealing with an energy detector, but the outcomes are not quite right, at least when we restrict ourselves to the simplest forms of energy detection requiring no transformations. Such problems are multiplied when we turn to pure tones and "frozen" (nonstochastic) noise. Neither class of stimuli exhibits any statistics at all. One is narrow-band, the other broad-band. Yet, listeners have clear difficulties with both, and in effect treat frozen noise as though it were fully stochastic when masking another noise (Raab & Goldberg, 1975). In fact, if off-frequency listening is controlled, even pure tones seem to follow Weber's law in the region 30 db or more above absolute threshold (Moore & Raab, 1974; Viemeister, 1972). Evidently Weber's law emerges from the dynamics of the detection process in these important test cases.

DETECTION THEORY IN A PASSIVE POISSON NETWORK

The mixed bag of successes and nettlesome problems resulting from stimulus-defined treatments of auditory energy detection, led us some time ago to consider the properties of primitive transmission networks. The first attempt (McGill, 1967) employed stimulus energy to control the mean rate of a Poisson counting process linked to its driver by a linear connection somewhere in the ear. The attempt produced a number of interesting results, including one or two that turned up in other contexts, and it generated one important insight.

We found that the Poisson transmission line is relatively transparent to signal/noise distributions of driving energy. The counting distribution, though a discrete point process, has essentially the same detection properties as the driver (except, of course, for pure tones and other nonstochastic stimuli). Hence, Poisson transmission inherits most of the successes and most of the headaches of signal detection based on energy analysis of the stimulus. Our expectation was that a Poisson transmission line would help us deal with a number of vexing problems posed by nonstochastic stimuli. It did that but in the end it could not cope with new data on pure-tone intensity discrimination. Specifically, we expected that a Poisson transmission line would introduce statistical fluctuations into pure tones and thus help to explain pure-tone intensity discrimination. When experiments on the latter were done, the theory looked reasonably good, but the masking curves did not have the slope forecast by a Poisson process.

Noncentral Negative Binomial Distribution

In order to clarify these points, consider what happens when the wide-band signal/noise energy distribution (equation [8]) drives a Poisson counting process. First, the m.g.f. of a Poisson with a mean count of ax:

$$M_{ax}(\theta) = \exp\left[ax(e^{\theta} - 1)\right].$$

Here x is a particular (driving) energy and a is a constant matching energy units to counting. There is no real transformation in the system, just proportional counting. Then drive this Poisson process by the signal/noise energy distribution in equation (8):

$$M_j(\theta) = \int_0^{\infty} f_s(x) M_{ax}(\theta) \, dx, \tag{14}$$

where j will now take on discrete values $0,1,2,\ldots,\infty$; and $M_j(\theta)$ is the generating function of a doubly stochastic counting distribution (i.e., two random processes in sequence, the first driving the mean of the second). After suitable manipulation we arrive at a new generating function constructed as a weighted sum of negative binomial m.g.f.s. With this insight, we conclude that the sought-after distribution may be a Poisson-weighted sum of negative binomials — a discrete form of the stimulus energy distribution. The conclusion is tested and checks out. Accordingly, we find for the counting probability $p_s(j)$ that exactly j counts are recorded during the ear's integration time:

$$p_s(j) = \sum_{i=0}^{i=\infty} \left[w_{E/N_0}(i) \right] \cdot \left[\binom{i+j+\nu-1}{j} \left[\frac{1}{1+aN_0} \right]^{i+\nu} \left[\frac{aN_0}{1+aN_0} \right]^j \right]. \qquad (15)$$

The distribution in equation (15) may be described as a noncentral negative binomial (Ong & Lee, 1979). It was also developed by Pevina (1967) to depict laser-flash energy (i.e., photon counting) distributions when a sinusoidal (coherent) signal is embedded in a broad-band gaussian noise of the same center frequency (see Teich & McGill, 1976). In such physical applications equation (15) is called the Poisson transform of equation (8).

Equation (15) is no idle curiosity. If E is set equal to zero we get the counting distribution of pure noise under the assumptions we have imposed. Moreover, given these two expressions, we can then find the detection law of the counting process in the transmission line. It proves to be (McGill, 1967):

$$\frac{1}{\nu^{1/2}} \cdot \frac{E_{75}}{N_0} \simeq c \qquad (16)$$

at threshold, where c is a constant not far from unity. This is Weber's law, and virtually the same result as generated directly from stimulus energy.

When the driving energy distribution in equation (14) is replaced by a delta function, the counting distribution of any fixed-energy stimulus is seen to be the Poisson superposition of the transmission network. So if the latter were an appropriate model of auditory transmission, pure tones and sine waves in frozen noise would have essentially the same square-root detectability as the deVries–Rose law of visual intensity discrimination (see McGill, 1971). This led to considerable experimentation in the 1970s, producing clear-cut results that rejected either linear coupling from energy to counting, or the whole idea of a Poisson network, and, in all likelihood, both.

Failure of the Passive Poisson Network

Research showed that when the energy in a pure tone, E_s, just discriminably different from a weaker tone, E_0, is plotted against the latter in log coordinates over a range of E_0 from about 30 db above threshold to 80 db, the result is a straight line with a slope of about 0.9 in log coordinates. It is certainly not 0.5 as a Poisson process would require, but neither is it Weber's law as, for example, in equation (16) (see McGill & Goldberg, 1968a, 1968b). This oddity set off another flurry of research to determine just what might be going on. In the outcome, experiments revealed that when spread of excitation in pure tones is controlled by using weak masking noise with a notch or gap surrounding the test frequency, the near-miss disappears and unit slope emerges (Moore & Raab, 1974; Viemeister, 1972). Masking with frozen noise generates Weber's law purely and simply (Raab & Goldberg, 1975). Nothing in the theory of an energy-driven Poisson transmission line prepares us for such results.

The failure of the theory could hardly be clearer or more interesting because it suggests that the auditory transmission network must somehow be imposing a Weber's law format on nonstochastic input signals. Step by step, the interplay of theory and experiment has pushed us into withdrawal from the simple auditory adaptation of the Hecht–Barlow mechanism with which we began. Sensory psychology's classical dictum, which holds that all problems reduce ultimately to a proper definition of the stimulus, grows increasingly difficult to defend in auditory detection unless we are prepared to search for the stimulus in the heart of the transmission network. Alternatively, we might proceed by redefining the transmission system to allow for some form of amplification. The latter will sometimes generate detectability obeying Weber's law even when non–stochastic stimuli provide the inputs to the network. In the next section we show how this happens.

DETECTION THEORY IN AN AMPLIFYING NEURAL TRANSMISSION NETWORK

Birth-death Stochastic Process

Consider the ear and its transmission network as a mechanism for detecting weak signals by cascade multiplication or amplification over an undetermined number of stages. Multiplication is achieved via a stochastic birth process, one which at each stage gives birth to some multiple > 1 of the neural events it receives as inputs. At each stage there are also losses proportional to the ongoing level of activity. Thus, as the signal message passes through the network it is continuously transformed, growing within the network by the algebraic sum of such gains and losses.

The network is designed to amplify weak signals and limit intense signals. Otherwise the latter would grow exponentially paralyzing transmission in a multiplicative cascade. The trick here will be to counterbalance a transform of the driving stimulus against the expected exponential growth of the neural message in the network, so that the average size of the message remains roughly linear with stimulus energy; or remains some predetermined function of stimulus energy.

In a classical birth–death stochastic process, the probability of a specific count is defined by a well-known differential equation (see Bharucha–Reid, 1960, p. 87):

$$P'_n(t) = -(\lambda_n + \mu_n)P_n(t) + \lambda_{n-1}P_{n-1}(t) + \mu_{n+1}P_{n+1}(t), \quad n = 1,2,3, \ldots$$
$$P'_0(t) = -\lambda_0 P_0(t) + \mu_1 P_1(t), \tag{17}$$

The subscript n refers to the count at time t while λ_n and μ_n are the gain and loss parameters associated with state n. The derivative in (17) is taken with respect to time. We are saying that if the count is n at time $t + \Delta t$, it got there either because it was already there at time t and failed to change during Δt (first term); or it was a step below in state $n - 1$ and went up (second term); or it was a step above in state $n + 1$ and came down (third term).

These constraints portray a narrow-band stimulus message whose magnitude performs a random walk ending at time $t + \Delta t$ in a count that may be above or below its value an instant earlier.

To simplify matters further, and to introduce the idea of stage by stage multiplication, we further define:

$$\lambda_n = n \cdot \lambda,$$
$$\mu_n = n \cdot \mu. \tag{18}$$

Equation (18) implies that the tendency to multiply increases linearly with the count (not time), and losses are proportional to the count. This is stochastic multiplication typical of amplifier networks. We also take state zero, that is, a count of zero, to be an *absorbing state*. Transitions up from zero are forbidden:

$$\lambda_o = 0,$$
$$P'_0(t) = \mu P_1(t). \tag{19}$$

Our last set of restrictions embodies the idea that a flux of neural events set off in the ear can die out. If the counting process should ever drift into state zero, the message is lost. Finally, we put a subscript x on λ and μ to indicate that the initial size of gains and losses in transmission are functions of the input intensity x. The multiplication rate (or loss rate) depends both on the driving energy and the current state of the count.

Driving energy is labeled x. It may be either stochastic (narrow-band noise), or deterministic (tones; frozen noise). The effective level at the ear is ax where a is taken to be constant. The central idea of a counting model is that effective energy drives an impulse record of the stimulus. The relation between stimulus energy and expected impulse count is taken to be:

$$\ln (1 + ax) = (\lambda_x - \mu_x) \cdot t \qquad (20)$$

This is an energy transformation. The variable x measures stimulus energy and thus has a time dimension built into it. The parameter t on the right-hand side of equation (20) is the running time of the counting process. Generally it is longer than the duration of the stimulus. Energy accumulates on the left-hand side of the equation and a counting record of the energy accumulates on the right-hand side. The log transform keeps the network linear despite its tendency to amplify whatever it sees. Parameters λ_x and μ_x are the gain and loss rates of the auditory network when the driving energy is x.

In classical branching theory t is allowed to increase without limit and a fundamental theorem of branching states:

$$\lim_{t \to \infty} \left\{ \begin{array}{c} state\ zero \\ probability \end{array} \right\} \Rightarrow \mu_x / \lambda_x = \pi\ (x), \qquad (21)$$

where $\pi(x)$ is the so-called "extinction" probability (message lost). We do not in fact operate at this limit because the auditory system is thought to have a fixed, relatively short integration time. Accordingly, the extinction probability appears as a parameter of the network.

If the stimulus is weak, a substantial likelihood exists that the message will fail to get through whereas intense signals should be detected with a probability close to unity. Thus $0 \le \pi\ (x) \le 1$. The limit will be near 1 when stimulus energy approaches zero, and near zero when x grows very large.

Linear Birth–death Process

With these definitions and restrictions we can now write down the counting probability driven by an input of intensity x:

$$P(0) = \frac{\pi(x) \cdot \gamma(x)}{1 + \gamma(x)}, \tag{22}$$

$$P(j) = [1 - P(0)] \cdot \left[\frac{1}{1+\gamma(x)}\right]\left[\frac{\gamma(x)}{1+\gamma(x)}\right]^{j-1}, \quad j = 1,2,3 \ldots .$$

In equation (22) $\pi(x) = \mu_x/\lambda_x; \gamma(x) = \frac{ax}{1 - \pi(x)}$. Evidently this type of linear birth–death process gives rise to a modified (because of P(0)) Bose–Einstein counting distribution (see Feller, 1957, p. 59). In fact, if μ_x is taken to be zero, then $\pi(x) = 0$, and we have a pure birth process in which

$$P(j) \Rightarrow \left[\frac{1}{1+ax}\right]\left[\frac{ax}{1+ax}\right]^{j-1}.$$

This expression and equation (22) from which it is produced are *shifted* Bose–Einstein distributions spanning only the nonzero values of the count and reflecting the role of the zero count as an absorbing state.

A Bose–Einstein (B–E) distribution has classical geometric form. It is built from a single positive parameter, in this instance $\gamma(x)$, generally a measurement of magnitude. The tail of the B–E converges exponentially to zero. In this respect it resembles Rayleigh narrow-band noise (see equation [3]). Consequently, even at a level of considerable generality, before any particular linkage between λ_x, μ_x, and x has been specified, a birth–death cascade will generate multiplicative noise resembling acoustic noise. Perhaps this may explain why the detectability of signals in acoustic noise is so easy to forecast from the statistics of the stimulus.

The general form of the birth–death counting distribution, equation (22), suggests that the process has two distinct outcomes: a spike of probability at count zero indicating lost signals, and a Bose–Einstein counting distribution over the nonzero states reflecting signal messages that pass through the network successfully.

Connection to Driving Energy

Now return to:

$$\ln(1+ax) = (\lambda_x - \mu_x)t.$$

The log will have nonnegative values when $x \geq 0$ which implies that $\lambda_x \geq \mu_x$. The force driving the transmission is the birth component, $\lambda_x\,t$, of the process. Some part of that force is dissipated in losses that become incorporated into the death component, $\mu_x\, t$. We might also define an "immigration" component representing outside neural activity that somehow wanders into the network becoming a source of additive noise. Such intrusions are almost inevitable. They can be incorporated into the model by allowing the gain parameter to approach an arbitrary limit as stimulus energy approaches zero. A major simplification occurs when the gain and loss parameters are set as follows:

$$\lambda_x\, t = (1 + ax)\, \ln\,(1 + ax)\,/\,ax, \qquad\qquad (23)$$

$$\mu_x\, t = \lambda_x\, t\,/\,1 + ax.$$

Equation (23) meets all prior specifications. The process will amplify weak stimuli and simultaneously limit intense stimuli. The gain parameter is equal to or greater than the loss parameter. Both parameters approach unity as stimulus energy approaches zero. Hence it is easy to introduce an adaptation level by altering this limit if we choose to do so. We keep the limit at unity here to avoid further complications.

The loss parameter, $\mu_x\, t,$ starts out equivalent to the system gain, guaranteeing a threshold below which no messages can be generated. As signal energy grows, the loss parameter falls off. Under very intense stimulation the transmission system becomes a pure birth process driven by the log intensity of the stimulus.

The main reason for the additional steps involved in constructing equation (23), however, is that they cause everything in the network to fall neatly into place, generating a particularly simple counting distribution:

$$\pi(x) = 1/1 + ax, \ \gamma(x) = 1 + ax; \qquad\qquad (24)$$

$$P\,(j) = \left[\frac{1}{2+ax}\right]\left[\frac{1+ax}{2+ax}\right]^{j}, \qquad j = 0,1,2,3\,\ldots$$

The counting distribution is now explicitly Bose–Einstein with parameter $1 + ax$. Our definitions have eliminated the separate spike of probability in state zero. The distribution now ranges down to a count of zero despite the latter's role as an absorbing state. As driving energy approaches zero, a residual internal noise is found, creating occasional false alarms at absolute threshold. If we set the critical number for detection at n, the probability of a false alarm can be found from the tail of the Bose–Einstein distribution in equation (24) with x approaching zero:

$$Pr \ (False \ Alarm) \ = \ \left[\frac{1}{2} \right]^n \qquad (25)$$

Accurate detection of a stimulus against this internal noise requires a critical number large enough to render the false alarms negligible.

We label equation (24) an *amplifier network counting distribution*. It constitutes our first tentative step beyond passive Poisson transmission. As observed earlier, the Bose–Einstein bears a striking resemblance to narrow-band acoustic noise. We may expect the amplifier network to impose such properties on information passing through it. Amplifier network counting distributions may thus be expected to have higher tails and larger variance than Poisson distributions. In the main this outcome is desirable since it suggests that Weber's law is built into the transmission network. But along with such advantages come new problems. In particular, normal approximations which perform so well at the stimulus level for estimating detectability, even with narrow-band noise, are no longer guaranteed to work. The high tails of a Rayleigh-driven Bose–Einstein counting process can sometimes mislead us. There are other problems as well.

AUDITORY OUTCOMES IN AN AMPLIFYING NEURAL TRANSMISSION NETWORK

The final sections of this chapter study the output of an amplifier network driven by typical auditory stimuli. We consider pure-tone intensity discrimination, and wide-band noise masking. Generally speaking, the outcomes are quite satisfactory. They yield solid (though imperfect) agreement with experimental data. Hence, a birth–death process (amplifier) network can serve as a useful guide in auditory and neurophysiological research, providing a new organizing principle for interpreting masses of data acquired along auditory pathways.

Pure Tones

The geometric distribution proves easy to work with in two-alternative forced-choice. Suppose we drive the amplifier network with two distinct-pure tones, identical in frequency but differing slightly in energy content. Call the weaker tone E_o and its counterpart, containing an energy increment, E_s. Hence $E_s \geq E_o$. For the probability that the signal tone generates a count exceeding the reference tone, we have:

$$P(S > N) = \sum_{k=0}^{k=\infty} \left[\frac{1}{2+aE_0}\right] \left[\frac{1+aE_0}{2+aE_0}\right]^k \cdot \left[\frac{1+aE_s}{2+aE_s}\right]^{k+1} .$$

Similarly, the probability that the counts are exactly equal proves to be:

$$P(S = N) = \sum_{k=0}^{k=\infty} \left[\frac{1}{2+aE_0}\right] \left[\frac{1}{2+aE_s}\right] \left[\frac{1+aE_0}{2+aE_0} \cdot \frac{1+aE_s}{2+aE_s}\right]^k .$$

When the counts are exactly equal, we are forced to choose one of the two alternatives as the signal. The reasonable course is to flip an unbiased coin. Hence the probability of a correct decision must be given by:

$$P(c) = P(S>N) + \frac{1}{2} P(S=N). \tag{26}$$

Insert the Bose–Einstein counting outcomes into equation (26). We find:

$$P(c) = \frac{3+2aE_s}{6+2aE_s + 2aE_0} . \tag{27}$$

This is the psychometric function for pure-tone intensity discrimination if decisions are based upon counts recorded in an amplifier network. When $E_s = E_o$, the probability of a correct choice is 0.5. As E_s grows relative to E_o, $P(c)$ approaches unity. In fact, suppose the reference tone E_o has sizable energy content. Then:

$$P(c) \Rightarrow \frac{E_s}{E_s + E_0} . \tag{27a}$$

Equation (27a) for the psychometric function proves to be identical with that governing intensity discrimination of narrow-band Rayleigh noise (see Green & McGill, 1970, equation [9a]; equation [11] in this chapter). Amplifier network transmission has converted the pure-tone counting record to narrow-band noise, and this network noise is indistinguishable from acoustic noise.

The threshold value of E_s / E_o, with the probability of a correct choice set at .75, is found to be 3; much larger than the experimental value of about 1.1. The narrow-band process is evidently incorrect. Excitation must spread into adjacent transmission channels from a focus at the stimulus frequency.

In view of the apparent conversion of pure tones to noise in the counting record, we can then invoke the stimulus theory of wide-band noise to illuminate the counting record for pure tones in an amplifier network (Green & McGill, 1970, equation [10]; see also equation [13] in this chapter):

$$\nu^{1/2}\left[\frac{E_{75}}{E_0} - 1\right] \cong 1. \tag{28}$$

The result is based on a wide-band normal approximation to the difference distribution of two independent noise energy samples having identical band width. (There are no problems with the approximation in these circumstances.) Notice that as the degrees of freedom parameter ν (measuring spread of excitation) increases, the ratio of pure-tone intensities must decrease at threshold. If spread is fixed we ought to see Weber's law, and experiments confirm that notched or band-stop noise produces just this outcome. If spread is uncontrolled, as it is in pure-tone intensity discrimination, the effect of increasing spread, as depicted in equation (28), is an increasing depression of the log–linear relation between E_s and E_o, below unit slope when both intensities are measured in db.

While these outcomes accord quite well with what we know of the data on pure-tone intensity discrimination, actual estimates of spread are fairly large — perhaps too large. Moreover, good data exist showing the near miss to Weber's law to be relatively impervious to center frequency and signal duration. It is difficult to square such findings with other measures of excitatory spread; critical bands, for example. But considering the rough and ready qualities of our model (orthogonal rectangular bands, uniform spread of excitation), its performance with pure tones must be accounted a considerable success.

Noise Intensity Discrimination

Wide-band noise intensity discrimination takes us to an entirely new conceptual realm when the locus of detection is an amplifier network rather than the noise stimulus itself. Our results, however, are remarkably similar to those found via stimulus energy analysis. The single notable change is an increased estimate of bandwidth caused by the noise associated with stochastic multiplication in the network.

In this instance we begin with a Rayleigh (narrow-band) noise driving the Bose–Einstein distribution in equation (24). The zero-state probability P(0) is then formulated as follows:

$$P(0) = \int_0^\infty \frac{f(x)}{2+ax}\, dx,$$

where

$$f(x) = \frac{1}{N_0}\, e^{-\frac{x}{N_0}}.$$

Hence,

$$P(0) = \frac{1}{2}\int_0^\infty \left| \frac{\frac{2}{aN_0}\, e^{\frac{-x}{N_0}}}{\frac{2}{a}+x} \right| dx.$$

This last expression is one of the many varieties of the exponential integral. Specifically,

$$P(0) = \frac{1}{2}\left(z\, e^z\, E_1(z)\right) = \frac{1}{2}\,\phi(z), \tag{29}$$

where $z = 2\,/\,aN_o$. The exponential integral $E_1(z)$ is tabled (cf., Abramowitz & Stegun, 1964, pp. 238–248), as indeed are certain values of the function $\phi(z)$. Extensive use of these relations necessitates preparing one's own tables. Fortunately it is a fairly easy task with a desktop computer. Such analysis reveals:

$$0 \le \phi(z) \le 1,$$
$$\text{as } 0 \le z \le \infty.$$
$$0 \le P(0) \le \frac{1}{2},$$

The upper limit on P(0) occurs when the driving energy x approaches zero, an already familiar fact. More generally:

$$\int_0^\infty f(x)\,\frac{(1+ax)^{k-1}}{(2+ax)^{k+1}}\,dx \;=\; P\,(k-1)\,-\,P\,(k), \qquad (30)$$

$$= \frac{1}{kaN_0}\left[1\,-\,(\frac{1}{2})^k\,-\,\sum_{j=0}^{j=k-1} P\,(j)\right].$$

This relation and the definition of *P(0)* in equation (29) permit iterative computation of successive values of the counting probability *P(k)* driven by narrow-band Rayleigh noise. A typical example is shown in Fig. 1.3 which illustrates the high tail of the noise-driven amplifier-network counting distribution. The RDBE distribution is identical to the K_o Bessel function-driven Poisson distribution found in a number of applications in biology and optics. All these applications (including our amplifier network) suggest closely related stochastic processes (see Teich & Diament, 1989).

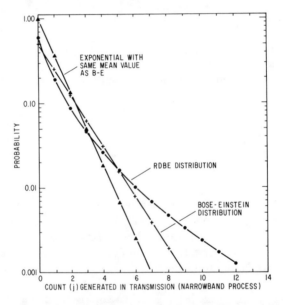

FIG.1.3 The Bose–Einstein counting distribution is a typical pure birth process. The effective driving energy, aN_0 is set equal to 1. The ordinate is logarithmic, making the B–E linear. Also shown for comparison is an exponential (continuous) curve deriving from the Rayleigh energy distribution of narrow-band acoustic noise. The curve differs only slightly. However, when the B–E is driven by this type of narrow-band noise, the resulting Rayleigh-driven Bose–Einstein (RDBE) counting distribution is seen to have a much higher tail, that is, larger variance, than its B–E parent. Hence the RDBE differs markedly from the B–E and its continuous equivalent, the Rayleigh energy distribution of narrow-band noise.

Having established the general appearance of the distribution, we now compute its mean and variance:

$$m_j = 1 + aN_0,$$

$$\sigma_j^2 = 2 + 3 \, (aN_0) \, (1 + aN_0).$$

(31)

The variance is quite large, much larger than its Poisson counterpart. This forecasts not only a further retreat from ideal energy detection, but an auditory bandwidth estimate likely to be considerably wider than that calculated via pure stimulus analysis. Both consequences are viewed here as highly desirable. They illustrate divergent interpretations of the same data based upon models that differ at key points. Our early successes with pure stimulus analysis of masking noise in auditory detection may have led us astray, lulling healthy skepticism by offering interpretations that were really very good despite many indications that they were also not quite on target.

Narrow-band noise transformed by a birth–death transmission network in the manner shown by Fig. 1.3 is evidently nongaussian, even when differences are formed between pairs of independent samples. The high tail causes serious trouble.

Wideband noise similarly transformed is another story. The convolution of many orthogonal rectangular noise bands invokes the central limit theorem and eventually swamps the high tails of individual narrow-band noise distributions. Accordingly at threshold we can set up a standard normal deviate for $P \, (S \geq N) = .75$ in two-alternative forced-choice:

$$\frac{0 - [\nu(1 + aN_s) - \nu(1 + aN_0)]}{\nu^{\frac{1}{2}}[2 + 3aN_0(1 + aN_0) + 2 + 3aN_s(1 + aN_s)]^{\frac{1}{2}}} \cong -.6745.$$

If we now let $\Delta N = N_s - N_o$, and discard terms of the form $2/aN_0$, the deviate boils down to:

$$\frac{\nu^{\frac{1}{2}} \Delta N / N_0}{[3 + 3 \, (1 + \Delta N / N_0)^2]^{\frac{1}{2}}} \cong -.6745.$$

It is here that the central limit theorem helps out. If ν is sufficiently large, so that $\frac{\Delta N}{N_o} << 1$, we can neglect terms of the order of $\frac{\Delta N^2}{N_0^2}$. Accordingly, since $\frac{\Delta N}{N_o}$ is approximately .1, we come finally to the detection law for intensity discrimination of wide-band noise when the latter drives a birth–death amplifier network:

$$(v/3)^{\frac{1}{2}} \cdot \frac{\Delta N}{N_0} \cong 1. \tag{32}$$

The outcome is remarkable in that analysis of the amplifier network leads to a result very similar to the one obtained directly from the stimulus (see equation [13]). The only real difference is a new estimate of the degrees of freedom parameter, now three times larger than its stimulus counterpart and reasonably close to Green's (1960) empirical detectability formula.

Typical experimental data show $\frac{\Delta N}{N_0}$ to be near .10. Hence v is estimated to be 300 in the psychometric function illustrated in Fig. 1.4. The slope of the latter is roughly half the slope found by Green (1960), and subsequently established on theoretical grounds by Laming (1986). Moreover, the estimated noise bandwidth of the amplifier network, assuming an integration time of the order of 200 ms, cannot be much wider than 1500 Hz, still a bit narrow.

Laming's running-derivative approach differs at least superficially from the amplifier network concepts presented here. The slope and bandwidth problems just cited would appear to give an advantage to Laming's methods and to cast at least a shadow of doubt on the energy transformations we have used.

But the amplifier network no longer requires us to remain strictly wedded to pure stimulus energy detection. Hence, a variety of transforms are open for consideration. For example, an additional power function operating on equation (23), defining the birth and death parameters, will in fact steepen our psychometric function and also increase the apparent bandwidth. Hence, we can come arbitrarily close to the performance we want, but until we have a better idea of the overall performance of amplifier networks, it is perhaps wise to keep things simple and to record discrepancies as they appear. This is one such. The slope of the pure-noise psychometric function resulting from equation (23) is too shallow and the estimated bandwidth is still too narrow. Everything else improves upon earlier versions.

Sine Waves In Noise

An analysis, parallel to our study of pure-noise intensity discrimination, has been carried out also for an amplifier network driven by a pure tone

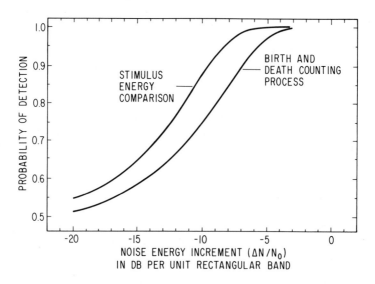

FIG.1.4 Comparison of two-alternative forced-choice psychometric functions emerging from stimulus analysis, and amplifier network analysis in noise-intensity discrimination. The *stimulus energy* curve is based on equation (11) with $\nu = 300$. The curve for a *birth and death counting process* is obtained from equation (32) with $\nu = 300$. Actually, they are nearly the same function translated by about 2.4db. In fact both curves can be found among the template psychometric functions in Fig. 1.2. The transformations involved in the amplifier network are then read off as an apparent decrease in effective stimulus band width (i.e., shift to the right in Fig. 1.2). Equation (32) enables us to reconstruct this shift and recompute the effective noise bandwidth based on a larger estimate of the degrees of freedom parameter.

embedded in band-limited noise. Many details are omitted here because we remain dissatisfied with the argument.

Psychometric functions developed from differences between independent Rayleigh-driven Bose–Einstein counting distributions pose unique difficulties if the critical masking band is insufficiently wide. The high tails of the counting distributions produce a normal approximation that limits the psychometric function at values less than unity. This peculiar asymptotic behavior is a property of the approximation, not of the counting process itself. Thus, when normal approximations become necessary in a signal/noise-driven amplifier network, a correction must be made so as to eliminate the spurious asymptote.

We have managed to subvert the entire problem when signals are embedded in a narrow-band noise. The amplifier network then generates an analogue of Marill's equation. But this exact solution has been developed only for a unit rectangular band ($\nu = 1$). As we have seen, stimulus data demand equivalent rectangular masking bands measured by $\nu = 5 - 10$ (see Jeffress, 1968). This is in the low range of degrees of freedom, beyond our current reach for an exact solution, and yet not quite up to numbers where the central limit theorem can be guaranteed; (but see Teich & Diament, 1989, Table II, the BI distribution; evidently an exact solution is reasonably close).

Given this caveat, we can produce an approximate psychometric function using what seems to us to be an appropriate correction of the normal approximation with relatively few degrees of freedom. The method involves bootstrapping from the exact narrow-band solution. First find a version of the normal approximation yielding close agreement with the exact psycho-metric function in the narrow-band case. Then apply this amended or corrected approximation to stimuli of moderate bandwidth. The resulting expression for the standard normal deviate corresponding to a tabled percentage of correct pairwise comparisons is the following:

$$\frac{E / N_0}{[(E/N_o)^{1.5} + 6(E/N_0) + 6\nu]^{\frac{1}{2}}} \cong d, \tag{33}$$

where d is a standard normal deviate running from zero to infinity. Equation (33) can be computed by systematically increasing values of E/N_o for a fixed ν. The result is then inserted into a program instruction converting normal deviates to probabilities, and the psychometric function is constructed easily on a PC or programmable calculator.

A well-controlled threshold measurement and a normal ear listening to a pure tone at 1000 Hz masked by wide-band noise, will begin to detect at signal-to-noise power ratios somewhere near 25. If we take the ear's tonal integration time to be about 150 ms, the threshold energy ratio calculates out at 25 • (.15) = 3.75. In pure stimulus analysis this threshold yields $\nu = 12$ for the corresponding degrees of freedom parameter. Here, the same parameter ($\nu = 12$) leads via equation (33) to a threshold energy ratio of approximately $E/N_o = 8.08$. Evidently the multiplicative noise in our amplifier network requires more energy for detection than an ideal energy detector would need. Hence, relatively low energy ratios found at threshold in signal detection experiments suggest even narrower bandwidths than those calculated from pure stimulus analysis.

Final Observations on Amplifier Networks

These results imply that an amplifier network will generate wider internal-noise bandwidths in noise-intensity discrimination and narrower band widths in signal detection than those computed from direct analysis of stimulus energy. This outcome is very desirable, and a strong endorsement of the type of transmission system we have been studying. It does seem, nevertheless, that our new estimates of critical bandwidth are perhaps a bit too narrow, just as our estimates of noise bandwidth from intensity discrimination are not quite wide enough.

All things considered, the indications of progress are obvious. We have been able to characterize an active detection network based upon the principle of stochastic multiplication. We have managed to do so without getting hopelessly lost in the myriad complexities of the auditory pathways. Abandoning total dependence on the stimulus, and constructing the functional outline of an amplifier network (a hybrid of stimulus, receptor, and transmission mechanisms) generates solutions for a variety of problems deemed either intractable or overwhelmingly complex when approached in the conventional stimulus-oriented way. Time will tell whether this system is the one we have been seeking.

REFERENCES

Abramowitz, M., & Stegun, I. (Eds.) (1964). *Handbook of mathematical functions*. Washington, DC: National Bureau of Standards, U.S. Dept. of Commerce.

Barlow, H. (1956). Retinal noise and absolute threshold. *Journal of the Optical Society of America, 46*, 634–639.

Barlow, H. (1957). Increment thresholds at low intensities considered as signal/noise discriminations. *Journal of Physiology, 136*, 469–488.

Barlow, H. B., Levick, W. R., & Yoon, M. (1971). Responses to single quanta of light in retinal ganglion cells of the cat. *Vision Research, 11, Suppl. 3*, 87–101.

Bharucha-Reid, A. (1960). *Elements of the theory of Markov Processes and their applications*. New York: McGraw-Hill.

Bouman, M. (1961). History and present status of quantum theory in vision. In W. Rosenblith (Ed.), *Sensory communication, 21*, pp. 377–401. Cambridge, MA: MIT Press and Wiley.

Çinlar, E. (1972). Superposition of point processes. In P. Lewis (Ed.), *Stochastic point processes: Statistical analysis, theory, and applications* (pp. 549–606). New York: Wiley.

Cox, D., & Smith, W. (1954). On the superposition of renewal processes. *Biometrika, 41*, 91–99.

Drenick, R. (1960). The failure law of complex equipment. *Journal of the Society of Industrial and Applied Mathematics, 8*, 680–690.

Feller, W. (1957). *An introduction to probability theory and its applications* (Vol. 7, 2nd ed.). New York: Wiley.

Green, D. (1960). Auditory detection of a noise signal. *Journal of the Acoustical Society of America, 32*, 121–131.

Green, D. (1967). Additivity of masking. *Journal of the Acoustical Society of America, 41*, 1517–1525.

Green D., & McGill, W. (1970). On the equivalence of detection probabilities and well-known statistical quantities. *Psychological Review, 77*, 294–301.

Hecht, S., Shlaer, S., & Pirenne, M. H. (1942). Energy, quanta and vision. *Journal of General Physiology, 25*, 819–840.

Hopfield, J. (1982). Neural networks and physical systems with emergent collective computational abilities. *Proceedings of the National Academy of Science, 79*, 2254–2558.

Jeffress, L. (1964). Stimulus-oriented approach to detection. *Journal of the Acoustical Society of America, 36,* 766-774.

Jeffress, L. (1968). Mathematical and electrical models of auditory detection. *Journal of the Acoustical Society of America, 44,* 187-203.

Laming, D. (1986). *Sensory analysis.* London: Academic Press.

Lawson J. L., & Uhlenbeck, G. E. (1950). *Threshold signals.* New York: McGraw-Hill.

Magill, J., & Soni, R. (1966). Photoelectric counting distributions for a noise-modulated system. *Physical Review Letters, 16,* 911-913.

Marill, T. (1956). Detection theory and psychophysics (Tech. Rept. No. 319, Oct. 30). Massachusetts Institute of Technology Research Laboratory of Electronics, Cambridge, MA.

McGill, W. (1967). Neural counting mechanisms and energy detection in audition. *Journal of Mathematical Psychology, 4,* 351-376.

McGill, W. (1968a). Variations on Marill's detection formula. *Journal of the Acoustical Society of America, 43,* 70-73.

McGill, W. (1968b). Polynomial psychometric functions in audition. *Journal of Mathematical Psychology, 5,* 369-376.

McGill, W. (1971). Poisson counting and detection in sensory systems. In E. Beckenbach & C. Tompkins (Eds.), *Concepts of communication* (pp. 257-281). New York: Wiley.

McGill, W., & Goldberg, J. (1968a). Pure tone intensity discrimination and energy detection. *Journal of the Acoustical Society of America, 44,* 576-581.

McGill, W., & Goldberg, J. (1968b). A study of the near-miss involving Weber's law and pure-tone intensity discrimination. *Perception and Psychophysics, 4,* 105-109.

Miller, G. (1947). Sensitivity to changes in the intensity of white noise and its relation to masking and loudness. *Journal of the Acoustical Society of America, 19,* 609-619.

Moore, B., & Raab, D. (1974). Pure tone intensity discrimination: Some experiments relating to the "near miss" to Weber's law. *Journal of the Acoustical Society of America, 55,* 1049-1054.

Nachmias J., & Steinman, R. (1963). Study of absolute visual detection by the rating scale method. *Journal of the Optical Society of America, 53,* 1206-1213.

Ong, S., & Lee, P. (1979). The non-central negative binomial distribution. *Biometrics Journal, 21,* 611-627.

Pevina, J. (1967). Superposition of coherent and incoherent fields. *Physics Letters, 24A,* 333-334.

Peterson, W., Birdsall, T., & Fox, W. (1954). The theory of signal detectability. *Transactions of the Professional Group on Information Theory (IRE), PGIT 2-4,* 171-212.

Pfafflin, S., & Mathews, M. (1962). Energy detection model for monaural auditory detection. *Journal of the Acoustical Society of America, 34,* 1842-1853.

Raab, D., & Goldberg, I. (1975). Auditory intensity discrimination with bursts of reproducible noise. *Journal of the Acoustical Society of America, 57,* 437-447.

Rice, S. O. (1944). Mathematical analysis of random noise. *Bell System Technical Journal, 23,* 282-332.

Rice, S. O. (1945). Mathematical analysis of random noise. *Bell System Technical Journal, 24,* 46-156.

Ronken, D. (1969). Intensity discrimination of Rayleigh noise. *Journal of the Acoustical Society of America, 45,* 54-57.

Rumelhart, D., Smolensky, P., McClelland, J., & Hinton, G. (1986). Schemata and sequential thought processes. In J. McClelland & D. Rumelhart (Eds.) *Parallel distributed processing,* (vol. 2, pp. 7-57). Cambridge, MA: MIT Press.

Ryan, A., Braverman, S., Woolf, N., & Axelsson, G. (1989). Auditory neural activity evoked by pure-tone stimulation as a function of intensity. *Brain Research, 483,* 283-293.

Saleh, B., & Teich, M. (1985). Multiplication and refractoriness in the cat's retinal-ganglion-cell discharge at low light levels. *Biological Cybernetics, 52,* 101–107.

Tanner, W. (1961). Application of the theory of signal detectability to amplitude discrimination. *Journal of the Acoustical Society of America, 33,*1233–1244.

Teich, M., & McGill, W. (1976). Neural counting and photon counting in the presence of dead time. *Physical Review Letters, 36,* 754–758.

Teich, M., Prucnal, P., Vannucci, G., Breton, M., & McGill, W. (1982a). Multiplication noise in the human visual system at threshold: 1. Quantum fluctuations and minimum detectable energy, *Journal of the Optical Society of America, 72,* 419–431.

Teich, M., Prucnal, P., Vannucci, G., Breton, M., & McGill, W. (1982b). Multiplication noise in the human visual system at threshold: 3. The role of non-Poisson quantum fluctuations. *Biological Cybernetics, 44,* 157–165.

Teich, M., & Saleh, B. (1988). Photon bunching and antibunching. In E. Wolf (Ed.), *Progress in optics XXVI* (pp. 1–104). Amsterdam: Elsevier Science Publishers.

Teich M., & Diament, P. (1989). Multiply stochastic representations for K distributions and their Poisson transforms. *Journal of the Optical Society of America A,6,* 80–91.

Viemeister, N. (1972). Intensity discrimination of pulsed sinusoids. The effects of filtered noise. *Journal of the Acoustical Society of America, 51,* 1265–1269.

Wolfram, S. (1985). Origins of randomness in physical systems. *Physical Review Letters, 55,* 449–452.

2 Behavioral Models of Signal Detection and Detection Models of Choice

Brent Alsop
University of Auckland, New Zealand

Nevin, Jenkins, Whittaker, and Yarensky (1977) and Davison and Tustin (1978) initiated a synthesis of two previously distinct areas within experimental psychology, namely, signal-detection theory (e.g., Green & Swets, 1974), and free-operant choice theory (e.g., Baum, 1974). This chapter continues this synthesis, moving closer to a parsimonious and integrated treatment of the effects of reinforcers and stimuli in signal-detection and free-operant procedures.

A SYNOPSIS OF PAST RESEARCH

In a typical signal-detection procedure the subject must choose between two possible concurrent response alternatives (e.g., "Yes" or "No"; peck left or peck right) following each presentation of one of two stimuli. Behavioral approaches to signal-detection performance have focused on this presentation of concurrently available response alternatives, stressing its procedural similarity to the standard free-operant concurrent-schedule procedure (Davison & Jenkins, 1985; Davison & Tustin, 1978; Nevin et al., 1977). Hence, Davison and Tustin (1978) developed their model of signal-detection performance from the standard model of concurrent-schedule performance, the generalized matching law (Baum, 1974), given by the equation:

$$\frac{B_1}{B_2} = c \left(\frac{R_1}{R_2} \right)^a,$$

(1)

39

where B denotes responses, R denotes obtained reinforcers, and the subscripts 1 and 2 denote the response alternatives. The bias parameter, c, measures any constant ratio preference for either alternative, irrespective of changes in the reinforcer ratio (Baum, 1974). The sensitivity parameter, a, measures the extent to which changing the reinforcer ratio affects the response ratio (Baum, 1974). Typically, such reinforcer-ratio changes produce less extreme changes in the response ratio than a one-to-one relationship demands (i.e., $a < 1.0$), a phenomenon known as under-matching (Baum, 1979; Wearden & Burgess, 1982).

Davison and Tustin (1978) suggested that responding following the presentation of either stimulus in a signal-detection procedure would be, in part, a function of the ratio of the reinforcers obtained on the concurrent response alternatives, as described by Equation 1. Following an S_1 presentation, this model predicts:

$$\frac{B_w}{B_x} = c \cdot d_s \left(\frac{R_w}{R_z} \right)^a, \tag{2}$$

and following an S_2 presentation:

$$\frac{B_y}{B_z} = c \cdot \frac{1}{d_s} \left(\frac{R_w}{R_z} \right)^a, \tag{3}$$

where B, R, a, and c are as shown. The subscripts w, x, y, and z, correspond to the cells of the signal-detection matrix (shown in Fig. 2.1) , which shows the various possible combinations of stimulus presented and response made. The discriminability between the stimuli appears as a further bias parameter, d_s. These equations predict that, if the subject cannot discriminate between S_1 and S_2 ($d_s = 1.0$), then performance following a presentation of either stimulus will be simply a function of the ratio of obtained reinforcers for the two responses (Equation 1). However, as S_1 and S_2 are made more discriminable ($d_s > 1.0$), responding following an S_1 presentation will be biased toward the B_w response (Equation 2; Fig. 2.1), and following an S_2 presentation biased toward B_z (Equation 3; Fig. 2.1).

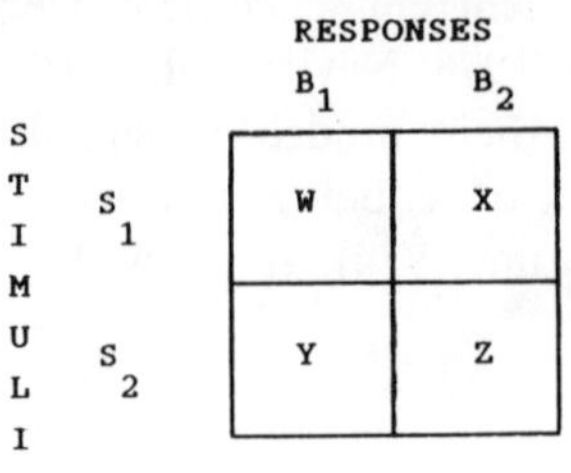

RESPONSES

		B_1	B_2
S T I M U L I	S_1	W	X
	S_2	Y	Z

FIG. 2.1 The signal-detection matrix of stimulus and response events using the w, x, y, and z notation to distinguish the four cells (Davison & Tustin, 1978).

Since its introduction, the Davison and Tustin (1978) model has successfully described performance in a variety of different experiments and procedures. These include reinforcement for errors procedures (Davison & McCarthy, 1980), intermittent versus continuous reinforcement procedures (McCarthy & Davison, 1982), and free-operant detection versus discrete-trial detection procedures (McCarthy, Davison, & Jenkins, 1982). As such, it has provided a quantitative and conceptual base for a major section of animal psychophysics.

Davison and Jenkins (1985) extended this merger of models of signal-detection and choice behavior. They noted that any choice experiment (e.g., a concurrent schedule) implicitly requires an identification of the various alternative responses and their respective contingencies. Therefore, the concepts of signal detection and discriminability might be useful to describe performance in standard free-operant procedures. To support this idea, Davison and Jenkins presented results from a study by Miller, Saunders, and Bourland (1980). Here, three groups of pigeons were trained on switching-key concurrent schedules. For each group the stimuli associated with the two schedules of reinforcement were lines of different orientation, but the disparity between the two line orientations differed across groups. In this manner, the discriminability between the concurrent alternatives could be manipulated by varying the stimuli signaling which schedule was available on the main key. For each group the ratio of reinforcers was varied across conditions, and the results were analyzed using the generalized matching law (Equation 1). The group trained with the greatest stimulus disparity (45°) gave results typical of concurrent-schedule performance; that is, negligible bias and a sensitivity parameter, a, of approximately 0.9. However, for the group trained with a stimulus disparity of 15°the obtained value of a was approximately 0.35, and for the group trained with a stimulus disparity of 0° the a value was approximately 0.17.

This relation between sensitivity to reinforcer ratios and stimulus disparity led Davison and Jenkins (1985) to offer an alternative model of concurrent-schedule performance which directly incorporated a discriminability parameter rather than a sensitivity parameter. They suggested that part of the problem confronting a subject in a concurrent schedule is to identify the relation between the responses emitted to the concurrent alternatives and the reinforcers obtained. When the separate response-reinforcer contingencies available in a concurrent schedule are difficult to discriminate (e.g., in some of Miller et al.'s [1980] switching-key concurrent schedules), performance will be less affected by changes in the ratio of reinforcers than in situations where the separate response-reinforcer contingencies are easy to discriminate. The Davison and Jenkins model (1985) takes the form:

$$\frac{B_1}{B_2} = c\left(\frac{d_r \cdot R_1 + R_2}{d_r \cdot R_2 + R_1}\right), \tag{4}$$

Where B, R, c, 1, and 2 are as earlier and the parameter d_r is said to measure the discriminability between the two response-reinforcer contingencies arranged in the concurrent schedule (Davison & Jenkins, 1985). When d_r is 1.0 (i.e., no discriminability between the response-reinforcer contingencies), the model predicts that the ratio of responding on the two alternatives will always equal the bias parameter, c, irrespective of the reinforcer distribution. As the discriminability between the response-reinforcer contingencies increases, d_r approaches infinity. When discriminability is perfect, the performance predicted by Equation 4 is the same as that predicted by the strict matching relation (Equation 1 with an a parameter of 1.0).

Davison and Jenkins (1985) demonstrated that this model described existing data as accurately as the generalized matching law. In fact, only at very extreme reinforcer ratios do the two models make noticeably different predictions. Davison and Jenkins argued that their model has advantages over the generalized matching law because the d_r parameter was conceptually easier to understand than the a parameter of the generalized matching law, and that it made more concrete predictions as to the types of experimental manipulation that should produce systematic parameter changes. Furthermore, they saw the parameter d_r as being closely related to the stimulus discriminability parameter, d_s, measured by the Davison and Tustin (1978) behavioral model of signal-detection performance (Equations 2 & 3). This allows a more parsimonious treatment of performance in both procedures.

Davison and Jenkins (1985) model of signal-detection performance simply replaces the generalized matching law (Equation 2) part of the Davison and Tustin (1978) model with the Davison and Jenkins expression for concurrent-schedule performance (Equation 4). Hence, following an S_1 presentation:

$$\frac{B_w}{B_x} = c \cdot d_s\left(\frac{d_r \cdot R_w + R_z}{d_r \cdot R_z + R_w}\right), \tag{5}$$

and following an S_2 presentation:

$$\frac{B_y}{B_z} = c \cdot \frac{1}{d_s}\left(\frac{d_r \cdot R_w + R_z}{d_r \cdot R_z + R_w}\right), \tag{6}$$

where all variables, subscripts, and parameters are as shown earlier. As in the Davison and Tustin (1978) model when d_s is 1.0 (i.e., no discriminability between S_1 and S_2), these equations simplify to equations for concurrent schedule performance.

However, Davison and Jenkins (1985) overlooked a major logical flaw in this model. Equations 5 and 6 also predict that the value of d_r has no effect on the value of d_s. Even when d_r equals 1, behavior should still be biased toward the "correct" response alternative following each stimulus presentation. This is not a reasonable prediction. If the subject cannot discriminate between the response-reinforcer contingencies during the choice phase of the signal-detection procedure, common sense dictates that subjects should respond indifferently between the alternatives regardless of the discriminability between the stimuli.

To overcome this problem, a new behavioral model of signal-detection performance is presented in this chapter, similar in approach to that proposed by Davison and Jenkins (1985). Following an S_1 presentation, this new model can be written:

$$\frac{B_w}{B_x} = c\left(\frac{d_s \cdot d_r \cdot R_w + R_z}{d_s \cdot R_w + d_r \cdot R_z}\right), \tag{7}$$

and following an S_2:

$$\frac{B_y}{B_z} = c\left(\frac{d_s \cdot R_z + d_r \cdot R_w}{d_s \cdot d_r \cdot R_z + R_w}\right), \tag{8}$$

where all variables, subscripts, and parameters continue the same. In this model, both R_w and R_z reinforcers influence behavior in each of the four cells. The extent to which a particular reinforcer influences behavior in a particular cell is determined by simple combinations of the two discriminability terms. For example, behavior in the B_w cell is influenced by R_w reinforcers when the subject correctly discriminates the stimulus presentation and the response-reinforcer contingency, and also by R_z reinforcers when the subject incorrectly discriminates the stimulus presentation and incorrectly discriminates the response-reinforcer contingency (Equation 7). Behavior in the B_x cell is influenced by R_w reinforcers when the subject correctly discriminates the stimulus presentation, but incorrectly discriminates the response-reinforcer contingency. It is further influenced by R_z reinforcers when the subject incorrectly discriminates the stimulus presentation but correctly discriminates the response-reinforcer contingency (Equation 7). Equation 8 describes a similar relationship for the B_y and B_z cells.

Like the Davison and Jenkins (1985) model, when d_s equals 1.0, Equations 7 and 8 reduce to the model of concurrent-schedule performance given by Equation 4. However, when d_r equals 1.0, Equations 7 and 8 predict equal responding to B_w and B_x, and to B_y and B_z, respectively. Thus the new model overcomes the logical problems of the Davison and Jenkins (1985) model. Furthermore, it makes testable predictions at odds with the Davison and Tustin (1978) and Davison and Jenkins models. The new model predicts that the effects of varying the reinforcer ratio should decrease as stimulus discriminability increases, whereas the earlier models have maintained an independence between these two types of effect. While data exist showing that these effects are independent (McCarthy & Davison, 1980), other studies have produced more ambiguous results (McCarthy & Davison, 1984). Indeed, this very interaction appears to characterize performance in situations where a number of different stimuli are used as sample stimuli (Davison & McCarthy, 1987).

THE PRESENT EXPERIMENT

The present experiment (Alsop, 1988) investigated the relation between the measure of stimulus discriminability (d_s in Equations 2, et seq.) obtained from a signal-detection procedure, and the measure of response-reinforcer contingency discriminability (d_r in Equation 4, et seq.) obtained from a switching-key concurrent-schedule procedure, when similar differences in stimulus disparity were arranged. It also provided a systematic set of signal-detection conditions varying both stimulus discriminability and the reinforcer ratio against which the three models of signal-detection performance (Davison & Tustin, 1978; Davison & Jenkins, 1985; and the new model) could be compared.

Six pigeons were trained on a number of discrete-trial matching-to-sample conditions where the stimuli to be discriminated were two intensities of white light. The reinforcer ratio (R_w/R_z) for the two types of correct response (B_w & B_z) were varied across conditions, but the stimulus presentation probability was held constant at 0.5. The pigeons were also trained on a number of free-operant switching-key concurrent schedules. The same two intensities of white light used in the signal-detection conditions were also arranged as the stimuli associated with each of the VI schedules available on the main key of the concurrent schedule. The ratio of reinforcers obtained on the two schedules (R_1/R_2) were varied across conditions and generally corresponded to the ratios arranged in the signal-detection procedure (R_w/R_z).

This entire procedure was repeated four more times, each time with a different pair of light intensities as the stimuli. This provided data from five sets of concurrent-schedule conditions and from five sets of signal-detection conditions, matched for discriminative stimuli. No direct physical measure of the light intensities were obtained, but the five pairs were ranked in terms of physical disparity by measures taken from a light-sensitive resistor which could be fastened across the face of the key. This ranking is shown in Table 2.1, with the sequence of experimental conditions and the arranged reinforcer ratios in each condition. For both types of procedure the reinforcers were arranged interdependently, in the manner of Stubbs and Pliskoff (1969), and the arranged overall reinforcer rate was always two per minute. The concurrent schedule used a 3-s changeover delay. It differed slightly from the usual switching-key concurrent schedule in that, following each reinforcer, the schedule available on the main key was randomly selected. The subject was free to switch immediately. This was designed to prevent any win-stay, lose-shift strategy developing at a low level of discriminability. All the results presented here were calculated from the mean data across subjects and the parameter estimates were calculated using an iterative curve-fitting computer program. The individual data are given in Alsop (1988).

CONCURRENT-SCHEDULE RESULTS

The results from the five sets of conditions using the switching-key concurrent schedule (A to E) were analyzed using the generalized matching law (Equation 1) and the Davison and Jenkins (1985) model of concurrent

TABLE 2.1
The Sequence of Experimental Conditions[1]

Set of Conditions	Arranged Ratio of Reinforcers (S1:S2)					Rank Stimulus Difference
	8:1	4:1	1:1	1:4	1:8	
CONC A	2	4	5	3	1	1
SDT A	33	8	7, 6*		32	
CONC B	10		11		9	2
SDT B	12		14		13	
SDT C	15		20		16	4
CONC C	17		19		18	
SDT D	21		23		22	5
CONC D	24		26		25	
SDT E	29		27		28	3
CONC E	30		31			

[1]The ranking of the five sets (A to E) of stimuli used in the concurrent schedule conditions (CONC) and signal-detection conditions (SDT) is shown, as is the arranged reinforcer ratio in each condition. During Condition 6* an extra light was added behind the key on S1 presentations. When subjects showed good discrimination of S1 and S2 this was removed and Condition 7 began.

schedule performance (Equation 4). Table 2.2 shows the estimates of sensitivity (a in equation 1) from the generalized matching law fits, and the estimates of log d_r from the Davison and Jenkins model for each set of conditions. The order of the sets of conditions, using either of these parameters, was identical to that obtained from the initial ranking using physical disparity.

Miller et al. (1980) obtained a values of 0.17 when the same stimulus was used to signal both concurrent schedules, a result Davison and Jenkins (1985) suggested was due to the subjects' adopting a win-stay, lose-shift strategy. Randomly ($p = 0.5$) selecting which schedule was available on the main key following each reinforcer prevented the subjects in the present experiment from also adopting such a strategy. In Set A, which arranged identical stimuli as S_1 and S_2, the estimates of both the a value and log d_r value were zero (Table 2.2). The maximum value of a obtained in the present experiment was only 0.6 (Set D), compared with the values greater than 0.9 reported by Miller et al. (1980). However, the results from the signal-detection part of the present experiment will indicate that even more discriminable stimuli than those used in Set D could be arranged, in which case even greater concurrent schedule a values or d_r values should have been obtained.

SIGNAL-DETECTION RESULTS

The data from each set of signal-detection conditions (A to E) were analyzed, using the Davison and Tustin (1978) model (Equations 2 & 3), the Davison and Jenkins (1985) model (Equations 5 & 6), and the new model (Equations 7 & 8). The estimates of d_s and a from the Davison and Tustin analysis are shown under Analysis 1 in Table 2.3 , the estimates of d_s and d_r from the Davison and Jenkins analysis are shown under Analysis 1 in

TABLE 2.2
Results of Data Analyses from the 5 Sets of Concurrent-schedule Conditions[1]

	Equation 1			Equation 2		
	a	log c	Av. Dev	log d$_r$	loc c	Av. Dev.
Set A	0.00	− 0.01	.04	0.00	− 0.01	.04
Set B	0.27	0.02	.06	0.31	0.02	.06
Set E	0.27	0.03	.01	0.33	0.03	.01
Set C	0.47	0.01	.00	0.57	0.02	.01
Set D	0.60	− 0.02	.03	0.75	− 0.01	.03

[1]The generalized matching law (Equation 1) and the Davison and Jenkins (1985) model of concurrent-schedule performance (Equation 4) were used.

TABLE 2.3
Results of 3 Analyses Conducted on the Data from the 5 sets of
Signal-detection Conditions[1]

	Analysis 1			Analysis 2	Analysis 3	
	$\log d_s$	a	Av. dev	$\log d_s$	$\log d_s$	Av. dev
Set A	0.00	1.00	.05	0.00	0.00	.14
Set B	0.11	0.99	.08	0.13	0.11	.14
Set E	0.28	0.84	.04	0.28	0.28	.04
Set C	0.59	0.73	.14	0.58	0.59	.14
Set D	1.02	0.60	.12	1.02	1.02	.20
				$a = 0.83$	$a = 0.83$	
				Av. dev = .14		

[1]The Davison and Tustin (1978) model of signal detection performance (Equations 2 & 3). A description of the analyses appears in the text.

Table 2.4, and the estimates d_s and d_r from the new model are shown under Analysis 1 of Table 2.5. The logarithm (base 10) of the d_s and d_r parameters are shown, as this provides a more useful scale for subsequent figures. For all three analyses, ordering the sets of conditions using the stimulus discriminability estimates (d_s) gives the same order as the ranking provided in Table 2.1. For the Davison and Tustin analysis, the log d_s estimates range from no discriminability (log d_s = 0, set A) to a log d_s of 1.02 (Set D). For the Davison and Jenkins analysis, the log d_s estimates ranged from 0 (Set A) to 0.89 (Set D). For the new model analysis, the log d_s estimates ranged from 0 (Set A) to 1.44 (Set D).

However, there were also systematic changes in the estimates of log d_r from the Davison and Jenkins (1985) and a from the Davison and Tustin (1978) model across the sets of conditions. As the stimulus discriminability

TABLE 2.4
Results of 3 Analyses Conducted on Data from the 5 Sets of
Signal-detection Conditions[1]

	Analysis 1			Analysis 2	Analysis 3	
	$\log d_s$	$\log d_r$	Av. dev	$\log d_s$	$\log d_s$	Av. dev
Set A	0.00	2.61	.02	0.00	0.00	.03
Set B	0.16	1.99	.03	0.13	0.13	.03
Set E	0.25	1.13	.02	0.27	0.26	.02
Set C	0.61	0.98	.03	0.66	0.69	.03
Set D	0.89	0.60	.03	1.17	1.18	.04
				$\log d_r = 1.27$	$\log d_r = 1.27$	
				Av. dev = .04		

[1]The Davison and Jenkins (1985) model of signal-detection performance (Equations 5 & 6) were used. A description of the analyses appears in the text.

TABLE 2.5
The Results of 3 Analyses Conducted on the Data from the 5 Sets of Signal-detection Conditions Using the New Model[1]

	Analysis 1			Analysis 2	Analysis 3	
	$log\ d_s$	$log\ d_r$	Av. dev	$log\ d_s$	$log\ d_s$	Av. dev
Set A	0.00	2.74	.02	0.00	0.00	.03
Set B	0.17	1.81	.03	0.17	0.17	.03
Set E	0.32	1.17	.02	0.32	0.31	.03
Set C	0.83	1.40	.04	0.81	0.83	.04
Set D	1.44	1.21	.03	1.41	1.41	.03
				$log\ d_r = 1.35$	$log\ d_r = 1.35$	
				Av. dev = .04		

[1]A description of the analyses appears in the text. See Equations 7 & 8.

increased, these estimates of the effect of varying the obtained reinforcer ratio decreased (Tables 2.3 & 2.4). The data from individual subjects also showed this trend. This result, while predicted by the new model, must be reconciled with some previous data. McCarthy and Davison (1980) found no effect of stimulus discriminability on a. However, they used only two different levels of stimulus discriminability, one with a mean log d_s across subjects of 0.4, and the other of 1.5. The present experiment uses more levels of stimulus discriminability, some much lower than 0.4, ranging from 0.0 to approximately 1.0. Also, with the benefit of hindsight, the a values they reported were rather low (mean a values of 0.48 and 0.5 respectively), when compared with the range of typical concurrent schedule a values of 0.7 to 0.9. The lowest a value obtained in the five sets of conditions analyzed in the present experiment was 0.6 (Table 2.3, Set D).

The new model does not appear to show this interaction, or at least not to the same extent. The parameter estimates of log d_r obtained when this new model was fitted to the data from the present experiment are shown in Table 2.5 (Analysis 1). For comparison, the log d_r values obtained for each stimuli pair are plotted as a function of the corresponding log d_s value for both the new model and the Davison and Jenkins model in Fig. 2.2. The covariation of the two parameters was less pronounced for the new model. For the Davison and Jenkins parameter estimates the trend was monotonic with the lowest value of log d_r (0.6) obtained in Set D. For the new model the lowest value occurred at Set E with a log d_r value of 1.17. While there was still a much larger parameter estimate of log d_r for Set A when analyzed using the new model, it should be noted that further increases in a log d_r parameter past a value of approximately 1.5 predict quite small differences in behavior allocation.

The presence or absence of an interaction between stimulus and reinforcer parameters is of some concern. One of the attractive features of the

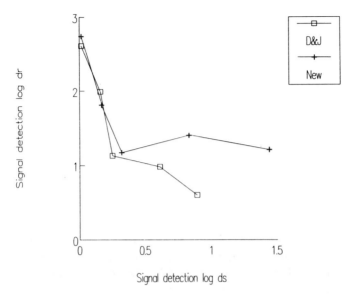

FIG. 2.2   The estimates of response-reinforcer contingency discriminability (log d_r) plotted as a function of the corresponding estimates of stimulus discriminability (log d_s) calculated using the Davison and Jenkins (1985) model (Equations 5 & 6) and the new model (Equations 7 & 8) for each of the five sets of signal-detection conditions.

Davison and Tustin (1978) model (Equations 2 & 3), and, by association, the Davison and Jenkins (1985) model (Equations 5 & 6), has been the independence of the effects of reinforcers and the effects of stimulus discriminability. Without this independence, these models require that two free parameters vary in order to accommodate changes in one experimental variable. Such an interaction decreases the utility of the models and, more generally, parameter invariance should be one of the goals of the quantitative analysis of behavior (Nevin, 1984).

Therefore, two further analyses were conducted to assess the effects of these changes in d_r and a. These analyses considered the usefulness of each of the models if a constant value of d_r or a was assumed.

Analysis 2

In Analysis 2, the model was fitted to the data from all five sets of conditions at the same time. Each set of conditions had a free parameter to measure d_s, but was constrained to only one free parameter across all the sets to measure d_r. This calculated a best overall d_r. For the Davison and Tustin (1978) model (Table 2.3), the best overall a value across the five sets was 0.83, and the estimates of log d_s were similar to those obtained when both parameters were allowed to vary for each set of conditions in Analysis 1. For the Davison and Jenkins (1985) model (Table 2.4), the best overall log d_r value was 1.27. However, the parameter estimates for log d_s were noticeably different for Set D and, to some extent, for Set C. The new model (Table 2.5) gave a log d_r value of 1.35 with little change to the parameter estimates of d_s. For each model the average deviation obtained for this analysis was within the range obtained in Analysis 1.

Analysis 3

In Analysis 3, each model was fitted to one set of conditions at a time, but d_r was fixed to the value obtained from Analysis 2. Fitting the Davison and Tustin (1978) model (Table 2.3) with the fixed a parameter of 0.83 produced some relatively poor fits to the data from some sets of conditions, as shown by the increases in the value of the average deviation compared with those obtained in Analysis 1. While the fits for the Davison and Jenkins (1985) model (Table 2.4) had similar average deviations to those obtained in Analysis 1, the parameter estimates of log d_s had changed for Sets C and D to accommodate the constant d_r parameter. In contrast to these two models, when the new model assumed a constant value of d_r there was little change in either the estimates of log d_s or the average deviations from those obtained in Analysis 1 (Table 2.5).

The new model appears to be a better descriptor of signal detection performance than either the Davison and Tustin (1978) or the Davison and Jenkins (1985) models for a variety of reasons. First, it overcomes the logical problems of the Davison and Jenkins (1985) model when d_r equals 1.0. Second, the parameter measuring the effects of the reinforcers in the choice phase (d_r) is invariant with changes in stimulus discriminability, or at least this can be assumed with little loss in terms of either goodness-of-fit or accuracy of parameter estimation. Third, the three models form a hierarchy of decreasing conceptual complexity. The Davison and Jenkins model is less complex than the Davison and Tustin model in that both stimuli effects and reinforcer effects in the former model can be viewed as measuring a similar type of process (i.e., discriminability), and they use a similar metric. The new model simplifies the Davison and Jenkins model even further as, in the new model, the action of these parameters is treated in a consistent manner (Equations 7 & 8). Additionally, Davison (this volume) proposed an identical signal-detection model to account for performance in procedures using more than two discriminative stimuli. He found that neither the Davison and Tustin model nor the Davison and Jenkins model could readily be extended to deal with this more complex situation.

It remains to compare each of the estimates of stimulus discriminability (log d_s) obtained when a pair of stimuli was used in the signal-detection procedure with the corresponding estimate of response-reinforcer contingency (log d_r) obtained when the same pair of stimuli was used to define the two schedules in the concurrent-schedule procedure. This relation is shown in Fig 2.3, where the signal-detection log d_s estimates calculated using the new model (Analysis 1, Table 2.5) have been plotted against the corresponding concurrent-schedule log d_r values (Table 2.2). Fig. 2.3 shows a smooth, orderly relation between these two parameters. Typical "matching" performance (e.g., Baum, 1979) does not suddenly appear at some minimum level of discriminability. The continued increase in the log d_r parameter at quite high levels of stimulus discriminability (i.e., Set C to Set D) is consistent with the type of underlying process implicit to a discrimination-based account of concurrent-schedule performance.

However, the function is not linear, and certainly does not show a one-to-one relationship between the parameter estimates obtained from these two procedures. Rather, the function was concave down (Fig. 2.3). Using the Davison and Jenkins (1985) analysis produces a similar pattern. The larger increase from Set A to Set B for the concurrent schedule d_r estimates than for the signal-detection d_s estimates was unexpected. This may be due to some procedural difference. For example, in the signal-detection procedure, the presentations of stimuli are separated by at least 3 seconds. However, in the switching-key concurrent schedule the subject has

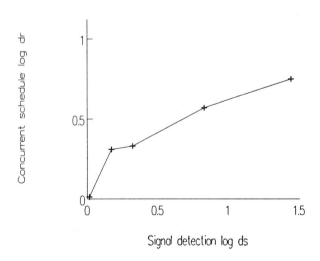

FIG. 2.3   The estimates of response-reinforcer contingency discriminability (log d_r) calculated from the sets of concurrent-schedule conditions plotted against the estimates of stimulus discriminability (log d_s) calculated from the sets of signal-detection conditions.

the opportunity to switch between the stimuli signaling the two schedules of reinforcement, providing relatively immediate comparison of the two stimuli. Furthermore, in the concurrent schedule, choices are taking place in the continuous presence of the sample stimulus, whereas in the signal-detection procedure each choice is made after the stimulus is removed. Previous research suggests this procedural difference may lead to differences in discriminability; for example, McCarthy, Davison, and Jenkins (1982) demonstrated that stimulus discriminability in a signal-detection paradigm was greater when the sample stimuli were present during the choice phase, than if they were removed during the choice phase.

SUMMARY

The behavioral model of signal detection presented in this chapter (Equations 7 & 8) offers a simple description where the effects of stimuli and reinforcers interact to affect performance in a signal-detection task. This model has empirical, conceptual, and logical advantages over the behavioral models of signal detection proposed by Davison and Tustin (1978) and by Davison and Jenkins (1985). Furthermore, it can logically be extended to account for performance in signal-detection procedures with reinforcement for errors, in free-operant detection procedures, in multiple schedules of reinforcement, and in single schedules of reinforcement (see Davison & Jenkins, 1985). Davison demonstrates its development and applicability in the area of complex stimulus control in the next chapter.

The model of concurrent-schedule performance incorporating the concept of response-reinforcer contingency discriminability (Equation 4) was proposed by Davison and Jenkins (1985) as an alternative to the generalized matching law (Equation 1). As analytical tools, the two models perform equally well. However, the model of signal-detection performance adopted in this chapter (Equations 7 & 8) demands Equation 4 as the model of concurrent schedule performance. Equations 7 and 8 cannot reduce to the generalized matching law. Therefore, the proposed integration of signal-detection and concurrent-schedule models becomes a necessity.

Caveat

Since these data were presented at Harvard in 1987, two further sets of experimental conditions have been conducted. Both arranged pairs of light intensities more disparate than those in Set D. The next most disparate pair of stimuli (mean log d_s = 1.28, Davison and Tustin analysis) provided data consistent with those results presented in this chapter. Analysis of the signal-detection performance typically showed a further decrease in the effects of changes in the reinforcer ratio with this increase in stimulus discriminability; that is, a mean a value of 0.5 from the generalized matching law analysis and a mean log d_r or 0.62 from the Davison and Jenkins (1985) analysis. The new model did not show this decrease in the parameter measuring the effects of changes in the reinforcer ratio giving a mean log d_r of 1.61.

The data from the most disparate pair of stimuli (mean log d_r = 1.66, Davison and Tustin analysis) are not easily reconciled with the results from the other sets of conditions. While stimulus discriminability increased, all subjects' behavior showed a marked increase in the effects of variation in the reinforcer ratio. The mean a value was 1.22 from the Davison and Tustin analysis, the log d_r was 2.48 from the Davison and Jenkins (1985) analysis, and the log d_r was 3.23 from the new model. Fig. 2.4 shows the estimates of log d_r plotted as a function of the estimates of log d_s from the new model analysis with the data from all seven sets of signal-detection conditions. The crosses (Fig. 2.4) show the results for all six subjects. The relation between these estimates is U-shaped; that is, higher estimates of log

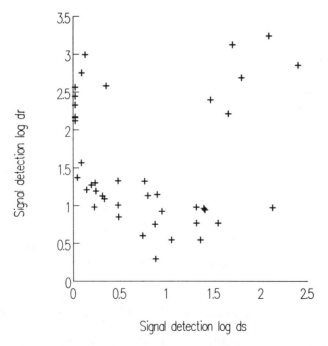

FIG. 2.4   The estimates of response-reinforcer contingency discriminability (log d_r) plotted as a function of the corresponding estimates of stimulus discriminability (log d_s) calculated using the new model (Equations 7 & 8) for each of the five sets of signal-detection conditions for each subject (pluses) and for the data from McCarthy and Davison (1984) (squares).

d_r are obtained when measured stimulus discriminability is very low or very high. A reanalysis of the results from the controlled procedure of McCarthy and Davison (1984) show a similar pattern. Individual subjects' parameter estimates from their study are plotted in Fig. 2.4 with open squares.

None of the models presented in this chapter can account for these results. The nonmonotonic nature of the relationship between the effects of stimuli and the effects of reinforcers suggested by the last set of conditions creates difficulty for any model. I must conclude that the new model appears to be a good descriptor of performance over a wide range of stimulus disparities in that log d_r is roughly invariant with changes in log d_s, but when stimulus disparity is extremely large, and, perhaps, very small, this constancy is not maintained. While it is tempting to invoke some secondary process (e.g., attention) to explain these boundary effects, at present such an invocation would be more speculation than explanation.

ACKNOWLEDGMENTS

I wish to thank Michael Davison for his assistance with this chapter. The financial support provided by the University Grants Committee, by way of equipment grants to Davison and my postgraduate scholarship, is gratefully acknowledged. Thanks also to the staff and students of the operant lab, especially Dianne McCarthy and Douglas Elliffe, for helping to run the experiments and for many interesting discussions.

REFERENCES

Alsop, B. (1988). *Detection and choice.* Unpublished doctoral dissertation, University of Auckland.

Baum, W. M. (1974). On two types of deviation from the matching law: Bias and undermatching. *Journal of the Experimental Analysis of Behavior, 22,* 231–242.

Baum, W. M. (1979). Matching, undermatching, and overmatching in studies of choice. *Journal of the Experimental Analysis of Behavior, 32,* 269–281.

Davison, M., & Jenkins, P. E. (1985). Stimulus discriminability, contingency discriminability, and schedule performance. *Animal Learning & Behavior, 13,* 77–84.

Davison, M., & McCarthy, D. (1980). Reinforcement for errors in a signal-detection procedure. *Journal of the Experimental Analysis of Behavior, 34,* 35–47.

Davison, M., & McCarthy, D. (1987). The interaction of stimulus and reinforcer control in complex temporal discriminations. *Journal of the Experimental Analysis of Behavior, 39,* 331–336.

Davison, M. C., & Tustin, R. D. (1978). On the relation between the generalised matching law and signal detection theory. *Journal of the Experimental Analysis of Behavior, 29,* 331–336.

Green, D. M., & Swets, J. A. (1974). *Signal-detection theory and psychophysics.* New York: Wiley.

McCarthy, D., & Davison, M. (1980). Independence of sensitivity to relative reinforcement rate and discriminability in signal detection. *Journal of the Experimental Analysis of Behavior, 34,* 273–284.

McCarthy, D., & Davison, M. (1982). Independence of stimulus discriminability from absolute rate of reinforcement in a signal-detection procedure. *Journal of the Experimental Analysis of Behavior, 37,* 371-382.

McCarthy, D., & Davison, M. (1984). Isobias and alloiobias functions in animal psychophysics. *Journal of Experimental Psychology: Animal Behavior Processes, 10,* 390-409.

McCarthy, D.,, Davison, M., & Jenkins, P.E. (1982). Stimulus discriminability in free-operant and discrete-trial detection procedures. *Journal of the Experimental Analysis of Behavior, 37,* 199-215.

Miller, J. T., Saunders, S. S., & Bourland, G. (1980). The role of stimulus disparity in concurrently available reinforcement schedules. *Animal Learning and Behavior, 8,* 635-641.

Nevin, J. A. (1984). Quantitative analysis. *Journal of the Experimental Analysis of Behavior, 42,* 421-434.

Stubbs, D. A., & Pliskoff, S. S. (1969). Concurrent responding with fixed relative rate of reinforcement. *Journal of the Experimental Analysis of Behavior, 12,* 887-895.

Nevin, J. A., Jenkins, P., Whittaker, S. G., & Yarensky, P. (1977). *Signal detection and matching.* Paper presented at the meeting of the Psychonomic Society, Washington. DC.

Wearden, J. H., & Burgess, I. S. (1982). Matching since Baum (1979). *Journal of the Experimental Analysis of Behavior, 33,* 339-348.

3

Stimulus Discriminability, Contingency Discriminability, and Complex Stimulus Control

Michael C. Davison
University of Auckland, New Zealand

In the development of the Experimental Analysis of Behavior, a great deal of effort has been expended on two historically separate questions. One question has been how the consequences of behavior affect subsequent behavior—the study of reinforcement control. The other has been how antecedent stimuli that signal differing contingencies affect behavior—the study of stimulus control. Studies of reinforcer control have generally provided either no explicit antecedent stimuli, or have provided antecedent stimuli that are assumed to be highly distinctive, and have studied parametric variations in reinforcer frequencies. Studies of stimulus control have generally arranged maximally differing reinforcer conditions (e.g., multiple variable-interval extinction) and tested the control by small differences in exteroceptive stimuli. While this characterization by no means embraces all the research literature in these areas, it is sufficiently general to highlight the absence of research specifically designed to quantify the joint effects of stimulus and reinforcer control on behavior.

Within the reinforcer-control literature, one area of endeavor has been the search for an empirical description of the ways in which changing reinforcer parameters (such as rates, delays, and amounts) affect the relative allocation of behavior between two response alternatives. The empirically based generalized matching law (Baum, 1974), was found to be a good description of relative behavior allocation in many situations, and it provided a reasonably wide domain of parameter invariance. The relation is written:

$$\frac{B_1}{B_2} = c \left(\frac{R_1}{R_2}\right)^a ,$$

(1)

where B and R denote behavior and reinforcer frequencies and the subscripts denote the two alternatives. The parameter a is called sensitivity to reinforcement (Lobb & Davison, 1975) and measures the degree to which changes in response–allocation ratios follow changes in obtained reinforcer ratios. The parameter c is called bias, and it measures a proportional preference for one alternative over the other caused by constant and unequal values of other choice-affecting variables present during the experiment (Baum). Sensitivity appeared reasonably constant over a number of manipulations of theoretically extraneous variables (such as deprivation, overall reinforcer rate, species, and so on). But it is clear now that we are fast reaching the limit of the assumed (and necessary) invariance. Sometimes dual-sensitivity models are required (Davison, 1982; Prelec, 1984); absolute reinforcer magnitude affects sensitivity to reinforcer–magnitude ratios (Davison & Hogsden, 1984; Logue & Chavarro, 1987); absolute reinforcer *rate* affects sensitivity to reinforcer–rate ratios (Davison, 1988); absolute reinforcer rate affects sensitivity to reinforcer–rate ratios (Alsop & Elliffe, 1988); and sensitivity to reinforcer delay ratios is not independent of absolute delay of reinforcement (Davison & Temple, 1973; Logue & Chavarro, 1987; Wardlaw & Davison, 1974; Williams & Fantino, 1978). The bias parameter, measuring a constant proportional preference for one alternative over another, has *seemed* to have a rather larger area of invariance, but logically this cannot be correct. A bias (a nonunit value of c) simply results from a constant, unequal, pair of choice-affecting variables (e.g., different reinforcer durations) influencing behavior with a particular sensitivity. If that sensitivity is not constant (e.g., with changes in reinforcer rate), then bias cannot be constant.

The experiment that most strongly brought home the circumscribed generality of the generalized matching law was reported by Miller, Saunders, and Bourland (1980). They showed that sensitivity to reinforcer frequencies in concurrent VI VI performance was not invariant with changes in the physical stimuli signaling the response alternatives. While, in retrospect, no one would have expected such an invariance, we really had not troubled ourselves with such possibilities. The Experimental Analysis of Behavior has always been more concerned with looking for generalities, rather than in finding differences. This is an excellent strategy if, and only if, we refrain from deifying the small generalities that we discover, and continually remind ourselves that a discovered invariance must not be allowed to constrain a field of endeavor. In my view, the generalized matching law has never been a law, only an interesting possibility. Because of the failures of parameter invariance discussed herein, it is clearly time to see whether we can do better. When Miller et al. reported their research, we had no quantitative model for linking discriminative-stimulus effects to the value of sensitivity. Their result offered two options: (1) to quantify the relation between sensitivity and stimulus difference, or (2) to conceive of a quantitative model, different from generalized matching, which can make such a result understandable. I am glad that we did not choose the former option and deify sensitivity still further.

Stimulus-control research had shown a notable lack of effective quantification, and research in this area seems clearly to be declining in popularity. Because of the obvious problems in interpreting the transition measures obtained from traditional generalization testing in Extinction, many of us had hoped to see an increase in the use of "steady-state" or "maintained" generalization procedures. A reasonable number of such experiments has been reported, and some very effective use has been made of such methods. Some quantitative models have been suggested (e.g., Blough, 1975), but none of these models seems to hold sway currently.

A second approach to the quantification of stimulus control has developed from the methods of signal-detection research. Signal-detection theory attempted to make use of properties of 2-response by 2-stimulus matrices to devise independent measures of *response bias* (the tendency of the subject, often under differential reinforcement conditions, to emit relatively more of one of the available responses) and *discriminability,* a measure of how well the subject is telling the difference between stimuli. While a great deal of research had explored the properties of detection-theory measures of discriminability, and has generally found them satisfactory, signal-detection theory failed to deal effectively with response bias. The problem here is that normative SDT has tried to define ideal ways in which the subjects might behave (e.g., maximizing percentage correct, or the probability of reinforcement, and so on). Empirical results have generally shown that the subjects were not doing any of these rational things, or at least not anything simple and rational. Further, it has been shown that SDT bias measures are not independent of SDT discriminability measures (McCarthy & Davison, 1984).

Because of the failure of the bias aspect of SDT, and the success of the empirical matching law, it occurred to a number of researchers that the matching law, or the generalized matching law, might provide a reasonable bias function for SDT. Nevin (1969) reviewed Green and Swets's book on signal detection and reported some matching-type analyses of signal-detection data. Then, Nevin, Jenkins, Whittaker, and Yarensky (1977) presented a strict-matching model of detection data at a conference (see also Nevin, Jenkins, Whittaker, & Yarensky, 1982), and Davison and Tustin (1978) published a generalized-matching model for signal detection. From Davison and Tustin's (more general) model, the generalized matching law provided two algebraically independent measures of response bias (log B) and discriminability (log d). Following the matrix of events in Fig. 3.1, the model was:

For performance following the presentation of S_1:

$$\frac{B_w}{B_x} = c \cdot d \cdot \left(\frac{R_w}{R_z}\right)^a , \tag{2}$$

and following the presentation of S_2:

$$\frac{B_y}{B_z} = \frac{c}{d} \cdot \left(\frac{R_w}{R_z}\right)^a . \tag{3}$$

The parameter a is sensitivity to reinforcement, c is bias (often referred to as *inherent bias*), and d is termed *discriminability* and measures the degree to which the subject discriminates the signaling stimuli independent of the degree of bias caused by differences in reinforcer frequencies, magnitudes, and so on, for the two responses, *B1* and *B2*. Because d is a ratio measure (ranging from 1 to ∞), we shall often report the measure log $d,$ which we also term discriminability.

Equations 2 and 3 seemed to have all the correct properties, and were supported by much subsequent research. They can be multiplied to give a bias function independent of $d,$ and divided to give a stimulus function which is independent of both reinforcer effects and inherent bias (c). The equations were extended to reinforcers-for-errors procedures, reinforcer amount variation, and so on. The approach seemed entirely satisfactory, and McCarthy and I started to foreshadow a new golden era of stimulus-control research.

Research reported subsequent to Davison and Tustin's (1978) paper have forced a reformulation of their signal-detection model. Since the model was dependent on the generalized matching law to describe the biasing effects of reinforcers, if the generalized matching law failed, so would the detection model. I have already discussed some empirical problems with the generalized matching law. There are logical problems, too. The research reported

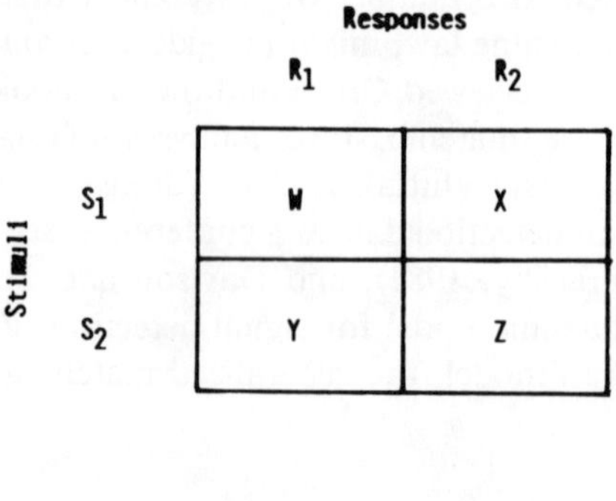

Responses

	R_1	R_2
S_1	W	X
S_2	Y	Z

Stimuli

Fig. 3.1   The matrix of events in a 2-stimulus, 2-response signal-detection procedure.

by Miller et al. (1978) showed that the putative constant sensitivity to reinforcement (*a* in Equation 1) was not constant; though, more confusingly, the generalized matching law does not unambiguously imply whether any operations (and if so, what operations) should affect sensitivity to reinforcement. Further, there seemed to be logical problems with the Davison–Tustin model as applied to signal-detection performances. For instance, why was the sensitivity-to-reinforcement measure a different type of measure from the measure of discriminability when, according to the model, both reinforcers and stimuli had similar effects on behavior? These difficulties seem to require a new model, one in which the sensitivity-type parameter clearly implied the operations of which it was a function. From these considerations, while previously we had considered our research as offering a model of bias to signal-detection theory, we now began to ask whether the notions of discriminability developed by SDT could help us with the understanding of reinforcer effects.

The $d_s - d_r$ model offered by Davison and Jenkins (1985) was developed in response to these concerns. The model is:

$$\ln S_1: \frac{B_w}{B_x} = c\, d_s \left(\frac{d_r R_w + R_z}{d_r R_z + R_w}\right),$$

(4)

$$\text{and in } S_2: \frac{B_y}{B_z} = \frac{c}{d_s}\left(\frac{d_r R_w + R_z}{d_r R_z + R_w}\right).$$

(5)

In this model, a contingency-discriminability model replaces the generalized matching law, so effectively *a* is replaced by d_r, named contingency discriminability. This is a similar measure, both logically and mathematically, to d_s. It measures how well the subject is telling the obtained response-reinforcer contingencies apart. Davison and Jenkins showed how this model could be used to describe many aspects of schedule-controlled behavior, both with and without discriminative control. Again, the model appeared very satisfactory (Davison & Jenkins), and logically such a model, in which discriminative stimuli and reinforcers are seen to act on behavior in similar ways, appears more parsimonious.

The research that I will discuss here began as an attempt to generalize the signal-detection models to procedures in which more than just two stimuli signaled the two response alternatives. The aim was to collect sufficient data to allow us to generalize from the 2-stimulus 2-response to the *n*-stimulus 2-response case. We did three experiments, and I shall report here brief analyses of all three. The data from both the temporal-discrimination and the color discrimination experiments have already been published (Davison & McCarthy, 1987, 1989, respectively).

3 EXPERIMENTS

Experiment 1: Color Discrimination

In this experiment (Davison & McCarthy, 1989), we could arrange up to eight color stimuli set 5 nm apart using a monochromator. We used what might be called a steady-state signal-detection procedure, or a multiple-stimulus 2-response detection procedure. Pigeons maintained at 85% body weight were used. Each nanometer value was presented equally often. A peck on the center key, where the color patch was presented, turned the color patch off, and illuminated the two side keys white. Over the major part of the experiment, if the stimulus had been in the range 559–574 nm, a right-key peck was occasionally reinforced, and if it had been in the range 579–594 nm a left-key response was occasionally reinforced. Using a dependent-scheduling procedure, we varied the reinforcer frequencies for the two responses. In other conditions, which also contribute to the present data set, we varied the number of stimuli comprising each set.

The 19 experimental conditions available when this was written provided in total 98 independent left-right response-ratio measures in the presence of the discrete colors comprising the stimulus sets.

Fig. 3.2 shows the probability of emitting a right-key response as a

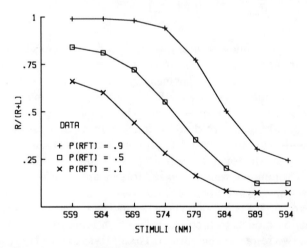

Fig. 3.2 Experiment 1. The relative frequency of emitting a right-key response as a function of the color (nanometers) displayed on the center key. The data for three probabilities of right-key reinforcers are shown. Right-key responses could be reinforced if the color was 574 nm or less, and left-key responses could be reinforced if the color was 579 nm or greater.

function of the stimulus presented for three of the eight conditions in which four colors made up each of the two stimulus sets. Only the two extreme right-reinforcer probability conditions and the equal reinforcer-probability condition are shown. We had clear control by the color value, with the functions changing monotonically.

Fig.3.3 shows some of the data obtained when four colors comprised each stimulus set and the reinforcer ratio for left-versus right-key responses was varied. The data have been plotted on log-ratio coordinates as is appropriate for the Davison–Tustin model. For many of the color values, the data often did not appear to be linear on these axes, as required by the Davison–Tustin (1978) model. While they could be forced into linear functions, the clear systematic deviations from these make it clear that the Davison–Tustin model cannot describe these data. The overall slopes of the functions seem to change according to which stimulus we are looking at, but not in any particular way, and certainly not in a manner that is symmetrical with the origin.

Experiments 2 and 3: Temporal Discrimination

Davison and McCarthy (1987) provided two further sets of data in which sets of stimuli were discriminated in a signal-detection task. Davison and McCarthy modeled these data using the Davison–Tustin model, and reported that sensitivity to reinforcement was not independent of discriminability. In Experiments 2 and 3, essentially the same procedure was used as

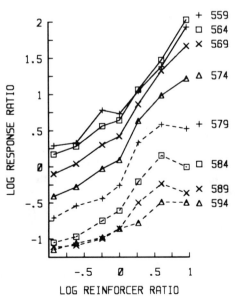

Fig. 3.3 Experiment 1. Log right-key/left-key choice ratios for the eight colors presented on the center key as a function of the log right-key/left-key overall reinforcer ratios obtained. Right-key responses could be reinforced if the color was 574 nm or less, and left-key responses could be reinforced if the color was 579 nm or greater.

in Experiment 1, but the pigeons were required to discriminate 1 stimulus duration (the fixed duration, or FD) from a set of 12 durations (the variable-duration or VD stimulus set). In both Experiments 2 and 3, the set of 12 durations comprised equally frequent presentations of durations from 2.5 to 57.5 s in steps of 5 s. A left-key peck following one of these was occasionally reinforced. In Experiment 2, the fixed duration (after which a right-key peck was occasionally reinforced) was 5 s. In Experiment 3, the fixed duration was 20 s. A probability gate set at 0.5 determined on each trial whether the fixed duration, or one of the set of 12 variable durations, was presented. In both Experiments 2 and 3 we varied the relative frequencies of reinforcers for the two correct responses over eight experimental conditions, providing 104 independent measures of relative frequencies of emitting left and right responses in each discrete temporal stimulus.

Fig. 3.4 shows part of the data plotted on log–ratio coordinates, that is, as appropriate to the Davison–Tustin model. Fig. 3.4 highlights the effects of stimulus discriminability on sensitivity to reinforcement (the slopes of the fitted lines), which are features of the data set that we will hope to reconstitute from an improved model more appropriate for complex detection.

Notice that in both Experiments 2 and 3, sensitivity to relative-reinforcer frequency was greatest at, and around, the FD value, and decreased with increasing physical distance from the FD value. The results, therefore, were rather different from those from the color-discrimination experiment (Fig. 3.5), in which the data were more clearly nonlinear and the general slopes of the functions changed less systematically with changes in discriminability.

3 MODELS

The Davison–Tustin and Davison–Jenkins models are not at all easy to generalize from the 2-stimulus to the n-stimulus detection procedures. In their analysis of the temporal-discrimination data (Experiments 2 and 3), Davison and McCarthy (1987) assumed that the measures R_w and R_z were the total reinforcer rates for the left-and right-key responses. This seems reasonable given that there are no interactions between the performances in the presence of the individual stimuli. But there clearly *are* interactions, and the overall reinforcer ratio affects performance differently in the presence of each stimulus (Fig. 3.4). Further, if performance in the presence of one stimulus is analyzed, and a log d value is obtained, to which pair of stimuli this log d belongs is quite unclear. These problems occur with both the Davison–Tustin (1978) and the Davison–Jenkins (1985) models.

To overcome these problems, we will take the logic and ideas of the

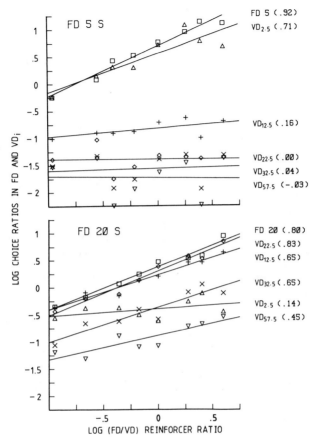

Fig. 3.4   Experiments 2 and 3. Log choice ratios for the FD duration and a selection of durations comprising the VD set as a function of the overall log reinforcer-frequency ratio. The slopes of the straight lines fitted to the data are shown in parentheses.

Davison–Jenkins (1985) model and apply them in a rather more systematic way than did Davison and Jenkins. This approach, in fact, independently provided the same signal-detection model for two stimuli and two responses that Alsop suggested (chap. 2 in this volume). Alsop's reasons for favoring that model are clear and logical. The research reported here adds further support and generality to that model.

As in the Davison–Jenkins (1985) model, the present model starts off with the notion of $d_s - d_r$ space. d_s (stimulus discriminability) and d_r (contingency discriminability) are two dimensions of the Yes–No signal-detection space, and these two dimensions intersect when $d_s = d_r = 1$. The model assumes that each stimulus/response/reinforcer combination arranged in a signal-detection experiment is discriminable from other such

RESPONSES

	B_1	B_2	B_3
	dr_{12}	dr_{23}	
S_1 ds_{12}	$/1$	$/dr_{12}$	$/dr_{13}$
S_2 ds_{23}	$/ds_{12}$	$/ds_{12}/dr_{12}$	$/ds_{12}/dr_{13}$
S_3	$/ds_{13}$	$/ds_{13}/dr_{12}$	$/ds_{13}/dr_{13}$

Fig. 3.5 The operation of part of the Euclidean model in a 3-response, 3-stimulus signal-detection matrix,. Responses are designated by B and stimuli by S, and d_r and d_s are contingency and stimulus discriminability measures respectively. The subscripts refer to rows (or columns) of the matrix. Thus, d_{r23} is the contingency discriminability between the B_2 and B_3 response/reinforcer consequences. The figure shows only the effects that reinforcers for cell B_1 in the presence of S_1 have on the other cells of the matrix. Reinforcers delivered in other cells have distributed effects according to the same principles.

combinations as a function of the joint stimulus and contingency discriminabilities of the two combinations. The greater the joint discriminabilities, the less will a reinforcer delivered for one stimulus/response combination affect performance in the other combination. However, if stimulus discriminability is low, a response reinforced in the presence of that stimulus will lead to the same response being emitted in the other stimulus (a stimulus error). If contingency discriminability is low, a response reinforced in the presence of one stimulus will also increase the emission of the alternative response in the presence of that stimulus (a contingency error). In this way, each combination of antecedent stimuli and the subject's responses can be located in $d_s - d_r$ space, the response set d_r units apart and the stimuli d_s units apart. Let us assume that these dimensions are orthogonal, and that they define a plane. Remember, though, that d_s and d_r are measured on a ratio scale, so distances in $d_s - d_r$ space are multiplicative rather than additive (it will be appropriate, therefore, to report log d_s and log d_r values). Fig. 3.5 shows a matrix for a general 3-stimulus and 3-response detection procedure to help show the working of the model.

In the initial model, I assumed that the effects of a reinforcer in a cell of the matrix on other cells falls with the reciprocal of the ratio-distance between the location of that experimenter-defined stimulus, response, and reinforcer location in $d_s - d_r$ space and the other available cells. Fig. 3.5 shows just one of the nine possible processes that will occur in that example. In this figure, d_{s13} denotes the discriminability between stimuli 1 and 3, and d_{r13} denotes the discriminability between the response-reinforcer contingencies on keys 1 and 3. According to the model, a reinforcer delivered for B_1 in the presence of S_1 has a direct and full effect on responding in that cell. It also has indirect and graded effects on responding in all other cells according to the distance between the location of the reinforcer and each cell. Equally, a reinforcer delivered for B_3 in the presence of S_3 will have similar effects in the other cells. For instance, the additive effect in the cell for B_1 given S_1 will be the effect in cell B_3,S_3 divided by d_{s13} and by d_{r13}. Notice that the model given in Fig. 3.5 does not conserve reinforcers. That is, the apparent sum of reinforcers is greater than the number delivered. This problem is purely cosmetic and results from making the model didactically simple for explanatory purposes. As pointed out by Davison and Jenkins, to ensure that reinforcers are neither created nor destroyed, each discriminability parameter should be divided by itself plus one.

The model shown in Fig. 3.5 is a city-block model in which the effects of a reinforcer fall off according to the distance from the original cell to the d_r degraded cell, and from the d_r degraded cell to the d_s degraded cell. In general, the degraded effect of reinforcers in cell (i,j), R_{ij}, on responding in cell (k,l) is given by $R_{ij}/d_{sik}/d_{rjl}$. Naturally, for cells located on the same key, or in the presence of the same stimulus, no discrimination can be made, and d_s or $d_r = 1.0$. Notice that this model is a city-block or peripheral-distance model in logarithmic terms ($\log d_s + \log d_r$).

The models discussed here make one further assumption. It is that ratios of responses emitted in a stimulus will match or equal the ratio of summated reinforcer influences for those cells. This assumption existed as a mathematical assumption in previous models (Davison & Tustin, 1978; Davison & Jenkins, 1985) and in the generalized matching law (Baum, 1974). In all three cases, behavior ratios strictly matched reinforcer ratios degraded in some way.

The model assessment is not easy. Because the stimuli were set up at equal physical distances apart (Experiment 1), and at arithmetically increasing distances (Experiments 2 and 3), the d_{sij} values will not be equal. Thus, we need 7 (Experiment 1) and 12 (Experiments 2 and 3) free discriminability parameters. Apart from the multitude of d_s parameters, we also need a value for d_r to deal with the contingency discriminability for the two responses, and for completeness we need an inherent bias parameter, c.

It is clear that the first, city-block, model is just one of a potentially infinite set of psychometric similarity models (Cross, 1965; Garner, 1974; Gregson, 1975). The general equation for such models is the Minkowski metric which, applied in the present case, gives the overall discriminability between two cells of the matrix ($\log d_{ij}$) in two-dimensional space according to the metric value, p:

$$\log d_{ij} = [(\log d_i)^p + (\log d_j)^p]^{1/p}.$$

If $p = 1$, the equation gives the city-block metric. This is Model 1 used here. While p could be any number, two other metrics have reasonably clear psychological implications. The first is $p = 2$, the Euclidean metric in which the distance between two points is measured along the hypotenuse. This is Model 2. The last, and limiting case, is when $p = \infty$. This is called the "supremum metric" (Gregson, 1975), and it implies that in a two-dimensional discrimination, only the greater one-dimensional distance (d_s or d_r) is effective. Thus, in the supremum metric, and in a two-dimensional discrimination, reinforcer discriminability should overwhelm stimulus discriminability when the former is greater, and the reverse should happen when the former is smaller.

In order to use the general Minkowski metric model, we must first recognize that the distance between the points in metrical space must lie in the range 0 to ∞ not in the range of d_s and d_r (1 to ∞). Thus, the hypotenuse ($p = 2$), for instance, must be calculated from the logged d_s and d_r parameters (as shown in the equation), but the value used in the detection model itself is the antilog of the hypotenuse value calculated from the Minkowski metric.

Data Analysis Procedures

In Experiment 1, there are 9 free parameters (7 d_s parameters, d_r, and bias), and in Experiments 2 and 3 there are 14 (12 d_s parameters, d_r, and bias). To fit the models and obtain the best parameter estimates, I was fortunate to have available a multidimensional nonlinear curve-fitting program developed by Peter Killeen (personal communication). I do not feel at ease with such large numbers of free parameters in a model, but I justify the approach on two grounds: (1) this number is completely dictated by the logic of the situation, and (2) the number of data is, at worst, nearly eight times larger than the number of free parameters. This ratio should be compared with the usual generalized-matching fits that obtain two free parameters from five data points. I hope also to be able to show some post hoc justifications from the subsequent data analyses.

The data fitted were the probabilities of emission of right-key responses in each stimulus. Logged ratios were not used as this procedure tended to overfit to extreme data (possibly data with large binomial variance), and thus to predict poorly data in which response choices were more equal. Also, the data from Experiments 2 and 3 contained some infinite ratios or log ratios which necessarily could not contribute to a parameter estimation.

For each data set, and each model, 6,000 iterations were carried out, sufficient to ensure that parameter estimates were stable. I also constructed an ad hoc measure of the relative importance of each parameter's contribution to accounting for the data set. This was done by successively changing each parameter (with the others at their best estimate) to 75% and then to 125% of the ratio (not logarithmic) estimate. The total absolute change in the error sum of squares for each pair of such variations was calculated as a percentage of the best-fit error sum of squares. Clearly, if such variations produce little change in the error sum of squares, the parameter may not be precisely estimated. Such a measure seems to be a reasonable yardstick of the importance of a parameter estimate in describing a data set, but, because of differences in the original sum of squares between data sets, it may not be a reasonable indicator across data sets. I also calculated the average error of the fit, and the variance in the data set accounted for by the predictions as a percentage. Because the relation between the obtained data and the predicted data must have a slope of 1.0 after finding the best parameters, the variance accounted for can be used to compare fits across data sets.

Results

The results of the parameter estimations are summarized in Table 3.1. In variance accounted for terms, the fit of all three models to the three data sets was excellent, never being less than 95% for the grouped data (for the individual subjects in Experiment 1, the smallest VAC was 88%, city-block and Euclidean models).

In Experiment 1, the discriminability values between the stimuli did seem to follow rather closely the pigeon color-naming function, with higher discriminabilities in the range 579–589 nm (Wright & Cumming, 1971). This result, therefore, provides some post hoc justification for the correct operation of the model. In Experiments 2 and 3, a second post hoc justification for the model is that discriminabilities generally fell with increasing temporal duration, as we would expect. There was one obvious problem estimate (the discriminability between 37.5 s and 42.5 s in Experiment 2). This was not caused by a programming error, but, happily, it was a very poorly estimated parameter value. The d_s measures from Experiments 2 and 3 do not map perfectly onto each other, though, cumulatively, they are rather similar over the range of 0 to 30 s. This lack of identity probably results from the differing design of the two experiments which gave areas of systematic data variation in two different, and each quite localized, regions, and also, as a result, other areas in which the estimates of d_s were imprecise.

A very clear result was that the fits of the models improved from the city-block, through the Euclidean, to the supremum models. This is hard to see (Table 3.1) in variance accounted for terms (generally, there was a 1% increase), but is clear in the error sum of squares which fell 23% for the Experiment 1 data, 45% for Experiment 2, and 28% for Experiment 3.

TABLE 3.1

Logarithmic Parameter Estimates and Goodness of Fit Statistics for the City-block, Euclidean, and Supremum Models[1]

	Experiment 1: Color discrimination		
		Model	
nm	City	Euclid	Supremum
d_s estimates:			
559–564	0.17(1)	0.08(2)	0.08(2)
564–569	0.30(5)	0.29(6)	0.28(9)
569–574	0.29(11)	0.28(14)	0.25(19)
574–579	0.21(42)	0.19(59)	0.18(77)
579–584	0.49(15)	0.45(20)	0.41(30)
584–589	0.47(5)	0.46(6)	0.41(9)
589–594	0.31(1)	0.36(1)	0.33(2)
dr	1.04(11)	1.25(11)	1.34(14)
bias	– 0.02(97)	– 0.03(115)	– 0.04(131)
VAC	97	97	98
Av. Dev.	0.0403	0.0381	0.0365
Err. SOS	0.287	0.241	0.220

	Experiment 2: Temporal discrimination, FD 5 s versus VD 30 s		
		Model	
seconds	City	Euclid	Supremum
d_s values:			
2.5–FD	0.05(7)	0.03(19)	0.04(26)
FD–7.5	0.98(14)	0.92(14)	0.86(27)
7.5–12.5	0.45(7)	0.64(4)	0.78(2)
12.5–17.5	0.24(3)	0.39(2)	0.49(2)
17.5–22.5	0.39(2)	0.48(1)	0.58(1)
22.5–27.5	0.00(1)	0.00(1)	0.00(2)
27.5–32.5	0.00(0)	0.00(2)	0.00(3)
32.5–37.5	0.00(0)	0.00(2)	0.00(3)
37.5–42.5	1.38(0)	1.49(0)	1.92(0)
42.5–47.5	0.21(0)	0.00(1)	0.00(1)
47.5–52.5	0.27(0)	0.00(2)	0.00(1)
52.5 – 57.5	0.00(0)	0.00(2)	0.00(1)
dr	1.22(10)	1.22(20)	1.26(33)
bias	– 0.35(43)	– 0.37(68)	– 0.38(94)
VAC	97	98	98
Av. dev.	0.0302	0.0263	0.0238
Err. SOS	0.231	0.165	0.126

(continued)

70

TABLE 3.1 *(Continued)*

Experiment 3: Temporal discrimination, FD 20 s versus VD 30 s

	Model		
seconds	*City*	*Euclid*	*Supremum*
d_s values:			
2.5–7.5	0.82(3)	0.74(4)	0.58(9)
7.5–12.5	0.38(7)	0.34(10)	0.31(20)
12.5–17.5	0.26(10)	0.22(17)	0.24(28)
17.5–FD	0.00(14)	0.00(25)	0.00(32)
FD–22.5	0.13(29)	0.10(32)	0.10(51)
22.5–27.5	0.36(24)	0.31(34)	0.28(59)
27.5–32.5	0.36(19)	0.33(26)	0.29(46)
32.5–37.5	0.13(12)	0.13(11)	0.11(22)
37.5–42.5	0.21(8)	0.20(11)	0.17(20)
42.5–47.5	0.16(4)	0.14(6)	0.11(8)
47.5–52.5	0.09(1)	0.00(2)	0.01(4)
52.5–57.5	0.08(0)	0.04(2)	0.00(2)
dr	0.89(18)	1.09(16)	1.22(17)
bias	− 0.11(105)	− 0.12(116)	− 0.13(152)
VAC	95	95	96
Av. dev.	0.0447	0.0414	0.0399
Err. SOS	0.338	0.280	0.242

[1]Percentage changes in error sum of squares for 50% parameter variations are shown in parentheses. VAC is the percentage of data variance accounted for by the model, Av. Dev. is the mean deviation of the data from the predictions, and Err. SOS is the error sum of squares.

Parameter values were always more precisely estimated (greater changes from forced parameter variations) for the supremum versus the other models.

Some parameter values were better estimated than others. As would be expected, parameter values from stimuli close to the intersection of stimulus sets were estimated most precisely simply because it was at these locations that relative reinforcer variations produced the greatest systematic variance. This is unfortunate, but it must be borne in mind that these experiments were not done to test the present models, rather they were done from a more traditional stimulus-control or temporal-discrimination framework. We shall later consider more adequate designs for research on the sort of models we are considering here.

The estimated parameter values appear to be sensible. First, focusing on the supremum model only now, log d_r values of 1.22 to 1.34, in combination with log d_s values between 0.2 and 0.5, translate to a values of around 0.8, and the estimates were remarkably similar across the data sets.

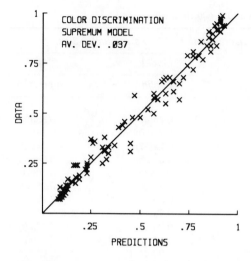

Fig. 3.6 Experiment 1. Obtained proportions of right-key responses as a function of predicted proportions of right-key responses using the supremum model parameters shown in Table 3.1. The straight line shows the locus of perfect prediction.

Another way to evaluate the model is to determine whether the original data functions can be recaptured from the fitted models. Figs. 3.6, 3.7, and 3.8 show the obtained group data plotted as a function of the predicted data for the three experiments using the best-estimated parameter values. The data were clearly well predicted, but some systematic deviations are apparent in Fig. 3.8 (temporal discrimination with a fixed duration of 20 s), and a poor distribution of data is evident in Fig. 3.7, a direct result of the experimental design used.

Fig. 3.9 shows, for Experiment 1, the predicted psychometric functions for relative reinforcer frequencies of .1, .5, and .9. The obtained data, shown in Fig. 3.1, were very similar. The analysis of the data from both

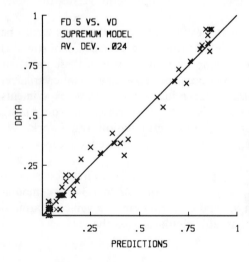

Fig. 3.7 Experiment 2. Obtained proportions of right-key responses as a function of predicted proportions of right-key responses using the supremum model parameters shown in Table 3.1. The straight line shows the locus of perfect prediction.

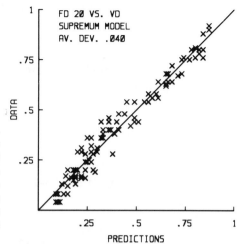

Fig. 3.8 Experiment 3. Obtained proportions of right-key responses as a function of predicted proportions of right-key responses using the supremum model parameters shown in Table 3.1. The straight line shows the locus of perfect prediction.

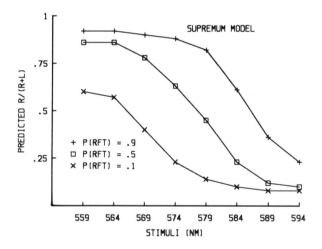

Fig. 3.9 Experiment 1. The predicted relative frequency of emitting a right-key response as a function of the color (nanometers) displayed on the center key. The predictions for three probabilities of right-key reinforcers are shown. These predictions should be compared with the data shown in Fig. 3.2.

Experiments 2 and 3 showed decreasing discriminabilities with longer temporal intervals. A further analysis showed that the weighted best parameters from these two experiments taken together accounted for 93% of the variance in Experiment 2 and 92% of Experiment 3. These weighted parameter estimates from the fits to Experiments 2 and 3 were used to predict log-response ratios for each stimulus duration as would be appropriate for a Davison–Tustin analysis, and straight lines were fit to these predictions as they were to the data in Fig. 3.4. Fig. 3.10 shows the results. Exactly the same sort of sensitivity changes with stimulus value were predicted as were seen in the data themselves.

In summary, then, the models appeared to work very well indeed, though it must be accepted that the data that we had to work with were not optimal for testing such models.

The Supremum Model and 2-stimulus Discrimination

As I stated before, the city-block model as used here is the same model as that suggested independently by Alsop when it is applied to a 2-stimulus

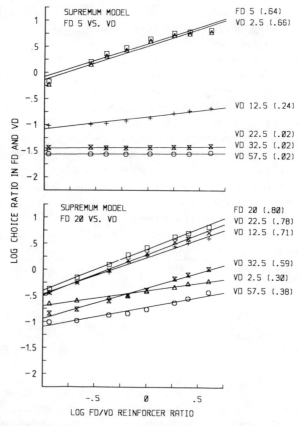

Fig. 3.10 Experiments 2 and 3. Predicted log-choice ratios for the FD duration and a selection of durations comprising the VD set as a function of the overall log reinforcer-frequency ratio. The slopes of the straight lines fitted to the predictions are shown in parentheses. These predictions should be compared with the data shown in Fig.3.4.

2-response detection task. The best of the three models analyzed here was the supremum model. In that model, only the larger of d_s or d_r affected the reallocation of reinforcers. Notice, however, that the supremum model operates in exactly the same way as the city-block model for the calculations of confusions (or generalizations) *within each* (d_s or d_r) *dimension*. That is, the only calculations that differ between the city-block and the supremum models are calculations of two-dimensional confusions that involve both different stimuli and different responses (diagonals in Fig. 3.5). Therefore, for a 2-stimulus 2-response application, the only calculation that differs between the models is the effect of R_w reinforcers on the z cell, and the effect of R_z reinforcers on the w cell in Fig. 3.1. As a result, with moderate values of both stimulus and contingency discriminability, empirical data may not allow a choice to be made between the city-block and the supremum models. Some situations, however, might be able to discriminate between the two models. For instance, if d_s was very large, $B_w/B_x => R_w/(R_w/d_r) = d_r$, a situation in which R_z does not affect response allocation in the presence of S_1. Since d_r is normally arranged to be as high as possible, with d_s lower, such situations have not often been parametrically investigated. Alsop's work may provide the appropriate data. Additionally, our own lab lore has determined that it is often difficult to get reasonable bias functions when discriminability is very high and subjects make few errors. This "result" may indicate that the supremum metric is indeed being used by our subjects.

To support the possibility that subjects use the supremum metric, Cross (1965) mentioned evidence from Harlow (1945), and from Warren (1953, 1954) that monkeys responded in complex discrimination tasks in a manner that corresponded with the supremum metric. Generally the performance in the complex discrimination was no better when cues redundant with color (in these cases) were provided. More recent evidence (Chase & Heinemann, 1972) seems to provide evidence both for and against the supremum metric. They trained three birds on a redundant light-intensity noise-intensity discrimination and then conducted generalization tests. There was considerable control by noise-intensity variation for subjects trained with small light-intensity differences, but rather little for subjects trained with large light-intensity differences. This latter result certainly supports the supremum metric. However, for the subjects trained with small light-intensity differences, the slopes of luminance gradients changed across noise-intensity variations, which argues against the supremum metric. But my interpretation of these data could be in error because they were plotted as probabilities of responding, and the raw data were not given.

SUMMARY

The three models for complex discrimination in a signal-detection situation developed here clearly all describe the available data well. It is, of course, premature to choose between them without a great deal more research. The form that this research should take is critical. The problem with the available data is that the procedures we used in these experiments were, in the case of Experiment 1, rather typical of maintained generalization experiments, and in the case of Experiments 2 and 3, designed to give some information about temporal control. Thus, both experiments were far from satisfactory in producing data with the nicely spread systematic variance necessary for the assessment of the models described here.

The problem of insufficient systematic variance can be overcome rather easily by effective experimental designs, though these will bear little relation to traditional stimulus-control designs. The following designs might be considered:

1. The obvious design of measuring the discriminability between pairs of stimuli, and determining whether they predict effectively in a complex discrimination. We have indeed followed this path in subsequent work in the color-discrimination experiment.
2. Arrange a pseudorandom sequence (Hunter & Davison, 1985) of reinforcer frequencies across a set of stimuli, so that for some stimuli reinforcers are delivered for the right response, and for others they are delivered for the left response. Then move the pseudorandom sequence across the set of stimuli over experimental conditions. This should provide systematic data variance unrelated to the value of the stimulus.
3. Drive ramps, or moving steps, or sinusoids across the set of stimuli in successive experimental conditions. Again, this should spread the systematic variance across the stimulus set, though the systematic variance for the extreme stimuli comprising the set might be difficult to obtain.

The results of such research efforts will show whether a model of complex stimulus control using the approach described here is attainable.

ACKNOWLEDGMENTS

I thank the New Zealand University grants committee for numerous grants that allowed the research reported here to be undertaken. I also thank Brent Alsop and Dianne McCarthy for their comments on drafts of this chapter.

REFERENCES

Alsop, B., & Elliffe, D. (1988). Concurrent-schedule performance: Effects of relative and overall reinforcer rate. *Journal of the Experimental Analysis of Behavior, 49,* 21–36.

Baum, W. M. (1974). On two types of deviation from the matching law: Bias and undermatching. *Journal of the Experimental Analysis of Behavior, 22,* 231–242.

Blough, D. S. (1975). Steady state data and a quantitative model of operant generalization and discrimination. *Journal of Experimental Psychology: Animal Behavior Processes, 104,* 3–21.

Chase, S., & Heinemann, E. G. (1972). Choices based on redundant information: An analysis of two-dimensional stimulus control. *Journal of Experimental Psychology, 92,* 161–175.

Cross, D. V. (1965). Metric properties of multidimensional stimulus generalization. In D. I. Mostofsky (Ed.), *Stimulus generalization* (pp. 72–93). Stanford, CA: Stanford University Press.

Davison, M. (1982). Performance in concurrent variable-interval fixed-ratio schedules. *Journal of the Experimental Analysis of Behavior, 37,* 81–96.

Davison, M. (1988). Concurrent schedules: Interaction of reinforcer frequency and reinforcer magnitude. *Journal of the Experimental Analysis of Behavior, 49,* 339–349.

Davison, M., & Hogsden, I. (1984). Concurrent variable-interval schedule performance: Fixed versus mixed reinforcer durations. *Journal of the Experimental Analysis of Behavior, 41,* 169–182.

Davison, M., & Jenkins, P. E. (1985). Stimulus discriminability, contingency discriminability, and schedule performance. *Animal Learning and Behavior, 13,* 77–84.

Davison, M., & McCarthy, D. (1987). The interaction of stimulus and reinforcer control in complex temporal discrimination. *Journal of the Experimental Analysis of Behavior, 48,* 97–116.

Davison, M., & McCarthy, D. (1989). Effects of relative reinforcer frequency on complex color detection. *Journal of the Experimental Analysis of Behavior, 51,* 291–315.

Davison, M. C., & Temple, W. (1973). Preference for fixed-interval schedules: An alternative model. *Journal of the Experimental Analysis of Behavior, 20,* 393–403.

Davison, M. C., & Tustin, R. D. (1978). On the relation between the generalized matching law and signal-detection theory. *Journal of the Experimental Analysis of Behavior, 29,* 331–336.

Garner, W. R. (1974). *The processing of information and structure.* New York: Wiley.

Gregson, R. A. M. (1975). *Psychometrics of similarity.* New York: Academic Press.

Harlow, H. F. (1945). Studies in discrimination learning by monkeys: Discrimination between stimuli differing in both color and form, only in color, and only in form. *Journal of General Psychology, 33,* 225–235.

Hunter, I., & Davison, M. (1985). Determination of a behavioral transfer function: White-noise analysis of session-to-session response-ratio dynamics in concurrent VI VI schedules. *Journal of the Experimental Analysis of Behavior, 43,* 43–59.

Lobb, B., & Davison, M. C. (1975). Preference in concurrent interval schedules: A systematic replication. *Journal of the Experimental Analysis of Behavior, 24,* 191–197.

Logue, A. W., & Chavarro, A. (1987). Effects on choice of absolute and relative values of reinforcer delay, amount, and frequency. *Journal of Experimental Psychology: Animal Behavior Processes, 13,* 280–291.

McCarthy, D., & Davison, M. (1984). Isobias and alloiobias functions in animal psychophysics. *Journal of Experimental Psychology: Animal Behavior Processes, 10,* 390–409.

Miller, J. T., Saunders, S. S., & Bourland, G. (1980). The role of stimulus disparity in concurrently available reinforcement schedules. *Animal Learning and Behavior, 8,* 635–641.

Nevin, J. A. (1969). Signal-detection theory and operant behavior: A review of David M. Green and John A. Swets' "Signal-detection theory and psychophysics." *Journal of the Experimental Analysis of Behavior, 12,* 475–480.

Nevin, J. A., Jenkins, P., Whittaker, S. G., & Yarensky, P. (1977, November). *Signal detection and matching.* Paper presented at the meeting of the Psychonomic Society, Washington, DC.

Nevin, J. A., Jenkins, P., Whittaker, S. G., & Yarensky, P. (1982). Reinforcement contingencies in signal detection. *Journal of the Experimental Analysis of Behavior, 37,* 65–79.

Prelec, D. (1984). The assumptions underlying the generalized matching law. *Journal of the Experimental Analysis of Behavior, 41,* 101–107.

Wardlaw, G. R., & Davison, M. C. (1974). Preference for fixed-interval schedules: Effects of initial-link length. *Journal of the Experimental Analysis of Behavior, 21,* 331–340.

Warren, J. M. (1953). Additivity of cues in a visual pattern discrimination by monkeys. *Journal of Comparative and Physiological Psychology, 46,* 484–486.

Warren, J. M. (1954). Perceptual dominance in discrimination learning by monkeys. *Journal of Comparative and Physiological Psychology, 47,* 290–293.

Williams, B. A., & Fantino, E. (1978). Effects on choice of reinforcer delay and conditioned reinforcement. *Journal of the Experimental Analysis of Behavior, 29,* 77–86.

Wright, A. A., & Cumming, W. W. (1971). Color-naming functions for the pigeon. *Journal of the Experimental Analysis of Behavior, 15,* 7–17.

4 Discrimination of Temporal Same–Different Relations by Pigeons

J. Gregor Fetterman
Arizona State University

To what extent are nonhumans capable of learning discriminations based upon abstract relations between stimuli (e.g., a same-different rule)? This question has generated a great deal of controversy over the years (e.g., Spence, 1937), and controversy continues to surround the issue of relational learning in animals (e.g., see Carter & Werner, 1978; D'Amato, Salmon, & Colombo, 1985; Premack, 1978,1983). The evidence indicates that pigeons have considerable difficulty learning relational concepts such as the same–different rule (see Carter & Werner, 1978, for a review), whereas monkeys trained on tasks like those used with pigeons (e.g., matching-to-sample — MTS) appear to base discriminative responses upon a generalized conceptual rule (e.g., D'Amato & Salmon, 1984).

Apparently at odds with the literature on relational learning in pigeons are some recent findings by my colleagues and me (Dreyfus, Fetterman, Smith, & Stubbs, 1988; Fetterman & Dreyfus, 1986, 1987; Fetterman, Dreyfus, & Stubbs, 1989; Stubbs, Dreyfus, & Fetterman, 1984) indicating that pigeons can learn discriminations that appear to be based upon abstract stimulus relations. In these experiments, pigeons were trained to make different choice responses, depending on which of two successive stimulus durations was longer, with the specific durations changing from trial-to-trial. This task was readily learned, and in light of considerations to be discussed, we believe that relational comparisons are involved. In this chapter, I will review some of these data, present the results of several recent experiments that appear perplexing in the context of our initial findings, and suggest an approach that incorporates the discrepant findings, based in part on a signal-detection framework.

Fetterman and Dreyfus (1986,1987) introduced a new method for the study of animal timing behavior, whereby pigeons were presented with a pair of successive stimulus durations, and then reinforcement was provided for different choice responses, depending on whether the first (t_1) or second (t_2) duration was longer. This procedure is the two-alternative forced-choice (2AFC) method of human psychophysics (Gescheider, 1985). The durations of the stimuli changed over trials (range of 1 to 32 s) such that approximately 700 combinations were presented, so that discrimination could not be based exclusively on the absolute value of either stimulus. All pigeons achieved a high level of discrimination performance, with the typical animal responding correctly about 85% of the time.

Fig.4.1 presents some of the data reported by Fetterman and Dreyfus (1987, Experiment 2). The figure shows the data for one pigeon. Each

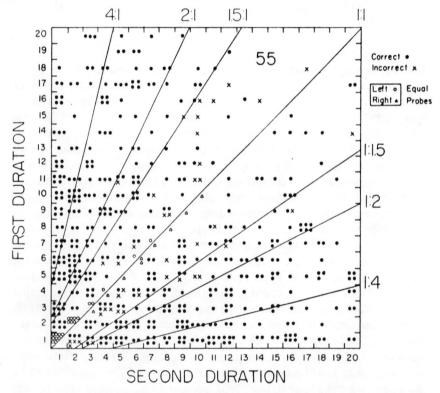

FIG. 4.1 The figure shows the performance of a single pigeon. Each symbol represents the outcome of an individual trial with filled circles indicating incorrect responses and Xs incorrect responses. The points are plotted in imaginary cells at the intersection of the first and second durations (from Fetterman & Dreyfus, 1987; Experiment 2).

symbol represents the outcome of a single trial with circles indicating correct responses and x's incorrect responses. Although individual durations ranged from 1 to 32, data are not included from trials in which the duration of either stimulus was greater than 20 s, because such trials occurred infrequently (see Fetterman & Dreyfus, 1987, for details on the method of arranging durations). The symbols are placed in imaginary squares corresponding to each duration pair. For example, there are three circles in the upper left when 20 s was followed by 3 s, indicating the pigeon was correct on each of three trials. Generally, accuracy decreased as the ratio of the stimuli approached 1:1 (major diagonal), as suggested by the mixture of filled circles and x's in the different regions of the matrix.

Fig.4.2 summarizes the matrix data of four pigeons by showing the average probability of responding "$t_2 > t_1$" as a function of the ratio of the first to second duration. The points plotted at the midpoints of the duration ratio categories represent the average duration pair ratio for each category. Each ratio category included duration pairs that differed in the absolute values of the stimuli (see Fig.4.1). For example, the category 4:1 > t_1/t_2 > 2:1 included the pairs 28 and 8 s, 14 and 4 s, 7 and 2 s, and so on. This psychophysical presentation indicates that performance changed as an orderly function of the ratio of a duration pair. The probability of responding "$t_2 > t_1$" was appropriately near zero when the t_1/t_2 ratio was greater than 2:1, increased as this ratio approached 1:1, and approximated 1.0 at small t_1/t_2 values (less than 0.5). This result implies discriminative control by the ratio of a duration pair, a conclusion abetted by analyses reported by Dreyfus et al. (1988).

Fetterman, Dreyfus, and Stubbs (1989) modified the duration comparison task so that different choices were reinforced according to whether a duration pair ratio was less or greater than a criterion ratio, for example whether the first stimulus was more or less than twice the duration of the

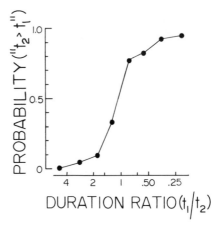

FIG. 4.2 Probability of reporting the second duration longer the first as a function of the ratio of the duration pairs. The data are averaged over four pigeons. (adapted from Fetterman & Dreyfus, 1987; Experiment 2).

second. Criterion ratios of 1:4, 1:2, 1:1 (i.e., shorter–longer), 2:1, and 4:1 were used in different conditions of the experiment. As has been shown, the specific durations changed across trials with more then 900 unique pairs included, and pairs less than and greater than the criterion ratio occurred equally under each condition. Levels of sensitivity, as measured by A′ (Grier, 1971) were comparable (about .85) across the different criterion ratios, whether the task involved a "simple" shorter–longer judgment (1:1 condition), or whether it involved the seemingly more complex judgment of one duration as twice or four times another.

The animals' facility with these tasks was surprising for several reasons. First, as noted, pigeons' abilities for abstraction of the kind implied by these data are highly suspect. The consensus has been that pigeons are not capable of learning such relational concepts. Second, the results were surprising in the context of recent work on short-term memory in pigeons. Duration tasks necessarily take place over time, and the duration comparison task is of particular interest in this regard because the first stimulus duration was always delayed from choice by the duration of the second stimulus. There are well-established limits to the short-term remembering of temporal events (e.g., Church, 1980; Spetch & Wilkie, 1983), yet the pigeons' performance was comparable whether durations were relatively short or relatively long, and hence whether a shorter or longer delay intervened between the first stimulus and the ensuing choice response (see Dreyfus et al.,1988, and Fetterman & Dreyfus, 1987, for detailed analyses). We have discussed this issue elsewhere in some detail (Fetterman & Dreyfus, 1987), and have concluded that it is difficult to say where perception of an event ends and memory for its temporal properties begins. This "direct" view of memory (e.g., Wilcox & Katz,1981) has much in common with that of White (chap.10 in this volume).

The research described in this chapter provides an extension of prior work on the learning of temporal relations by pigeons. It was motivated by questions about pigeons' abilities to acquire a temporal same–different concept, and by a desire to make closer contact with the research on relational learning involving the same-different rule. Most recent work on relational learning in animals has employed color, form, or pictorial sample stimuli, and animals are typically required to respond to different choice alternatives according to a categorical relation of sameness or difference between sample and choice stimuli.[1] In contrast, we have used durations as

---

[1]This is the "nonsymbolic" or identity version of MTS. With "symbolic" MTS (SMTS) the relation between sample and correct choice stimuli is arbitrary. For example, an animal might be trained to respond to vertical and horizontal lines after red and green samples. Duration tasks, such as the pair comparison procedure, necessarily involve the symbolic choice arrangement.

the stimuli and required animals to base choices on the relative magnitudes of the stimuli (i.e., shorter–longer). Thus, there are several potentially relevant distinctions between our work and other research on relational concepts in pigeons. Our tasks involve a prothetic (Stevens & Galanter, 1957) or continuous stimulus dimension with reinforcement based on the relative magnitudes of the stimuli. Colors, forms, pictures, and the like, on the other hand, constitute metathetic or categorical dimensions, and in these procedures animals must respond on the basis of a categorical relation between sample and choice stimuli (or between the two stimuli of a pair, as in the case of Santiago & Wright, 1984). It is difficult to say whether these distinctions are important for the pigeon, but there is evidence to suggest that they matter for humans (e.g.,Creelman & Macmillan, 1979).

The experiments employed a modified version of the duration comparison task, one in which reinforcement for different choices depended on whether the durations of the stimuli were the same or different. The research served the purpose of extending work with this discrimination procedure to a new temporal concept, and also of making contact with the work on relational learning involving the same–different rule.

EXPERIMENT 1

Three pigeons were given daily sessions in a standard three-key operant chamber; each session contained approximately 150 trial periods. Trials began with the center key lit white. A peck to this key changed the key color to red. The first and second durations of a pair were associated with red and green lights on the center key, respectively; the change in key color from red to green occurred independently of behavior. The offset of green was accompanied by the onset of the amber side key lights. A response to one side key was correct if the durations of the stimuli were the same (e.g., 4 s followed by 4 s) whereas a response to the alternate side key was correct if the durations of the stimuli were different (e.g., 4 s followed by 2 s *or* 2 s followed by 4 s). Correct responses were reinforced intermittently with 4-s access to mixed grain, followed by a 20-s intertrial interval (ITI) and a new trial period. Incorrect responses initiated the ITI directly, and a noncorrection procedure was used.

Duration pairs were constructed by combining the durations 1, 2, 4, and 8-s in all possible ways. The resulting stimulus combinations included 4 *same* pairs (1–1, 2–2, 4–4, and 8–8 s) and 12 *different* pairs (8–1, 1–8, 4–1, 1–4, 8–2, 2–8, 4–2, 2–4, 8–4, and 4–8 s). Sessions contained equal numbers of problems from the *same* and *different* categories, and pairs within each category were presented equally often. Reinforcement for the two choice responses was equal and controlled according to the method described by stubbs (1976). This arrangement resulted in food delivery for approximately 50% of the correct responses. Correct responses that did not result in food illuminated the feeder light for 0.5 s followed by the ITI. The animals were trained for approximately 40 sessions with the results to follow based upon data obtained over the last 5 sessions of training.

Results and Discussion

The same–different (S–D) task proved very difficult for the birds to learn. A' scores for Pigeons 76 and 84 were .70 and .61 respectively, values that reliably exceeded the chance level of .50. The performance of the third subject, Pigeon 80, was not reliably greater than chance.

The top three panels of Fig.4.3 (adapted from Fetterman, 1987) show the percentage of correct responses for individual pairs of durations. The six pairs of bars on the left of each panel represent performance for *different* pairs of durations, and the four individual bars on the right, *same* pairs. The *different* pairs are arranged so that each set of bars shows performance with the identical pair of stimulus durations, and where the longer stimulus was the first ($t_1 > t_2$; filled bars) or second ($t_2 > t_1$; unfilled bars) member of the pair. One obvious pattern for *different* pairs is that all birds were more accurate when $t_1 > t_2$ (14 of 18 comparisons.). This could be viewed as a *positive time-order error*. Pigeons 76 and 84 were reasonably accurate on the various *same* pairs, with the exception of the 4–4 s pair. Pigeon 80 was at or slightly below chance on all of the *same* pairs.

The bottom panel presents data, averaged over four pigeons, from Fetterman and Dreyfus (1986). They paired the durations 2, 4, 8, and 16 s and required pigeons to make one response when $t_1 > t_2$ and the alternate response when $t_2 > t_1$. The task was very similar to the one employed in the present experiment except that the discrimination involved a shorter–longer (S–L) as opposed to a S–D comparison of the stimuli. Two points of comparison are pertinent. First, subjects were clearly more accurate on the S–L than the S–D discrimination; accuracy scores for the S–L task averaged about 90% correct. Second, Fetterman and Dreyfus observed patterns in their data that suggested a *negative time-order error;* generally, their subjects were more accurate when the longer of two stimuli was presented second (unfilled bars), a pattern opposite to that observed in the present experiment.

Two of three pigeons "learned" the temporal S–D task by a criterion that equates learning with a performance that reliably exceeds chance. However this measure of learning does not tell us whether the pigeons acquired the S–D concept, or whether choices were based on stimulus-specific rules. The patterns of accuracy scores in Fig. 4.3 suggest the latter interpretation. All

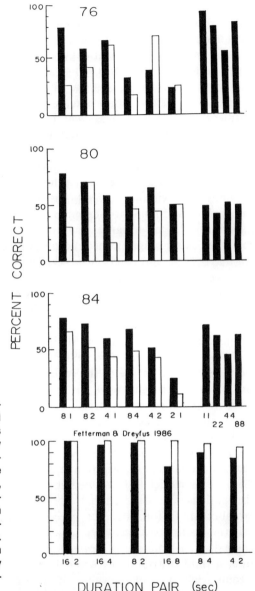

FIG. 4.3 Percentage of correct responses for individual pairs of durations. The pairs of bars on the left show accuracy for the two configurations of *different* pairs; the filled bars represent $t_1 > t_2$, and the unfilled bars represent $t_2 > t_1$. The bottom panel presents data from Fetterman and Dreyfus (1986). See text for details (from Fetterman, 1987; reprinted by permission of the Psychonomic Society).

birds displayed systematic "confusions" between pairs of stimuli, a result that indicates misapplication of an absolute choice rule. For example, accuracy for Pigeons 76 and 84 was substantially below chance when the durations 7 and 2 seconds were presented in either order, and accuracy on *same* pairs composed of 1 or 2 seconds was much greater than chance. This result indicates a strategy of responding "same" when both durations were short. Pigeon 76 apparently based some choices on the duration of the second stimulus alone. This bird tended to respond "same" whenever the second stimulus was 8 s, a strategy reflected in the accuracy scores for pairs with a second duration of 8 s (1–8, 2–8, 4–8, and 8–8 s).

It seems evident then that the birds did not acquire the temporal S–D concept, but instead responded on the basis of stimulus specific rules. Furthermore, accuracy was well below that observed on a seemingly comparable task involving shorter–longer comparisons of duration (Fetterman & Dreyfus, 1986, 1987), where the birds evidently mastered the S–L concept. At the outset, the differences in the structure of the two tasks seemed trivial. We fully expected that the animals would master the S–D discrimination without difficulty, as had been observed with related pair comparison discrimination tasks. But, as demonstrated by the results of Experiment 1, performance was profoundly affected by what could be construed as an insignificant procedural modification. Perhaps we should not have been surprised, however, because similar results have been obtained in human psychophysical experiments. For example, Creelman and Macmillan (1979) studied comparative judgments of pitch and found that accuracy was higher when the judgment involved a relative (higher–lower) as opposed to a categorical (same–different) comparison of tone frequencies. These results seem similar to those presented in Fig.4.3

The pigeon and human discrimination data indicate that subjects are not indifferent to the nature of the required comparison, and signal-detection analyses afford a framework for understanding these effects (see Noreen, 1980, for detailed comparisons of psychophysical methods and results within an optimal decision making framework). The "sensory difference" model is a signal-detectability account in which the observer is assumed to use the perceived difference (X_1-X_2) between sequential stimuli as the decision variable (e.g., Macmillan, Kaplan, & Creelman, 1977; Noreen, 1980). This model is illustrated in Fig.4.4, where underlying Gaussian distributions are assumed but not required for the analysis. For the two-alternative, forced-choice procedure (i.e., the S–L discrimination), only the distributions centered at $+t$ and $-t$ are relevant; in this case the single decision criterion is centered at zero. For the same–different procedure, a third distribution (centered at zero) must be added to take into account trials in which the values of the stimuli are the same (i.e., $t_1 = t_2$). In this case, the observer must establish two criteria (provided, of course, that we assume a *signed*, and not an *absolute* difference model), one at d_A, the other at d_B, and respond "same" whenever the sensory difference falls between these values, and otherwise respond "different."

The predictions of this model approximate observed performance for the human psychophysical data (e.g., see Creelman & Macmillan, 1979;

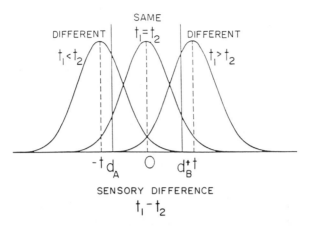

FIG. 4.4 Hypothetical processes underlying the temporal same–different discrimination. The variables, d_A and d_B, represent decision criteria. See text for details (adapted from Noreen, 1980).

Noreen, 1980). Its relevance in the present context is that it predicts the direction of observed differences in accuracy with S–D and two-alternative, forced-choice procedures (60% correct versus 88% correct for the data of Creelman & Macmillan, 1979). Unfortunately, point predictions are not possible for the present data without an estimate of discrimination accuracy with yet another paradigm, the "yes–no" or single stimulus procedure (see Noreen, 1980), and such data are not available for these subjects. But, we may employ the model portrayed in Fig. 4.4 as a heuristic device, and use it as a means of generating testable hypotheses about the basis of the differences in task performance.

The preceding analysis suggests several candidate hypotheses for the difficulty of the temporal S–D task. First, as conceptualized in Fig. 4.4, the task requires two decision criteria, so that the subject should respond "same" whenever the "sensory difference" falls above one cutoff (d_A) or below the other (d_B); otherwise the subject should respond "different." If this conceptualization is correct, subjects might have more difficulty with the S–D discrimination because of the need for a second decision criterion. A second potential source of difficulty is that S–D tasks require subjects to classify two configurations of the stimuli under a single response category, "different." In the case of the temporal S–D procedure, Fig. 4.3 indicated that the animals had considerable difficulty treating the two configurations ($t_1 > t_2$ and $t_2 > t_1$) as comparable instances of the category "different." Thus "confusion" or response competition might have been a causal factor.

Procedural modifications that might simplify the task may easily be deduced from this analysis. For example, *different* pairs could be constructed so that they contained only one configuration of the stimuli ($t_1 >$

t_2 or $t_2 > t_1$). This modification would eliminate the possibility of response competition, and also the need for multiple decision criteria. Alternatively, a three-category task (e.g., see Vickers, 1979) could be used in which different choices were associated with the three categories of stimuli. This three-response classification task might be easier than one that simply lumped the $t_1 > t_2$ and $t_2 > t_1$ categories, as in Experiment 1. Experiments 2 and 3 employed modifications of the "basic" temporal S–D task that assessed this analysis.

EXPERIMENT 2

The intent was to simplify the task in order to assess the analysis presented in Fig.4.4. The procedure was modified so that only the $t_1 > t_2$ configuration of *different* pairs was used. In Experiment 1, all three birds were more accurate with this arrangement of the stimuli (see Fig.4.3). This experiment also provided a within-subjects comparison of performance with S–D and S–L discrimination procedures. Two pigeons with extensive experience on the S–L task were transferred to the S–D task, allowing a direct comparison of performance on the two discrimination problems.

The method was virtually identical to that described for Experiment 1. The significant change of procedure involved *different* pairs, which now included but one configuration of the stimuli, those with $t_1 > t_2$. Table 4.1 lists the duration pairs used: 7 *same* and 24 *different* pairs. For the *different* pairs, note that only pairs with $t_1 > t_2$ are included, that values of the second stimulus are limited to those used to construct *same* pairs, and that the ratios of these pairs cover a substantial range, from 1.2:1 to 6:1. *Same* and *different* pairs occurred equally often, but *different* pairs were presented in such a way that each value of the second duration occurred equally (see Fetterman, 1987, for details and the logic of this method of problem selection). All birds were trained for 20 sessions, with the results to follow, based on data from the last 5 sessions of training.

TABLE 4.1
Duration Pairs Used in Experiment 2

Different pairs (s)	Same pairs (s)
6–1, 4–1, 2–1	1–1, 2–2, 4–4, 6–6
10–2, 8–2, 6–2, 4–2	8–8, 10–10, 12–12
12–4, 10–4, 8–4, 6–4	
16–6, 14–6, 12–6, 10–6, 8–6	
16–8, 14–8, 12–8, 10–8	
16–10, 14–10, 12–10	
16–12	

Three of the subjects had served in Experiment 1. Two additional birds, Pigeons 53 and 68, were transferred to the modified S–D task after approximately 100 sessions of training with S–L comparisons of duration. Under the S–L procedure, durations were arranged by a system where a timer pulsed a probability gate each 0.5 s; the probability of an output from the gate was .10. Individual durations lasted until there was an output from the gate, or until 32 pulses had occurred, providing a duration range for each stimulus of 0.5 to 16.0 s. This arrangement yielded more than 700 combinations of the two durations. Correct responses were chosen to facilitate transfer from the S–L to S–D discrimination. The correct response given $t_1 > t_2$ was the same for both tasks; following transfer, the response previously associated with $t_2 > t_1$ was correct when $t_1 = t_2$.

Results and Discussion

Sensitivity measures (A′) improved for two of the three pigeons from Experiment 1. The values of A′ in Experiment 2 were .78, .55, .58, .71, and .67 for Pigeons 76, 80, 84, 53, and 68, respectively. Analyses of performance on individual pairs of durations revealed few systematic "confusions" that would indicate control by absolute properties of the stimuli, as observed in Experiment 1. If anything, accuracy was related to the ratio of the two durations. For *different* pairs of stimuli, accuracy approached chance as the duration ratio approached 1:1 (see Fetterman, 1987, for further details).

Fig.4.5 presents transfer data by showing performance across individual sessions before and after the change from the S–L to S–D task. Both A' and percentage correct measures are shown for each subject for the last five sessions with the S–L task, and the first and last (separated by dashed lines) five sessions of training with the S–D task. The different symbols for the percentage correct measures identify the stimulus categories.

A′ scores decreased following the change from the S–L to S–D comparisons of the stimuli, but both birds discriminated at greater than chance level on the first transfer session. There was little change in discrimination sensitivity over the remaining 19 sessions of training, however. The bottom row shows that the change from S–L to S–D comparisons of duration produced a decrease in accuracy for both choices, even though the appropriate choice given $t_1 > t_2$ was constant for both tasks. There were changes in bias (indicated by differences in percentage of correct scores for the two choices) for Pigeon 53 over the course of training with S–D comparisons of the stimuli that indicate a shift in its decision criterion. Immediately following transfer, this pigeon was more accurate after pairs with $t_1 > t_2$ (unfilled circles), but accuracy was comparable for both categories of stimuli over the last five sessions of training. This change is

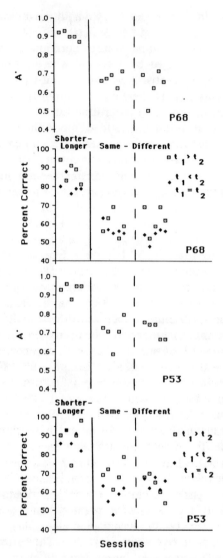

FIG. 4.5 Performance before and after transfer from a shorter–longer (S–L) to a same–different (S–D) temporal comparison task. From left to right, each panel shows performance over the last five sessions of the S–L task, and the first and last five sessions (separated by dashed lines) of training with the S–D task. The different symbols for percentage correct measures identify the stimulus categories (from Fetterman, 1987; reprinted by permission of the Psychonomic Society).

not surprising because substitution of $t_1 = t_2$ for $t_1 > t_2$ pairs would decrease the distance between the modes of the hypothetical distributionsalong the decision axis (see Fig.4.4). The changes for Pigeon 68 were not as clear in this regard, however.

Procedural modifications introduced in Experiment 2 produced marginal improvements in discrimination performance for two of three birds, a result that does not offer strong support for the analysis presented in Fig. 4.4. However, there were few instances of "confusion errors" that would illuminate an absolute strategy for choice responses. Whatever the basis of the discrimination, the modified S–D comparison was clearly more difficult than the closely related S–L task, a point made strongly by the transfer data of Fig.4.5.

EXPERIMENT 3

In this experiment, pigeons were trained on a three-category classification task in which different choice responses were reinforced given $t_1 > t_2$, $t_1 = t_2$ and $t_2 > t_1$. As Vickers (1979) noted, there is a close relation between this three-category task and tasks that require S–D comparisons of the stimuli. When prothetic stimuli are used, the former can be converted to the latter by requiring subjects to make the response "different" whenever the first stimulus is greater *or* less than the second.

Because these data have not been presented elsewhere, I will describe the procedure in some detail. Four pigeons were given daily sessions in a four-key operant chamber. These were not the same birds that served in Experiments 1 and 2. Three keys were located in a horizontal row about 22 cm above the chamber floor. The fourth, stimulus key, was mounted above the center key of the three-key array, about 28 cm above the chamber floor. The stimulus durations were presented on the top (stimulus) key and initiated by a peck to the white stimulus key light. The first and second durations of a pair were correlated with red and green lights, respectively, and the offset of the green light was accompanied by the onset of red, white, and green lights behind the left (L), center (C), and right (R) keys, respectively. Correct responses were mapped onto these keys in the order $t_1 > t_2$ (L), $t = t_2$ (C), and $t_2 > t_1$ (R). Correct responses produced 3-s access to mixed grain, followed by a 20-s ITI. Incorrect responses initiated the ITI directly. A correction procedure was used, but correction trials were not included in the data analyses. Conditions during correction trials were exactly as described for noncorrection trials, except that a duration pair was repeated until the appropriate choice response was emitted and reinforced. Once the scheduled reinforcer was obtained, a new duration pair was arranged on the next trial, according to the method to be described. Sessions ended after 80 reinforcers.

The pairs of stimuli were generated in the following way: First, a "base" duration was selected, with base durations ranging between 1.0 and 10.5 s in increments of 0.5 s, providing 20 different duration values. Each base duration value occurred equally often. The base duration was assigned as the first (t_1) or second (t_2) member of the pair, and each base duration occurred in each ordinal position an equal number of times. On *same* trials, the value of the opposing pair member was equal to the base duration. On *different* trials, the opposing stimulus duration was either 2.0, 2.5, or 3.0

times the value of the base duration. Thus, on *different* trials, one stimulus was at least twice but not more than three times the value of the other, and each problem ratio occurred equally. In implementing this algorithm for selection of *different* pairs of stimuli, some restrictions were placed upon particular combinations of extreme (shortest and longest) base durations and multipliers so that only a small fraction (about 15%) of trials contained individual durations that were by themselves predictive of the correct response. Each trial type ($t_1 > t_2$, $t_1 = t_2$, and $t_2 > t_1$) was arranged with equal probability.

All birds were trained initially on a two-alternative, forced-choice S–L discrimination in which duration pairs included either the $t_1 > t_2$ or $t_2 > t_1$, but not the $t_1 = t_2$ configuration of the stimuli. The birds were required to peck the left choice key given $t_1 > t_2$ and the right given $t_2 > t_1$. The center choice-key was always darkened and inoperative during this phase of training, which lasted for approximately 40 sessions. Once performance stabilized, equal pairs of stimulus durations were introduced, and three choice alternatives were provided after each stimulus pair, as has been described. Different choices were reinforced after $t_1 > t_2$, $t_1 = t_2$, and $t_2 > t_1$. Pigeon T became ill and did not participate in this part of the experiment.

Results and Discussion

Fig.4.6 shows the data from the initial phase of training by presenting the probability of responding "$t_1 < t_2$" as a function of the duration pair ratio. All four pigeons learned this task without difficulty and, as the figure indicates, choice probabilities changed as an orderly function of the ratio of a duration pair.

The introduction of equal pairs of durations produced a marked disruption in performance; on average, choice accuracy decreased from about 90% to 40% correct responses (note, however, the corresponding decrease in chance performance, from 50% to 33%). Discrimination performance recovered fairly rapidly, approaching an asymptote of about 60% correct responses (average of the three birds; range 55% to 65%) after approximately 35 sessions of training with the three-response classification task.

Fig.4.7 presents the major results of Experiment 3. This figure shows the probability of responding to each choice key (coded by different symbols) as a function of the ratio of the two stimulus durations. The probabilities were calculated from data summed over the last 7 sessions of training, and each panel shows performance for a single animal.

Performance varied appropriately with changes in the ratio of the two durations. Choice probabilities for the $t_1 > t_2$ and $t_2 > t_1$ alternatives approached 0 and 1.0, respectively, as the t_1/t_2 ratio decreased. In general,

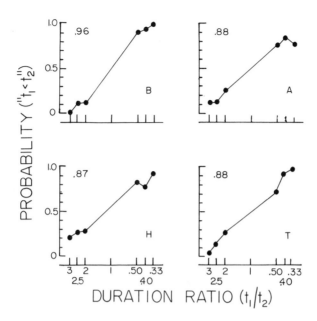

FIG. 4.6 Probability of reporting the second stimulus longer than the first as a function of the ratio of the two durations. The numbers in the upper left of each panel represent values of A'.

the animals discriminated *equal* pairs of durations from those in which the values of the stimuli were different. The modes of the distributions for the "$t_1 = t_2$" choice were appropriately located at the 1:1 duration ratio and, generally, choice probabilities decreased monotonically on either side of the mode. There were differences among individuals in the degree to which choices of the *equal* alternative were an orderly function of the duration ratio, with Pigeons B and A representing the two extremes (best and worst) of performance.

Fig.4.8 summarizes the psychophysical presentation of Fig. 4.7 by presenting choice probabilities in the form of a "confusion" matrix. This figure shows the probabilities of the different choices (rows) for each category of the stimuli (columns). This presentation allows us to see whether there were systematic patterns of choices, for example, whether the animals tended to "confuse" equal pairs with one or another of the *different* problem categories. There are three major findings. First, the values along the major diagonal (representing proportion correct for each choice alter-native) indicate that, in general, the animals were more accurate for the $t_1 > t_2$ and $t_2 > t_1$ (i.e., *different*) categories than for equal pairs of durations. This difference in performance may simply reflect the necessarily restricted range of duration ratios (1:1) included in the equal category, however. *Different* categories included multiple duration ratios that were more or less

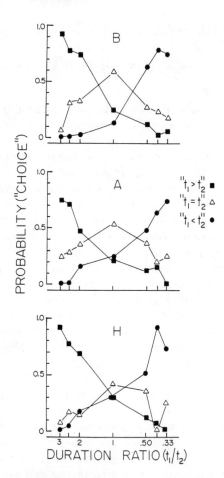

FIG. 4.7 Probability of responding to each of three choice alternatives as a function of the ratio of the two durations. Each panel shows performance for a single pigeon. The different symbols identify the choice alternatives.

discriminable from other duration pairs (see Fig.4.7). Second, confusion errors for the *different* categories primarily involved inappropriate choices of the *equal* ($t_1 = t_2$) alternative; the two *different* categories were rarely confused with one another. This result suggests that the discrimination was based on the ratio of the stimulus durations, or according to the difference (signed or absolute) between the durations. Finally, neither *different* configuration was "confused" with equal duration pairs more often than the other. There were no systematic biases (across birds) that would indicate the positive or negative time order errors found in earlier work with this duration comparison task (Dreyfus et al., 1988; Fetterman, 1987; Fetterman & Dreyfus, 1986, 1987).

Experiment 3 tested one implication of the "sensory difference" analysis portrayed in Fig. 4.4. By that account, the difficulty of the temporal S–D discrimination resulted from "confusion" or response competition because

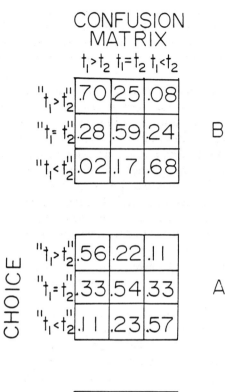

CONFUSION
MATRIX

FIG. 4.8 Summary probabilities of responding to the three choice alternatives (rows) for each stimulus category (columns). Each matrix shows the data for a single pigeon.

the birds were required to respond to complementary configurations of the stimuli ($t_1 > t_2$ and $t_2 > t_1$) as instances of a single category *different*. In Experiment 3, the complementary configurations were associated with spatially distinct choice alternatives, thereby (presumably) reducing or eliminating the possibility of response competition.

The data presented in Fig.4.7 demonstrated that the birds discriminated among the three stimulus configurations, and suggested that discrimination was based on the ratio of a duration pair, as with prior research (e.g., Fetterman & Dreyfus, 1987). Furthermore, by comparison with the appropriately defined chance performance (50% in Experiment 1, versus 33% in Experiment 3), discrimination accuracy for Experiment 3 was further "above the floor" than in Experiment 1. Estimates of accuracy that take into account the differences in chance performance may be obtained according to the following equation:

$$P_{AC} = (P_C - P_G) / (1 - P_G)$$

in which P_{AC} represents a "corrected" accuracy score, where the correction takes into account the probability of guessing correctly when choices are not under the control of the stimuli. P_C and P_G represent the observed probability of a correct response and the probability of guessing correctly, respectively. For chance performance, the value of this measure is zero (because the numerator goes to zero), whereas perfect performance yields a value of 1.0.

Taking the average performance of Pigeons 76 and 84 for Experiment 1 (Pigeon 80 did not learn the task), and the average of all birds for Experiment 3 as our estimates of P_C, we find the "corrected" accuracy score for Experiment 1 to be .18, and that for Experiment 3 to be .40. This comparison suggests that the seemingly more complex task of Experiment 3 was less difficult than the task of Experiment 1, as suggested by the analysis presented in Fig.4.4. However, the same analysis indicates that the S–L discrimination of Experiment 3 (see Fig. 4.6) was less difficult than the three-response classification task (Fig.4.7). Corrected accuracy scores for the two and three-choice procedures were .70 and .40, respectively. It appears that introduction of the "equal" category altered the nature of the discrimination.

GENERAL DISCUSSION

Taken together, the experiments reported in this chapter demonstrate that the temporal S–D discrimination is more difficult for pigeons than comparable discriminations based on the relative magnitudes of the stimuli (Dreyfus et al., 1988; Fetterman & Dreyfus, 1986, 1987; Fetterman et al., 1989; Stubbs et al., 1984). Performance on two variations (Experiments 2 and 3) of the "standard" (Experiment 1) temporal S–D task indicated that the "sensory difference" analysis (Fig. 4.4) was a step in the right direction, but this analysis does not appear to provide a complete account of the difficulty of the S–D discrimination. The modified S–D discrimination was more difficult than S–L comparisons of the stimuli (Experiment 2), and the three-response classification seemed *not* to be merely a phenotypical variant of the simpler S–L task; introduction of the "equal" category of stimuli affected performance in a way that suggested the task was fundamentally different for the animals (Experiment 3).

Our research with S–L comparisons of duration indicated that pigeons based choice responses on temporal relations between stimuli (Dreyfus et al., 1988), but such positive results are not common in research on the problem of relational learning in animals. A number of factors may contribute to the different results, but we believe the training context to be a critical factor. We have typically used many combinations of stimuli, whereas with MTS animals are generally trained with a small set of exemplars prior to the introduction of test stimuli. When but few stimuli are presented during training, the absolute features of the stimuli may over-shadow relational cues. The ever-changing pairs of stimuli with our procedure may prevent overshadowing of relational by absolute cues by "calling attention" to the one invariant feature of the task, the temporal relation between the stimuli. Had we used only two durations during training, as with MTS, it is likely that our animals would have based choices on individual durations because they (as well as the temporal relation) would have been predictive of the correct response. Wright, Cook, Rivera, Sands, and Delius (1988) provide data that bear on this speculation. Wright et al. trained pigeons on a simultaneous MTS task with computer-drawn color pictures as the stimuli. Two of their birds (trial-unique group) were trained with 152 different stimuli, and the birds saw each stimulus just once in any given session. A second pair of pigeons (two-stimulus group) was trained with only two different stimuli daily, as is standard practice with MTS. Both sets of birds were given transfer tests with novel stimuli after the task was learned to a criterion of 75% correct responses. The trial-unique birds showed substantial transfer to novel instances whereas the two-stimulus birds showed little transfer to new test stimuli. These results, like ours, suggest that concept attainment in pigeons is facilitated when large numbers of stimuli are employed.

It is not surprising that, whenever possible, animals respond to absolute properties of stimuli, and pigeons have demonstrated a remarkable capacity for such solutions to problems that also afford a "cognitive" strategy (e.g., Edwards & Honig, 1987; Vaughan & Greene, 1984). But sometimes animals do abstract complex relations, even under relatively impoverished training conditions. Hulse, Cynx, and Humpal (1984) trained starlings to discriminate between rhythmic and arrhythmic sound patterns (a series of four tones separated by intertone intervals). During training, a single rhythmic pattern was intermixed with multiple arrhythmic patterns generated from a list of 11 tone and intertone intervals. Following training, transfer tests were given in which the tempo of the patterns was altered through changes in the tone and intertone intervals. Transfer performance was very good, sug-gesting that the birds discriminated on the basis of the relation of the tone and intertone intervals, in spite of the limited number of stimuli presented during training. Perhaps there is something significant about temporal ratios of stimuli that facilitates abstraction of the kind that has been observed in our research and in the related research of Hulse and associates.

A second issue, and the focus of the present chapter, concerns the different performances engendered by S–L and S–D comparisons of temporal stimuli. As demonstrated by the data presented in this chapter, the latter discrimination is far more difficult for pigeons than the former, and these differences are clearly not due to variation in the method of training as discussed above. The version of the S–D task reported as Experiment 1 was adopted after some 100 sessions of training in which several hundred combinations of stimuli were intermixed; the animals showed no evidence of learning the discrimination under these circumstances.

The analysis pictured in Fig. 4.4 provided one framework for conceptualizing the differences in performance with S–L and S–D comparisons of duration, and this framework is very similar to one proposed for human psychophysical judgments in similar situations (e.g., Noreen, 1980; Vickers, 1979). Modifications of the basic S–D task produced a pattern of results that, to some degree, was compatible with the "sensory difference" analysis. However, neither the elimination of one configuration of stimuli (Experiment 2) nor the provision of a third choice alternative (Experiment 3) changed performance to the degree that might have been predicted solely from this analysis. Other factors appear to be involved.

Duration forms an intensive (prothetic) continuum, and comparisons of stimuli along prothetic continua naturally involve relative judgments (e. g., shorter–longer; brighter–dimmer, etc.). Same–different comparisons along prothetic continua may be difficult because they call for a categorical coding of the stimuli, and this process is opposed by the effects of stimulus generalization. For S–D tasks, it would be to the subject's advantage to "label" each of the stimuli, and base choices on the categorical relationship of the labels to each other. This transformation of the stimuli would alter the nature of the discrimination, changing an "analogue" comparison of stimuli into a categorical perception task (see Noreen, 1980, for a discussion of this point). But the data from this and other timing experiments (e.g., Spetch & Wilkie, 1983) indicate that the ratio–scale properties of stimulus durations are preserved, and that animals do not routinely "recode" temporal stimuli (see, however, Kraemer, Mazmanian, & Roberts, 1985, for evidence suggesting a categorical coding of duration).

The preceding discussion focused upon differences in discrimination depending on whether relative or categorical comparisons of prothetic stimuli were involved. The conclusion from the present and related experiments is that, with prothetic dimensions, relative comparisons of the stimuli yield higher estimates of sensitivity than do seemingly similar categorical comparisons. But we can also ask whether there are differences in performance between S–D comparisons of stimuli with prothetic and metathetic continua.[2] Farell (1985) reviewed the literature on human S–D judgments and noted that results differ, depending on whether "codable" (metathetic) or "uncodable" (prothetic) stimuli were used, and these differences were not artifacts of stimulus discriminability. The results from other pair comparison experiments with animals are instructive. Typically, these studies (e.g., Macphail, 1980; Santiago & Wright, 1984; White, 1974) have used colors, forms or pictures as the stimuli and based reinforcement for different choices according to whether a pair of stimuli are the same or different. Transfer tests are sometimes given as a measure of relational learning, but the point to be made here is the relative ease with which pigeons can learn these discriminations by comparison with the temporal S–D task. Same–different comparisons of metathetic stimuli appear far easier for pigeons to learn than S–D comparisons of duration, both with respect to the rate of learning and the asymptotic level of discrimination performance (e.g., see Wright et al. 1988).

SUMMARY

There are clear limits to pigeons' abilities to base discriminations upon relations between stimuli, and these limitations are similar to those observed in human psychophysical experiments. These limits seem due in part to factors implicated by signal-detection accounts, but also to specific combinations of stimulus dimensions and discriminative comparisons.

The present results should be replicated with other perceptual continua. For example, pigeons could be trained to compare the flicker rates of two stimuli, and to base comparisons on relative (faster–slower) or categorical (same–different) relations between the stimuli. The clear expectation, based on the present findings, is that the latter comparison would be more difficult than the former. In any event, the present and related research of Hulse et al. (1984) affords an alternative approach to the study of relational learning in animals, one that places same–different and identity learning in the broader context of a variety of stimulus relations to which pigeons and other animals may or may not be sensitive.

ACKNOWLEDGMENTS

Experiments 1 and 2 were conducted at Norwich University, Northfield, VT, and supported by a Dana Research Fellowship from Norwich University to J. G.

---

[2]Comparisons of discrimination performance for different stimulus dimensions must, of course, take into account the discriminability of the stimuli, and it is difficult to equate different tasks on this variable. Nonetheless, this question is pertinent to the issues at hand.

Fetterman. Experiment 3 and the preparation of this chapter were supported by a National Research Service Award postdoctoral fellowship (1 F32MH09306) from the National Institute of Mental Health (NIMH) to J.G. Fetterman, and by NIMH grant 1 R01 MH43233 to P. R. Killeen.

Thanks are extended to Michael Davison, Leon Dreyfus, Peter Killeen, and David MacEwen for comments on the manuscript. Peter Killeen generously provided laboratory space for some of the research reported in this chapter.

J. Gregor Fetterman is now at Department of Psychology, Indiana University-Purdue University at Indianapolis, 1125 East 38th St., Indianapolis, IN 46205.

REFERENCES

Carter, D. E., & Werner, T. J. (1978). Complex learning and information processing by pigeons: A critical analysis. *Journal of the Experimental Analysis of Behavior, 29,* 565–601.

Church, R. M. (1980). Short-term memory for time intervals. *Learning and Motivation, 11,* 208–219.

Creelman, C. D., & Macmillan, N. A. (1979). Auditory phase and frequency discrimination: A comparison of nine procedures. *Journal of Experimental Psychology: Human Perception and Performance, 5,* 146–156.

D'Amato, M. R., & Salmon, D. P. (1984). Cognitive processes in cebus monkeys. In H. L. Roitblat, T. G. Bever, & H. S. Terrace (Eds.), *Animal cognition* (pp. 149–168). Hillsdale, NJ: Lawrence Erlbaum Associates.

D'Amato, M. R., Salmon, D. P., & Colombo, M. (1985). Extent and limits of the matching concept in monkeys *(cebus apella). Journal of Experimental Psychology: Animal Behavior Processes, 11,* 35–51.

Dreyfus, L. R., Fetterman, J. G., Smith, L. D., & Stubbs, D. A. (1988). Discrimination of temporal relations by pigeons. *Journal of Experimental Psychology: Animal Behavior Processes, 14,* 349–367.

Edwards, C. A., & Honig, W. K. (1987). Memorization and "feature selection" in the acquisition of natural concepts in pigeons. *Learning and Motivation, 18,* 235–260.

Farell, B. (1985). "Same"–"different" judgments: A review of current controversies in perceptual comparisons. *Psychological Bulletin, 98,* 419–456.

Fetterman, J. G. (1987). Same-different comparison of duration. *Animal Learning and Behavior, 15,* 403–411.

Fetterman, J. G., & Dreyfus, L. R. (1986). Pair comparison of duration. *Behavioural Processes, 12,* 111–123.

Fetterman, J. G., & Dreyfus, L. R. (1987). Duration comparison and the perception of time. In M. L. Commons, J. E. Mazur, J. A. Nevin, & H. Rachlin (Eds.), *Quantitative analyses of behavior: Vol. 5. The effect of delay and of intervening events on reinforcement value* (pp. 3–27). Hillsdale, NJ: Lawrence Erlbaum Associates.

Fetterman, J. G., Dreyfus, L. R., & Stubbs, D. A. (1989). Discrimination of duration ratios. *Journal of Experimental Psychology: Animal Behavior Processes, 15,* 253–263.

Gescheider, G. A. (1985). *Psychophysics: Method, theory, and application* (2nd ed.). Hillsdale, NJ: Lawrence Erlbaum Associates.

Grier, J. B. (1971). Nonparametric indexes for sensitivity and bias: Computing formulas. *Psychological Bulletin, 75,* 424–429.

Hulse, S. H., Cynx, J., & Humpal, J. (1984). Cognitive processing of pitch and rhythm structures by birds. In H. L. Roitblat, T. G. Bever, & H. S. Terrace (Eds.), *Animal cognition* (pp. 183–198). Hillsdale, NJ: Lawrence Erlbaum Associates.

Kraemer, P. J., Mazmanian, D. S., & Roberts, W. A. (1985). The choose-short effect in pigeon memory for stimulus duration: Subjective shortening versus coding models. *Animal Learning and Behavior, 13,* 349–354.

Macmillan, N. A., Kaplan, H. L., & Creelman, C. D. (1977). The psychophysics of categorical perception. *Psychological Review, 84,* 452–471.

Macphail, E. M. (1980). Short-term visual recognition memory in pigeons. *Quarterly Journal of Experimental Psychology, 32,* 521–538.

Noreen, D. L. (1980). Optimal decision rules for some common psychophysical paradigms. *Proceedings of the Symposium in Applied Mathematics, 13,* 237–279.

Premack, D. (1978). On the abstractness of human concepts: Why it would be difficult to talk to a pigeon. In S. H. Hulse, H. Fowler, & W. K. Honig (Eds.), *Cognitive processes in animal behavior* (pp. 423–451). Hillsdale, NJ: Lawrence Erlbaum Associates.

Premack, D. (1983). Animal cognition. *Annual Review of Psychology, 34,* 351–362.

Santiago, H. C., & Wright, A. A. (1984). Pigeon memory: Same/different concept learning, serial probe recognition, acquisition, and probe delay effects on the serial-position function. *Journal of Experimental Psychology: Animal Behavior Processes, 10,* 498–512.

Spence, K. W. (1937). The differential response in animals to stimuli varying within a single dimension. *Psychological Review, 44,* 430–444.

Spetch, M. L., & Wilkie, D. M. (1983). Subjective shortening: A model of pigeons' memory for event duration. *Journal of Experimental Psychology: Animal Behavior Processes, 9,* 14–30.

Stevens, S. S., & Galanter, E. H. (1957). Ratio scales for a dozen perceptual continua. *Journal of Experimental Psychology, 54,* 377–411.

Stubbs, D. A. (1976). Response bias and the discrimination of stimulus duration. *Journal of the Experimental Analysis of Behavior, 25,* 243–250.

Stubbs, D. A., Dreyfus, L. R., & Fetterman, J. G. (1984). The perception of temporal events. In J. Gibbon & L. Allan (Eds.), *Timing and time perception* (pp. 30–42). Annals of the New York Academy of Sciences, Vol. 423.

Vaughan, W., & Greene, S. (1984). Pigeon visual memory capacity. *Journal of Experimental Psychology: Animal Behavior Processes, 10,* 256–271.

Vickers, D. (1979). *Decision processes in visual perception.* New York: Academic Press.

White, K. G. (1974). Temporal integration in the pigeon. *British Journal of Psychology, 65,* 437–444.

Wilcox, S., & Katz, S. (1981). A direct realistic alternative to the traditional conception of memory. *Behaviorism, 9,* 227–239.

Wright, A. A., Cook, R. G., Rivera, J. J., Sands, S. F., & Delius, J. D. (1988). Concept learning by pigeons: Matching-to-sample with trial-unique video picture stimuli. *Animal Learning and Behavior, 16,* 436–444.

5 Discriminability and Distinctiveness in Complex Arrays of Simple Elements

Werner K. Honig,
Dalhousie University, Halifax, Nova Scotia

The procedures used to assess the discriminability of stimuli in animal psychophysics require differential reinforcement; for example, correct identifications of a stimulus are rewarded, while false alarms or "misses" are not (Blough & Blough, 1977). Such differential reinforcement may well enhance the discriminability of the stimuli, as their differential association with reward would make them *distinctive.* Indeed, there is a history of research on acquired distinctiveness of cues (Lawrence, 1949; see Osgood, 1953, for a review). In the area of animal psychophysics, the issue of acquired distinctiveness of cues needs to be addressed. Ideally, it should be possible to separate the discriminability of stimuli from their associative value, in order to equate their distinctiveness. In practice, this is difficult, because the training procedures normally involve differential reinforcement. Even in cases where this can be avoided, as in a conditional discrimination (e.g., if the stimuli are the same, go left; if different, go right), the different responses associated with the stimuli may make them more distinctive and thus enhance their discriminability.

In addition to the specific effects of discrimination training on distinctiveness, there may be more general effects of an "attentional" nature (Mackintosh, 1977). In a well-known study, for example, Jenkins and Harrison (1960) showed that the dimension of tonal frequency gained stimulus control following interdimensional training, in which pigeons were first taught to discriminate the presence of a tone from its absence. Such general effects of discrimination training on the distinctiveness of stimuli again makes it very hard to "isolate" discriminability of the stimuli as a determinant of stimulus control.

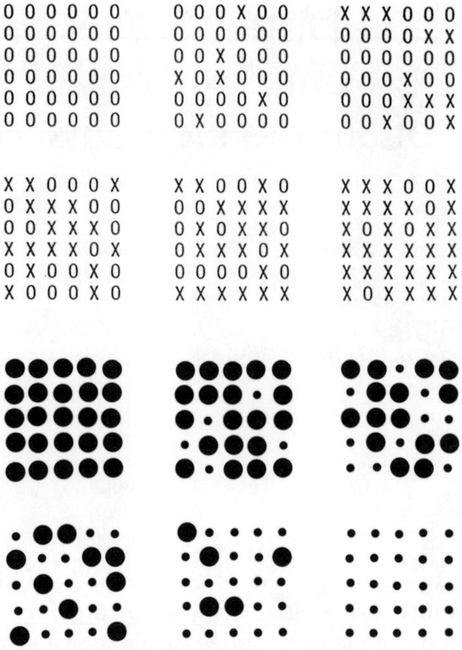

```
0 0 0 0 0 0      0 0 0 X 0 0      X X X 0 0 0
0 0 0 0 0 0      0 0 0 0 0 0      0 0 0 0 X X
0 0 0 0 0 0      0 0 X 0 0 0      0 0 0 0 0 0
0 0 0 0 0 0      X 0 X 0 0 0      0 0 0 X 0 0
0 0 0 0 0 0      0 0 0 0 X 0      0 0 0 X X X
0 0 0 0 0 0      0 X 0 0 0 0      0 0 X 0 0 X


X X 0 0 0 X      X X 0 0 X 0      X X X 0 0 X
0 X X X 0 0      0 0 X X X X      X X X X 0 X
0 0 X X X 0      0 X 0 X X 0      X 0 X 0 X X
X X X X 0 X      0 X X X 0 X      X X X X X X
0 X 0 0 X 0      0 0 0 0 X 0      X X X X X X
X 0 0 0 X 0      X X X X X X      X 0 X X X X
```

FIG. 5.1 Selected arrays of stimulus elements used for training and testing. These include six of the nine different proportions of Xs and Os. Elements that differed in color were presented in a similar manner. The six different proportions of large and small elements are all shown.

Some of these difficulties can be reduced with a different kind of training procedure, that offers a new approach to the problem of separating discriminability from distinctiveness. We are working with *arrays* of stimulus elements that differ on a stimulus dimension. These elements are presented in different proportions as a square pattern on a panel at which the pigeon pecks to obtain food. The *proportion* of the elements in the matrix provides the primary dimension of stimulus control. The elements themselves do not change in any particular training condition. However, different sets of elements can be used in their various proportions in different training conditions, and these can vary in their presumed discriminability. A set of red and blue elements would presumably be more discriminable than a set of red and orange elements.

Different kinds of discriminations can be acquired with arrays of this nature. *Numerosity discriminations* involve differential reinforcement of the different stimulus elements, while the *mixture discriminations* do not. In this way, we can separate the discriminability of the stimuli, which depends on their physical difference, from their distinctiveness, which is influenced by their association with reward. As we shall see, when the stimuli are made distinctive, differences in performance that can otherwise be attributed to discriminability are greatly reduced. The particular contribution of the procedures to be described here is that the general aspects of the training situations are the same in different problems, except for the differential association of particular stimulus elements with reward.

GENERAL PROCEDURES

In the research described here, we have trained pigeons on two kinds of maintained discriminations, using arrays of stimulus elements. These are discriminations of *relative numerosity* and of *stimulus mixture.* Both involve the same patterns of two different elements, which are projected onto the pigeon's response panel. The two elements appear in different proportions in square arrays, or matrices. For example, 36 small dots in a square matrix can be all red, all blue, or some proportion of each (see Honig & Stewart, 1989). This relative proportion (or relative numerosity) of elements defines the dimension on which stimulus control is established. Fig. 5.1 provides two sets of arrays which are typical of the kind used for our research. The elements shown here differ in form or in size, and are readily reproduced in black and white. We have in fact more often used small, colored circular patches, or "dots" (blue, green, red, and orange). The arrays of 36 colored elements correspond closely to those made up of Xs and Os, as pictured in Fig. 5.1. The dots are 4 mm in diameter on the response screen, and spaced 11 cm apart, center to center. In these arrays of 36 elements, the proportion of a particular element is 1.0, .83, .69, .58, .50, .42, .31, .17, or .0. When the elements differ in size, there are only 25 in the array, and the proportions are 1.0, .80, .60, .40, .20, and .0. Several randomized arrangements of each mixture are available. Since they are square, each array can be presented in several orientations.

The pigeon pecks directly at the stimulus display, which is back-projected onto a hinged panel that is about 7 cm square. One array is presented at a time. A negative trial ends after 20 s without reinforcement. A positive trial ends with the first peck after 20 s, which is reinforced but not counted. Typically, a session is comprised of four blocks of trials in which each instance of the different proportions of the elements is presented at least once. In several procedures, one or two positive arrays are presented more frequently in order to provide a reasonable proportion of positive trials. Trial order is randomized within blocks.

MIXTURE-NEGATIVE DISCRIMINATIONS

In the *mixture-negative discriminations,* the two kinds of elements are equally associated with reinforcement. Trials with uniform arrays of elements, such as all-blue and all-red, end with reinforcement, while all combinations of elements (i.e., mixtures) are negative. Both of the positive uniform arrays are presented twice in each block of 11 trials; each of the negative mixed arrays is presented once. The mean rate of responding to the two uniform arrays is used as a reference value. Responses to each of the mixed arrays are divided by this reference value to provide a discrimination index, or DI. (This is indicated as the "proportion of responses" in the figures.) A low value indicates a good discrimination between the mixed and the uniform arrays.

Mixtures of Red and Blue Dots

Three pigeons were trained in the mixture discrimination in which the uniform arrays of red dots and blue dots were positive, and the different degrees of stimulus mixture were all negative. The birds were trained for 12 sessions of four blocks of trials.

Results.   The birds readily learned this discrimination, and they acquired it at rather similar rates. The mean data are shown in Fig. 5.2 for the three blocks of four training sessions. A U-shaped negative gradient was obtained, with a steep slope between the uniform and the mixed arrays, even when the proportion of "minority" elements in the mixed arrays was not large. The birds were therefore very sensitive to the degree of stimulus mixture. The mean discrimination index for the "most mixed" array was close to .03 for the third block of trials.

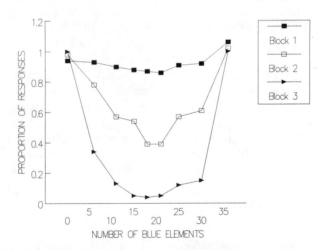

FIG. 5.2 Acquisition of the mixture discrimination with blue and red elements. The mean data from three subjects are shown. These were obtained from three blocks of four sessions. (The data presented here appears in the *Journal of Experimental Psychology: Animal Behavior Processes*, Vol. 17.)

Mixtures of Red and Orange Dots

The mixture discrimination was replicated with red and orange elements, which are physically and perceptually more similar than red and blue. Four new pigeons were used. The procedures were the same as those carried out with red and blue dots, except for the difference in the stimulus elements.

The pigeons acquired this discrimination more slowly than the mixture discrimination with red and blue elements. The mean data are shown in Fig. 5.3, for the first and second blocks of four sessions, and for the averages of two subsequent blocks of four sessions each. By the last two blocks of sessions, responding to the "most mixed" arrays was at levels similar to those obtained with red and blue dots. The asymptotic forms of the gradients are very similar. However, the gradients based on red and orange elements reflect 40 sessions of training, rather than 12.

Mixtures of Elements Differing in Form

This experiment was undertaken to determine whether the mixture discrimination acquired with red and blue dots would transfer to elements that differ in form. This is possible in principle with the mixture problem, as the dimension of stimulus mixture can be abstracted from the specific elements that comprise the arrays. The three birds already trained with red and blue dots were retrained with similar arrays of 36 Xs and Os (see Fig 5.1). After they learned to peck reliably at the uniform arrays, they were

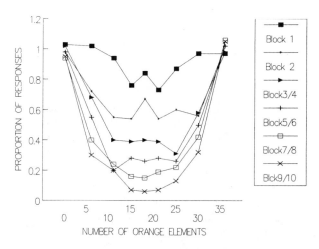

FIG. 5.3 Acquisition of the mixture discrimination with red and orange elements. From blocks 3 through 10, the data from sets of two blocks have been combined to reduce crowding. (The data presented here appears in the *Journal of Experimental Psychology: Animal Behavior Processes,* Vol. 17.)

trained for 12 sessions on the mixture–negative discrimination. Except for the difference in stimuli, the procedure corresponded to the mixture–negative discrimination with colors.

There was no transfer of the discrimination to different forms. The initial mixture gradients were flat. Moreover, 12 training sessions produced only a small reduction in responding even to the most mixed arrays. In order to make the discrimination easier, the patterns were modified. They consisted of 16 rather than 36 elements, which were larger than the original Xs and Os, and covered roughly the same total area on the response screen. However, even with these simplified arrays, acquisition of the mixture discrimination was slow and unsatisfactory. After 10 blocks of training sessions, the pigeons had only achieved a mean DI of about .50 with the 50% mixture. Furthermore, the gradients of two of the subjects were asymmetrical. (This was not the case with the gradients based on color.)

We then simplified the discrimination, hoping to take advantage of an "easy-to-hard" effect. The birds were retrained with patterns of 36 Xs and Os. However, the negative arrays each contained 50% of each kind of element — in short, only the "most mixed" arrays were contrasted to the positive, uniform arrays in training. Each session consisted of 16 positive trials with uniform arrays of Xs or Os, and 16 negative trials with 18 items of each kind. This was carried out for 26 training sessions. Then the original discrimination was reinstated with all of the different degrees of stimulus mixture.

The three subjects acquired the simplified discrimination reasonably well. Individual birds achieved DIs of .33, .24, and .13. When the original "full" mixture discrimination was reinstated, responding was primarily reduced at first with the 50% mixture used in the simplified training procedure. After that, the negative gradients increased in slope. The gradients stabilized after two blocks of training sessions. These data are shown in Fig. 5.4. The gradients differ from those based on mixtures of different colors. They are more V-shaped than U-shaped. In fact, they are almost linear. The question arises whether this difference in form is due to the nature of the elements used in the arrays, or to the special training procedure, in which the "intermediate" degrees of stimulus mixture were not used. The gradients from the last block of training sessions with the simplified arrays of 16 elements were compared with the gradient from the first block of training sessions (with 36-element arrays) following the special training procedure. Except for a marked reduction in responding at the "most mixed" value following special training, those two gradients were quite similar; in fact, they crossed several times. The linear form of the mixture gradients obtained with forms appears, therefore, not to be an effect of the special training procedure. It is due to the discriminability of the elements. For pigeons, the "minority" elements seem to be more discriminable when

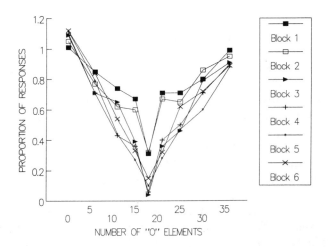

FIG. 5.4   Acquisition of the mixture-negative discrimination with different forms (X and O), following a special training procedure. Data for six blocks of four sessions are shown.

elements differ in color than when they differ in form. When colors are used, a steep gradient is obtained with a "floor" that reflects a low rate of responding.

Mixtures of Elements Differing in Size

The degree of difference between colors can be ordered, at least on an ordinal scale. This is difficult with forms. Differences in size are readily quantified, and we extended our research on mixture–negative discriminations accordingly. The stimulus patterns were the arrays of 25 large and small dots. The large dots were 9 mm in diameter, while the small ones were 4 mm. The mixed arrays contained 20 dots of one size and five of the other, or 15 of one size and 10 of the other. The latter are the "most mixed" arrays (see Fig. 5.1).

Three new pigeons were used for this research. After they were trained to peck at the uniform arrays of large and small dots, and reached a stable rate of responding, the mixture problem was introduced. In each block of trials, each mixed array was presented once, while each uniform array was presented twice. Four blocks of trials comprised a session.

The birds acquired this discrimination so slowly that the problem was simplified by contrasting the uniform and the "most mixed" arrays, as we had done with the discrimination based on Xs and Os. The mixtures of 5 and 20 small and large dots were replaced by additional examples of the "most mixed" arrays of 10 of one kind and 15 of the other. This procedure was carried out for 14, 16, or 19 sessions for the different birds, at which time they acquired the discrimination reasonably well. The discrimination with the full range of mixture values was then reinstated, and the birds were trained for 12 further sessions.

As shown in Fig. 5.5, the pigeons performed well on the mixture discrimination after the special training procedure. The discrimination ratio based on the "most mixed" and the uniform arrays was about .10 for the third block of four sessions. However, since there are fewer training values on the mixture dimension when there are only 25 elements rather than 36, it is hard to compare the slopes of the gradients from this experiment with those obtained from the prior studies.

Since the degree of difference between stimuli can be scaled unequivocally on the size dimension, it was of interest to train the same subjects with mixtures of small and medium elements, rather than small and large. The medium elements were 6 mm in diameter, and they replaced the large elements in the arrays. All other aspects of the procedure remained the same.

Initial gradients obtained with the medium and small elements are also shown in Fig. 5.5. They are much flatter and not as orderly than those obtained with large and small elements. Although there was some initial transfer, there was no improvement with further training. In fact, the pigeons did less well during the second block of four sessions than the first block. Further research on the problem, not described here, failed to reveal any marked improvement in the mixture problem with small and medium elements.

Our findings with the mixture-negative procedures can be summarized in this way: The maintained discriminations are orderly and stable, once they

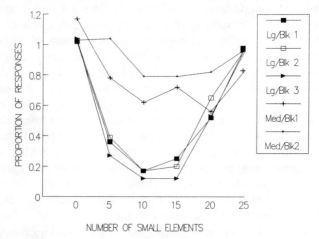

FIG. 5.5 Acquisition of the mixture-negative discrimination with large and small dots, in three blocks of four sessions each. Transfer of the discrimination to arrays of small and medium dots is also shown.

have been acquired. These discriminations are sensitive to the degree of difference between the stimulus elements, which in behavioral terms translates into their discriminability. The discrimination is acquired more quickly with a larger difference between the elements (blue vs. red as against orange vs. red, and large vs. small as against medium vs. small). Different forms seem to be especially hard to discriminate. The presence of odd elements in the array had less of an effect in reducing responding when the elements differed in form than when they differed in color, even when the birds were responding very little to the "most negative" degrees of stimulus mixture.

MAINTAINED NUMEROSITY DISCRIMINATIONS WITH A UNIFORM POSITIVE ARRAY

The mixture-negative discrimination is a maintained discrimination procedure, in which both kinds of elements are equally associated with reinforcement. Therefore, the pigeon has to discriminate among different combinations of elements with the same associative value. In the *maintained numerosity discrimination* the same patterns of stimulus elements can be presented; however, only the uniform array of one element is positive, while all the other arrays, including the uniform array of the other element, are negative. The elements are therefore differently associated with reinforcement. In other respects, the mixture–negative and maintained numerosity discriminations are identical. With this latter procedure, we have obtained reliable discrimination gradients that decline as a function of the number of negative elements in the arrays.

This so-called "Single S + " procedure has been carried out with red and blue elements, with Xs and Os, and with dots that differ in size. The first two discriminations could be compared directly, as the numbers of elements in the arrays were the same, and the procedures differed only with respect to the stimuli. Different groups of four pigeons each were trained on this task. In each randomized block of trials, the uniform positive array (all blue or red dots, or all Xs or Os) was presented four times, and each negative array was presented once, including the uniform negative array. Otherwise, the training procedures were the same as in the mixture discrimination. The positive stimuli (blue or red, and X or O) were counterbalanced across subjects.

Results

The pigeons readily acquired these maintained discriminations. The data are shown in Fig. 5.6 for three blocks of four training sessions. Even in the

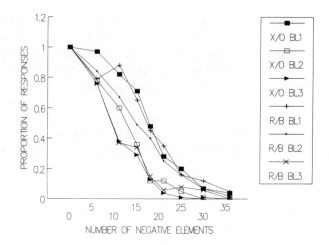

FIG. 5.6 Acquisition of relative numerosity discriminations involving a single positive, uniform array. Data are shown [for three blocks of four sessions] with arrays of red and blue elements, and Xs and Os.

first block of trials, an orderly, rather steep, gradient was obtained with both problems, and the gradients based on color and form were almost identical. In the course of training, the gradients became yet somewhat steeper. In the second block, the gradient obtained with Xs and Os was somewhat steeper than the gradient based on colored elements. The gradients obtained for the third block of sessions were again very similar. These findings clearly differ from those obtained with the stimulus mixture procedure, which required special training when forms were to be discriminated as the stimulus elements.

Different Sizes of Dots

The patterns were arrays of 25 large and small dots, or medium and small dots. For two pigeons, the large or medium dots were positive, and the small dots were negative. The other two were trained with the opposite discrimination. Each session consisted of four blocks of trials, in which the uniform positive array was presented three times, and each negative array was presented once. The discriminations were carried out for four blocks of four sessions each. During the first and fourth blocks, the arrays consisted of large and small dots. During the second and third blocks, the medium and small dots were presented.

The results are shown in Fig. 5.7. Orderly gradients were obtained from the outset of training. They became slightly steeper during the four blocks of sessions. The pigeons had no difficulty with either discrimination. The changes in slope in the course of training were due entirely to the continued

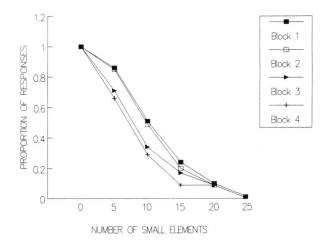

FIG. 5.7 Acquisition of a relative numerosity discrimination with a single positive, uniform array. In blocks 1 and 4, the arrays were composed of small and large elements. In blocks 2 and 3, the arrays were composed of small and medium elements.

experience with the discriminations, not to the sizes of the medium and large dots. This finding differs from the mixture gradients obtained with the same elements, which were very sensitive to the difference in size of the elements, so much so that the pigeons required a special training procedure when medium and small elements were used. In this respect the results are parallel to those obtained with Xs and Os. Special training was required when those forms were used for the mixture problem, but the numerosity discrimination was learned quite readily.

These results suggest that when the elements in complex patterns are differentially associated with reinforcement, they become *distinctive*. The differences in discriminability between colors and forms, so clearly observed in the mixture gradients, are eliminated in the relative numerosity discriminations. Furthermore, the pigeons had no difficulty with the numerosity discrimination when it involved medium and small dots. The differential association between the stimulus elements and reinforcement, which enhances their discriminability, reduces any difference in the slopes of the numerosity gradients.

MAINTAINED DISCRIMINATIONS WITH MORE THAN 1 POSITIVE VALUE

The maintained discrimination with a single, uniform positive array may not be the most appropriate training procedure for comparison with the mixture-negative discrimination. For one thing, only one value on the dimension is positive in the former, while two values (the uniform arrays) are positive in the latter. Furthermore, the range between the positive array and the "most negative" array is much greater in the numerosity discrimination, as it extends across the whole continuum. The corresponding range of the mixture negative procedure is only half as great, from each of the uniform arrays to the most mixed array. It is therefore of interest to compare numerosity discriminations that involve different ranges of adjacent numerosity values, to determine how this affects the slopes of the gradients. In this research the same numerosity values were used as before. Several adjacent proportions, including one uniform array, were positive. The other numerosity values, including the other uniform array, were negative. This procedure limited the range of the negative proportions, but the elements were still differentially associated with reinforcement.

Different Numbers of Positive Values

The different proportions of 36 blue and red elements were used in training, except for the 50% mixture. The continuum of relative numerosity was partitioned to provide a range of positive and a range of negative values in successive phases of the research. (1) The uniform array of one kind of element was the single positive value. This is the "single S+" procedure. (2) Two positive values: one uniform array and the adjacent value with 30 elements of one kind and six of the other. (3) Four positive values: all displays with more elements of one kind were positive; the other four proportions were negative. (4) Six positive values: All arrays were positive, except for the uniform negative array, and the adjacent proportion of 30 negative and 6 positive stimuli. The pigeons were trained with each of these different partitions of the continuum over several blocks of four sessions each. Each session contained four blocks of trials. The different proportions of elements were presented once in each block, except for the single S+ procedure, in which the positive array was presented four times. Red and blue were counterbalanced as the positive elements.

Results. Results from the sixth block of training sessions are shown in Fig. 5.8 for each of these procedures, except for the "Single S+" procedure, which was run only for five blocks of sessions. The data from the last block are shown for that condition. For each session, the level of responding to the uniform array of positive elements was assigned the value of 1.0, and the remaining response totals were converted to a proportion of that value. These proportional values were averaged for each block of sessions for each bird, and then averaged for the four birds to provide mean gradients.

The pigeons generally responded at equal rates to each of the proportions in the positive range. Within the negative range, the gradients reflect the proportions of negative elements. The negative parts of the several gradi-

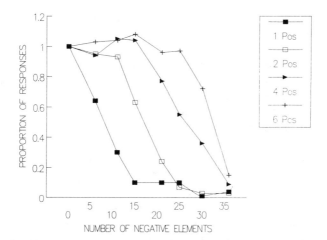

FIG. 5.8   Data from the sixth block of training sessions in each of four maintained discriminations with 36 red and blue elements. Different phases of training involved different numbers of "adjacent" proportions of positive elements as the positive arrays. These were the single uniform array, and 2, 4, or 6 proportions of positive elements.

ents, beginning with the "most negative" of the reinforced arrays, are quite similar in slope. The scope of the negative range had little effect upon the negative parts of these gradients. Admittedly, when this scope extended over only three values (with 11, 6, or 0 positive elements) the gradient was somewhat steeper than in the other conditions, but otherwise they are quite parallel. Within the positive range, the pigeons responded at similar rates to the various proportions of red and blue dots, although these contained different numbers of negative elements. Sloping gradients were obtained only within the negative range, starting generally with the last reinforced value in the positive range.

Different Kinds of Stimulus Elements

Research with a range of positive numerosity values has also been carried out with different kinds of stimulus elements. In the work presented here, the positive range always included the four proportions in which the positive element was the more numerous. The remaining arrays, in which the positive element was in the minority, were negative.

One group of four pigeons was trained with red and blue elements; one group with red and orange elements, and one group with Xs and Os. The first group was also trained with arrays of 64 red and blue dots. The procedures were similar to those described in the previous section: There were four blocks of trials in each session, and the positive element was counterbalanced across subjects in the different procedures.

Results.   The data are presented in Fig. 5.9 for the fourth block of four sessions in each discrimination, at which point the data were quite stable. The gradients obtained with red and blue dots (both in arrays of 36 and 64 elements), and with different forms are quite similar. The red-orange numerosity gradient differs from the others, in that the declining slope begins within the range of reinforced values. However, the slope of the gradient among the negative proportions is almost the same as the slope obtained from the other gradients.

Discussion.   The data obtained from research with these numerosity discriminations suggest that the differences among gradients from the stimulus mixture discriminations cannot be accounted for by procedural factors. When several adjacent numerosity values are positive, so that the range of negative values is constrained, this does not materially affect the slopes of the gradients obtained within that range. It is not clear why responding within the ranges of reinforced proportions did not reflect the different proportions of negative elements (the single exception being the maintained discrimination with red and orange elements). With its bias toward pecking at stimuli that precede reinforcement, the pigeon may have "memorized" the range of positive proportions, but this notion does little more than offer a new description of the data.

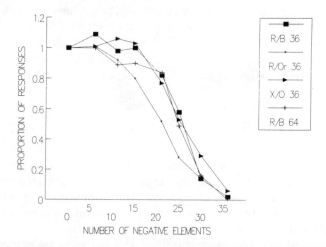

FIG. 5.9   Data from the fourth block of maintained discrimination sessions in which all arrays containing more positive than negative elements were positive, while the rest were negative. The elements were 36 red and blue dots, 64 red and blue dots, 36 red and orange dots, and 36 Xs and Os.

GENERAL DISCUSSION

Discriminability and Distinctiveness

The data in this chapter support a theme that has now been elaborated with a few variations: Control of behavior by stimulus elements in complex arrays is enhanced by differential association with reinforcement, and this renders the stimuli distinctive. Such associations are provided by the single S+ training procedures and by the "range discriminations," of which the single S+ procedure is actually a limiting instance. These discriminations are not markedly affected by the characteristics of the different kinds of elements, at least within the range of physical differences used for this research. In the stimulus mixture discriminations, the elements are all associated with reinforcement to the same degree. Their discriminability is not enhanced, and this procedure can therefore be used to assess the inherent differences in discriminability among different colors and sizes. It also reflects the low discriminability of different forms.

Relation to the Differential Outcomes Effect

The present findings appear to be related to the familiar differential outcomes effect (DOE). If a discrimination is carried out so that correct choices of two different positive stimuli are followed by different reinforcers, acquisition of the discrimination is greatly facilitated, and the memory for the initial or sample stimulus is much better, than it is when there is only one kind of reinforcer (see Peterson, 1984, for a review). Of particular interest here is a procedure of Peterson, Wheeler, and Trapold (1980). In a conditional discrimination, pigeons were trained with food reinforcement as the outcome following correct choices after one initial stimulus (horizontal or vertical lines), and explicit nonreinforcement (signaled by a tone) as the outcome for correct choices after the other initial stimulus (vertical or horizontal lines). The pigeons acquired the discrimination more quickly with the differential outcomes. Moreover, they were better able to maintain good performance over working memory intervals between the presentation of the initial stimulus and the choice stimuli.

This research was extended by Peterson (1984) to the comparison of colors and line orientations as sample stimuli in the acquisition of a conditional discrimination. Normally, conditional discriminations are learned much more slowly by pigeons when lines are used as samples. When the line orientations were made distinctive through differential association with reinforcement, the difference between lines and colors as sample stimuli was eliminated because the lines were more effective and memorable as sample stimuli. DeLong and Wasserman (1981) carried out similar research with a conditional successive discrimination procedure, in which only one test stimulus is presented, rather than two. Different probabilities of reinforcement (0.2 and 1.0) were associated with the samples (or initial stimuli) in some conditions. The discrimination was markedly better in this condition than it was in the same discrimination when the probability of reinforcement was 0.6 following either initial stimulus.

This research on the differential outcomes effect is relevant to the comparisons between mixture discriminations and maintained numerosity discriminations obtained with the same elements. The differential association with reward reduces differences in the discriminability of the stimuli. It makes the less discriminable elements distinctive, and facilitates the acquisition of the numerosity discrimination with elements that are otherwise not very discriminable. The mixture discriminations do not benefit from this enhancement of distinctiveness.

Discriminability of Stimulus Elements and the Limits of Stimulus Control.

Our conclusions present an apparent contradiction: From the differential performance in the mixture discriminations, we conclude that the different kinds of elements are not equally discriminable for the pigeons: red and blue are more discriminable than red and orange, both are more discriminable than Xs and Os, and different sizes of elements also differ in discriminability. Yet these "inherent" differences can be overcome by differential association with reinforcement. At some level, then, the pigeons must be able to discriminate between the different elements; otherwise, the associations with reinforcement and extinction would never be acquired. Clearly, it would be possible to make the differences between elements so small that the pigeon could not distinguish between them, even with optimal training procedures. We appear not to have reached this limit. The point is that *effective* stimulus control is modulated by differential associations among the elements with reinforcement contingencies. Our methods, involving complex arrays of small elements, have presumably not approached the limits of *potential* stimulus control. That aspect of the stimuli may best be studied with standard psychophysical methods, in which only one or two elements are presented at a time, and in which their characteristics are changed in small increments on a well-defined physical dimension.

Relation to Signal Detection.

The research described here is quite different from traditional work in the detection of particular punctate events. Such work is carried out with well-defined methods, in which single stimuli are presented briefly, and assessed by the subject with a choice response that indicates "yes" or "no."

The number of stimuli is limited, and bias is manipulated largely by controlling the probability of occurrence particular events. The method is generally symmetrical, in the sense that the stimuli are equally associated with reinforcement. This well-established but restricted procedure is being applied to complex and meaningful events; for example, the identification of tumors on X-ray photographs is described elsewhere in this volume. Such events may well involve meaningful or "affective" associations, like the differential associations with food among the stimulus elements described in this chapter. It would be assumed within the confines of signal-detection theory, that such associations affect bias, and that is certainly justified. But they may also affect discriminability, which is a matter that yet needs to be determined. It would be necessary first to imbue the stimuli in a signal-detection procedure with associative values, in order to make them distinctive, and then one could study their discriminability with standard signal-detection procedures. One could, for example, teach rats to associate two tones differentially with water and no water (or with two different liquid flavors), and then train them on a signal-detection task with the same tones where the reward for correct responding is food. The manipulation of distinctiveness as a variable within the area of signal detection could expand the scope and value of that powerful methodology in its applications to events in the "real world."

ACKNOWLEDGMENTS

The present research was supported by grant No. AO 104 from the Natural Sciences and Engineering Council of Canada. Karen Stewart was involved in all aspects of carrying out the work reported here, while Brent Alsop provided insightful comments on its relation to signal-detection theory, and on its presentation in this chapter.

REFERENCES

Blough, D. S., & Blough, P. (1977). Animal psychophysics. In W. K. Honig & J. E. R. Staddon (Eds.), *Handbook of operant behavior* (pp. 513–549). Englewood Cliffs, NJ: Prentice–Hall.

DeLong, R. E., & Wasserman, E. A. (1981). Effects of differential reinforcement expectancies on successive matching-to-sample performance in pigeons. *Journal of Experimental Psychology: Animal Behavior Processes, 7,* 394–412.

Honig, W. K., & Stewart, K. E. (1989). Discrimination of relative numerosity by the pigeon. *Animal Learning and Behavior, 17,* 134–146.

Jenkins, H. M., & Harrison, M. (1960). Effect of discrimination training on auditory generalization. *Journal of Experimental Psychology, 59,* 246–253.

Lawrence, D. H. (1949). Acquired distinctiveness of cues, I: Transfer between discriminations on the basis of familiarity with the stimulus. *Journal of Experimental Psychology, 39,* 770–784.

Mackintosh, N. J. (1977). Stimulus control: Attentional factors. In W. K. Honig & J. E. R. Staddon (Eds.), *Handbook of operant behavior* (pp. 481–513). New York: Appleton–Century–Crofts,

Osgood, C. E. (1953). *Method and theory in experimental psychology.* Oxford University Press.

Peterson, G. B. (1984). How expectancies guide behavior. In H. L. Roitblat, T. G. Bever, & H. S. Terrace (Eds.), *Animal cognition* (pp. 135-145). Hillsdale NJ: Lawrence Erlbaum Associates.

Peterson, G. B., Wheeler, R. L., & Trapold, M. A. (1980). Enhancement of pigeons' conditional discrimination performance by expectancies of reinforcement and nonreinforcement. *Animal Learning and Behavior, 8,* 22-30.

6 Memory Limitations in Human and Animal Signal Detection

Sheila Chase
Hunter College, City University of New York

Eric G. Heinemann
Brooklyn College, City University of New York

In previous volumes of this series, we described a general theory of memory and decision making that accounts for phenomena as diverse as probability learning, categorization, concept formation, and pattern recognition (Chase, 1983; Heinemann, 1983a; Heinemann & Chase, 1989). In this chapter we shall discuss how this theory is related to signal-detection theory (SDT), and attempt to account for some of the differences between the behavior predicted by SDT and that actually observed. (The problems discussed in this chapter concern "recognition" rather than "detection" but to facilitate communication we shall use the well-known terminology of SDT.) We shall limit our discussion here to decisions involving stimuli that induce sensations which vary along a single intensive dimension, such as loudness or brightness.

It is now clear that neither humans nor pigeons behave quite as described by SDT in the form presented by Swets, Tanner, and Birdsall (1961). For example, the basic measure of sensitivity, d', is affected by factors not treated by the theory. Four such factors will be considered here: (1) the occurrence of responses that are independent of stimulus value, guessing, (2) improvements in sensitivity that occur during discrimination training (Chase, Bugnacki, Braida, & Durlach, 1983; Heinemann & Avin, 1973; Swets & Sewall, 1963), (3) the dependence of d' for any particular pair of stimuli upon the range of stimulus values presented during the experiment (Braida & Durlach, 1972; Chase, 1983), (4) the dependence of d' on the position of the stimulus pair within the range (Braida & Durlach, 1972; Weber, Green, & Luce, 1977).

According to our theory, a relatively small amount of information is available at the time a decision is made. As the available information increases, performance approaches that of the optimal statistical decision maker, as specified in SDT. Changes in the information on which decisions are based are reflected in changes in observed sensitivity.

Our memory and decision model was originally developed to account for data obtained from experiments in which the stimuli were lights or sounds varying only in intensity and the observers were pigeons (Heinemann & Chase, 1975). In these experiments, two or more stimuli were presented repeatedly in random order for classification, a procedure referred to as the method of single stimuli. The pigeons initiated each stimulus presentation by pecking on a key located in the center of the response panel. After each stimulus presentation, the pigeons were required to peck at one of two or more choice keys which differed in location. Pecks at only one of the choice keys were considered correct on a given trial. In most of our experiments the correct choice was cued by the intensity of white noise or by the luminance of a rectangular translucent screen (*display key*) located above the row of choice keys. The trial ended when a choice key was pecked. A correct choice was followed by presentation of food; an incorrect choice, shortly thereafter, by another presentation of the same stimulus (*correction procedure*). Only results obtained on first presentations are considered here. Sessions usually ended when 80 or 100 correct choices had been made.

In the experiments to be reported here the number of stimuli to be classified varied from 2 to 13. In two-choice experiments, the proportion of responses to one of the keys was plotted against stimulus value. From these psychometric functions, or *choice curves, d'* may be obtained for pairs of stimuli by treating "hits" as responses to the high-intensity key given the more intense of the two stimuli and "false alarms" as responses to this key given the less-intense stimulus. For experiments involving more than two choices, *d'* was obtained using a technique described by Durlach and Braida (1969). In the latter experiments, percent correct and information transmitted were also used as measures of performance.

VARIABLES AFFECTING SENSITIVITY TO INTENSITY DIFFERENCES

If the stimuli to be categorized are two sounds of slightly different intensities, months of training may be required before there is any evidence that the pigeon is discriminating between the stimuli. Results of an experiment in which the difference between two levels of white noise was varied are shown in Fig. 6.1.

Fig. 6.1 shows how the proportion of trials on which the pigeon chooses one of the keys changes with training. At first this key is chosen almost

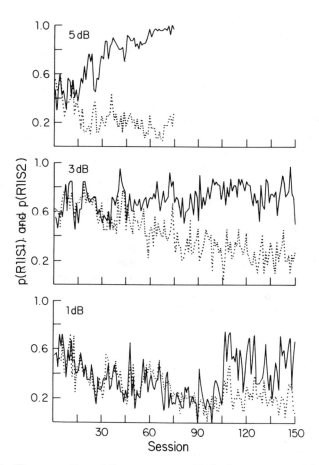

FIG. 6.1   The proportion of R_1 responses made in the presence of S_1 (solid line) and in the presence of S_2 (broken line). Each panel shows results for a single pigeon trained to discriminate between two levels of white noise differing by the amount shown in the panel (from Heinemann, 1983b).

equally often in the presence of each of the two sounds. As learning progresses, the curves separate (d' computed from these sets of "hits" and "false alarms" increases). The number of training trials over which performance remains at chance, called the *presolution period* (PSP), depends on the intensity difference, as does the asymptotic separation between the two curves. The larger the intensity difference, the shorter the presolution period and the greater the separation. Heinemann (1983b) has shown that this relationship is what one would expect if, during the presolution period, the observer were acting as a detector of the statistical association between the sensory events induced by the two stimuli and the outcomes of his behavior. As the difference between the average sensory effects induced by the stimuli increases, fewer trials (observations) are required to decide that the stimuli are differentially associated with the outcome of the decision. As a result of a sequential analysis (see Wald, 1947), the observer comes to "attend" to those aspects of the situation (complex of sensations) that are significantly associated with the outcomes of the two choices.

When humans serve as psychophysical observers, this presolution period can usually be bypassed simply by telling them which aspects of the situation are relevant. Even with humans, however, substantial training may be required before judgments become stable (Chase et al., 1983; Swets & Sewall, 1963).

In order to observe how a discrimination develops, Heinemann and Avin (1973) trained pigeons with a set of 10 sound intensities covering a range of 38 dB. The pigeons were rewarded for pecking on one key in the presence of any of the 5 lowest intensities, and for pecking on the other key in the presence of any of the 5 highest. Fig. 6.2 shows the proportions of responses to the high-intensity key as a function of stimulus intensity. Data are shown for 10-day blocks, with the first function plotted against the actual stimulus values and successive functions each moved to the right by an arbitrary amount. Note that for all birds the curve for the first 10-day block is quite flat. As training progresses, the curves steepen.

By the end of training, the proportion of responses to the key that was correct for the higher intensities resembles the psychometric functions obtained by Swets, Tanner, and Birdsall (1961) for human subjects. According to the version of SDT they present, the sensory effects induced on repeated presentations of a stimulus are normally distributed and of equal variance. In Fig. 6.3, seven such hypothetical sensory-effect distributions are shown. In the Heinemann and Avin (1973) experiment, the pigeon must decide which of the two key choices, R_1 or R_2, will be rewarded in the presence of the sensation experienced on a given trial. According to SDT, the proportion of trials on which each response is made in the presence of each stimulus depends on the difference between the sensory effects induced by that stimulus and the *criterion*, C, where C is a fixed value of sensory effect. R_1 is made if the sensory effect produced by the stimulus falls below the criterion; R_2 is made if it falls above the criterion. The steepness of the psychometric function, and hence d', depends on the variance of the sensory effect distributions. The position of the function along the stimulus axis depends on the position of the criterion.

Stimuli corresponding to sensory effect distributions that fall essentially to only one side of the criterion (here distributions 1 and 7) should yield R_2 proportions close to 0 and 1.0. As shown in Fig. 6.2, early in training errors occur in the presence of stimuli that are rarely misclassified at the end of training (here the 67 and 99 dB SPL sound intensities). Heinemann and Avin (1973) assumed that such errors are the result of "inattention" to the

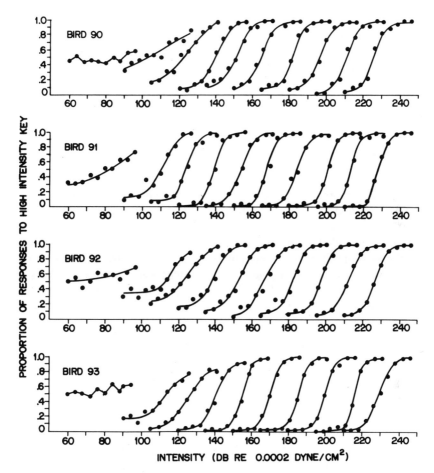

FIG. 6.2   Proportion of R_1 responses as a function of stimulus intensity, at various stages of training. Moving from left to right, the curves represent the results obtained on successive blocks of 10 days. The first curve is correctly placed in the coordinate system, the second curve has been moved to the right by 30 dB, and each of the remaining curves has been moved to the right 15 dB more than the immediately preceding one (from Heinemann & Avin, 1973).

relevant stimulus dimension, specifically, that on a fraction of the trials the subject's choice is not based on sound intensity. As can be seen in Fig. 6.1, key choice is independent of sound intensity during the presolution period. The first 10-day block undoubtedly includes choices made during the presolution period. It is therefore not surprising that the choice curve for the first 10-day block is quite flat. Even after the presolution period is over, however, the proportion of trials on which the pigeons choose the high-

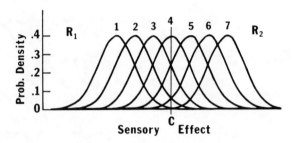

FIG. 6.3 Assumed distributions of sensory effects induced by repeated presentations of each of seven different stimuli.

intensity key in the presence of each of the end stimuli only gradually approaches 0 and 1.0. It appears that, even after the pigeon learns that sound intensity is relevant, it does not consistently base its choice on this dimension.

An experiment of Heinemann, Avin, Sullivan, and Chase (1969) showed that the asymptotes of the choice curves are affected by training conditions. These investigators trained pigeons to choose between two pecking keys on the basis of two levels of white noise intensity. The birds were then tested with 13 sound intensities covering a range from 65 to 100 dB SPL, a procedure referred to in the animal learning literature as a *generalization test,* since new stimuli are presented (usually without reward) and the probability of occurrence of previously trained behaviors is examined. The test data for birds trained with intensity differences of 29, 7, and 2.3 dB are shown in Fig. 6.4 . Here, as in the Heinemann and Avin (1973) experiment, the choice curves resemble the functions one would expect to obtain if the decision process were that described in Fig. 6.3. However, close inspection shows that the high-intensity key is chosen on a substantial number of trials on which one of the lowest intensities was presented. This is especially clear in the result for birds trained on the smallest intensity difference, 83 vs 85.3 dB (Row 3).

The form of the psychometric function may differ even more drastically from the ogival form predicted by SDT when training is done with two closely spaced stimuli, but the stimuli presented during the generalization test that follows training cover a very large range. Under these conditions the generalization curves obtained may be nonmonotonic, that is, choice proportions in the presence of stimuli at the lower and upper end of the continuum may approach 0.5. Curves such as these were obtained by Siegel and Church (1984), who trained rats to discriminate between two signal durations. Nonmonotonic stimulus generalization curves were also obtained by Ernst, Engberg, and Thomas (1971) for light intensities, and by Lawrence (1973) for sound intensities.

Monotonic choice curves with asymptotes above 0 and below 1.0 can be fit reasonably well using the SDT model described in Fig. 6.3, provided that the effects of inattention are taken into account. A *correction for inattention*

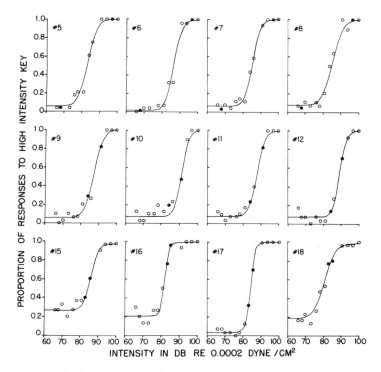

FIG. 6.4 Distribution of choices obtained during generalization tests following training to discriminate between levels of white noise differing by 29 dB (top row), 7 dB (middle row) and 2.3 dB (bottom row). Each panel shows results for one pigeon (from Heinemann, Avin, Sullivan, & Chase, 1969).

was used in fitting the smooth curves shown in Figs. 6.2 and 6.4. However, Heinemann and Avin (1973) found that even when measures of sensitivity were corrected for the presumed effects of inattention, sensitivity increased with training. This finding strongly suggests that factors other than improved attention are responsible for some of the increases in d' with training.

The rationale for the correction for inattention and the procedure for applying it are described fully in Heinemann et al. (1969). This correction may be applied to nonmonotonic functions as well (see Heinemann & Chase, 1975). While the correction is of some use as a complement to SDT (see also Blough & Blough, 1989; Church & Gibbon, 1983), it cannot fully extricate SDT from the difficulties that have been discussed.

In addition to depending on the amount of training, and the distance of the test stimuli from those used in training, estimates of sensitivity also depend strongly on the context in which the stimuli are presented. Here, context refers to the set of stimuli to which the observer is exposed in an absolute identification task.

The important effects of context on measures of sensitivity were high-lighted in 1956 by George Miller, who pointed out that humans can identify only about "7 plus or minus 2" unidimensional stimuli with perfect accuracy. Adopting the graphical presentation used by Miller, Fig. 6.5 shows the relationship between information transmitted (number of items correctly identified, expressed as a power of 2) and input information (number of equally probable items in the set to be identified). The data shown were obtained from pigeons, humans, and monkeys trained to identify luminance levels that would rarely be confused if they were presented in pairs (Chase, Murofushi, & Asano, 1985). The pigeons and monkeys were trained to make absolute identifications of three, seven, and nine stimuli. Absolute identification by humans of the nine stimuli used in the monkey experiment is shown for comparison purposes. Both the monkeys and the pigeons were able to identify three luminance levels virtually without error. For three stimuli information transmitted is 1.6 bits. As the number of stimuli was increased from three to five, information transmitted increased to 1.8 bits for the pigeons and to 2.0 for the monkeys. This value decreased slightly as the number of stimuli was increased to nine. Clearly, information transmitted does not increase indefinitely as the number of stimuli presented for identification increases. The dotted lines in this figure are functions predicted by our model.

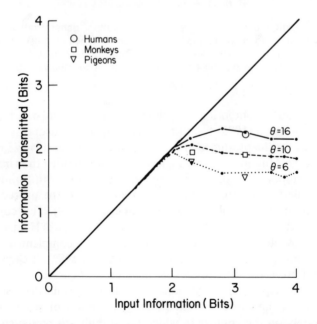

FIG. 6.5 Transmitted information as a function of input information. The theoretical curves differ in sample size. Perfect performance is shown by the diagonal line.

Since most errors in absolute identification involve confusions between adjacent stimuli, it is not surprising that more errors are made as the number of equally spaced stimuli within a fixed range is increased. What is surprising is the finding that, beyond a certain point, increasing the separation between adjacent stimuli does not improve performance. This phenomenon, the *range effect,* was first observed by Pollack (1952) who found little improvement in absolute identification of tones differing in frequency with a 20-fold increase in stimulus spacing. Braida and Durlach (1972) examined performance of human observers in an absolute identification task involving 10 intensities (equally spaced on a logarithmic scale) of a 1,000-Hz tone. As the range of stimulus intensities was increased from .225 to 3.6 log units, performance improved, but a further increase in the range from 3.6 to 5.4 log units had little effect on performance. Pigeons trained on an absolute identification task similar to that of Braida and Durlach, but involving nine light intensities, also failed to improve as the range was increased, in this case from 3.0 to 3.8 log units (Chase, 1983).

Not only is d' for a pair of stimuli affected by the range of the set of stimuli of which they are a part, but also by the position of the stimuli within the range. Stimuli near the ends of the range are identified more accurately than those in the center (Braida & Durlach, 1972; Eriksen & Hake, 1957). Such *anchor* or *edge effects* cannot be attributed completely to the fact that confusions involving the end stimuli are one-directional. Weber, Green, and Luce (1977) corrected their data for this factor and still found that the end stimuli were identified with greater accuracy. Within the SDT framework, Berliner, Braida, and Durlach (1977) and Berliner, Durlach, and Braida (1978) separated the effects of bias from those of resolution. Their analysis clearly showed that sensitivity to the intensity difference between adjacent stimuli, as indexed by d', depends on the position of the stimulus pair within the range. They suggested that the end stimuli act as anchors, and that the observers measure the distance of the various stimuli from these anchors with a noisy ruler. This notion was formalized by Braida et al. (1984) in their *perceptual anchor model of context coding.* When describing their performance in an absolute identification task, human subjects often refer to the end stimuli as reference points on which their judgments are based. However, the edge effect is not a phenomenon peculiar to human observers. Monkeys trained to make absolute identifications of light intensities also show greater sensitivity to stimulus differences near the ends of the range (Chase et al., 1985).

DESCRIPTION OF THE MODEL

Although our model of memory and decision processes was not designed to account for psychometric functions with asymptotes other than 0 or 1.0, or for changes in d' as a function of variables that should have no effect on the internal representation of the stimuli, it does so quite well. The model, as it applies to decisions involving stimuli varying only in intensity or duration, will be outlined briefly. A number of simplifying assumptions are made in this presentation of the model. A more detailed description of the model and illustrative data can be found in previous volumes of this series (Chase, 1983; Heinemann, 1983a; 1983b; Heinemann & Chase 1989). Some of the processes and the parameters to be described may seem arbitrary to a reader unfamiliar with these chapters. However, in most cases the processes postulated and parameters suggested are based on extensive empirical work, and on considerations that arise when the model is applied to several situations that are beyond the scope of this chapter, for example, situations that involve multidimensional stimuli, including those that give rise to the phenomena of *blocking* and *overshadowing* (Chase & Heinemann, 1972; Heinemann & Chase, 1975), and pattern recognition (Heinemann & Chase, 1989).

The model exists in the form of a computer program. Tests of the model are made by comparing simulated with actual behavior. The assumptions are:

1. After the pigeon has learned that input from particular sensory channels is relevant to the outcome of its behavior, information coming from these channels (during any particular trial) is placed into long-term memory (LTM) (see Heinemann 1983a, 1983b). This information is entered on a record which shows the sensation experienced, the response made, and the outcome of the response (e.g., whether or not reward followed). While a record resides in LTM, Gaussian noise is added to the value of the experienced sensation. Prior to the end of the PSP, the memory contains no information regarding the relevant stimuli. It does, however, contain information regarding the response and the outcome, in particular, whether or not the response made was followed by reward.

2. On each trial, a record is placed in a randomly selected location in memory, displacing the record previously in this location. The number of records contained in this memory is limited. The early stages of learning following the PSP thus consist primarily of the replacement of records that lack stimulus information.

3. When a stimulus is presented, a small sample of the records which show that a reward was received is drawn randomly from memory. Our computer simulations and data suggest that the number of records in the sample is between 3 and 15. The response made depends completely on the present sensation, which we shall refer to as the *current input,* and the information available in this sample of records from LTM. When a sample contains some records with stimulus information as well as some that lack

such information, only the former are used. We tentatively assume that, following the presolution period, samples are drawn until a sample is obtained that includes at least one record that contains stimulus information. Resampling does not go on indefinitely, however. After perhaps 10 unsuccessful attempts to find stimulus information, the choice is made on the basis of response/reward information alone.

4. The decision process is illustrated in Fig. 6.6. The figure shows four records that provide stimulus information. The Gaussian distributions each represent a previously experienced sensation. The value of the retrieved sensation, for example, the remembered loudness, can be thought of as fluctuating during the decision process, in which case the distributions shown in Fig. 6.6 represent momentary loudness values.

In our simulations, the remembered sensation values are specified as points on a decision axis that is scaled in standard units (i.e., standard deviation units). Gaussian noise is added to the values retrieved from LTM (those forming the sample). The degree to which distributions associated with different response labels overlap depends on the separations among the stimuli used in training. However, note that, although three distributions in Fig. 6.6 bear the same response label, R_2, indicating that they represent remembered sensations induced by the same stimulus, the means of these distributions are different. That the memories of sensations induced by the same physical stimulus are here represented by distributions that have different means is a consequence of the assumption that remembered sensations stored in LTM are represented by Gaussian distributions, and

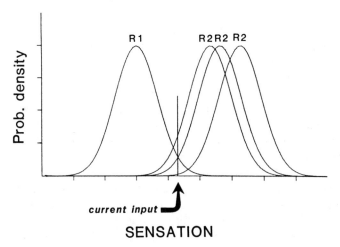

FIG. 6.6 A sample of four records retrieved from the LTM. The choice of response is based on the probability densities at the point labelled "current input." (See text.)

that each retrieved record represents a sensation selected at random from such a distribution. We assume that the Gaussian noise arises from several sources, among these are variability in the sensory effects produced by the stimuli, and variance added during storage and retrieval. For simplicity, all sources of variance are assumed to be independent and the variances are combined in this illustration and in our simulations.

To select a response, the probability density at the current input is obtained for each record and the densities are summed separately for each response. The response made is the one for which the sum of the probability densities is the highest. If this sum is less than some very small threshold value, (δ), then a new sample is drawn. If repeated resampling fails to provide stimulus information (a probability density greater than δ) then a "guess" is made, i.e., the choice made is based only on response/reward information.

THEORETICAL ACCOUNT OF FACTORS AFFECTING SENSITIVITY

According to our model the form of psychometric functions, as well as values of sensitivity that may be derived from these functions, is affected by the processes described herein. To simplify exposition, the various processes and their effects are described singly, but they often act together to produce particular effects.

(1) *Effects of inattention to the relevant stimuli on the asymptotes of the choice curves.* In a previous section of this chapter, we presented data indicating that, if psychometric functions are determined throughout the course of training, they typically have asymptotes well above 0 and below 1.0 early in training, but with continued training gradually approach functions that have asymptotes of 0 and 1.0. These data are compatible with the assumption, which underlies the correction for inattention, that at any particular stage of training some of the choices made are independent of stimulus value.

The account our model gives of this involves the following considerations: Early in training, the LTM is filled primarily with records that were stored during the PSP. These records contain only response/reward information. Thus, samples drawn from LTM shortly after the end of the PSP will contain no stimulus information on many trials, or will contain only a few records with stimulus information. Under these conditions, the functions will be close to horizontal lines. As training progresses, the average number of records that contain stimulus information increases, resulting in the increased separation between the upper and lower asymptotes of the psychometric functions shown in Fig. 6.2.

In more detail, choice functions based on response/reward information alone are horizontal lines, as are those obtained if each sample drawn has only a single record that contains stimulus information. With only a single such record in each sample, the response made will be the one associated with this record, regardless of which stimulus is presented for identification. In what follows, it will be convenient to refer to those records in each sample that contain stimulus information as the *effective sample*. Recall that, provided a sample contains at least one record with stimulus information, the choice of response will be based solely on the effective sample (Assumption 3). The probability that more than one response will be represented in the effective sample increases as the size of that sample increases. Fig. 6.7 shows the results of computer simulations of how the proportions of R_2 responses vary with stimulus value when judgments are based on effective samples of several different sizes and there are two possible choices. For a sample size of 1 the function is a horizontal line. For a sample size of 2 the probability of a correct choice is substantially improved; the asymptotes of this curve are near .28 and .72. A sample size of 18 yields asymptotes close to 0 and 1.0.

We turn next to nonmonotonic functions such as those obtained by Siegel and Church (1984). The account our model gives of these deviations from the performance predicted by SDT is based on the following considerations:

The nonmonotonic functions under discussion occur when the stimuli used in a generalization test include some that differ greatly from those used in training. When the means of all records in a retrieved sample are at least three standard deviations from the current input, then the probability density at the current input is treated as smaller than δ. When this occurs,

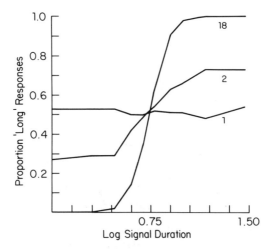

FIG. 6.7 Results of a simulation showing the effects of sample size on the psychometric function in a situation in which various signal durations are categorized as "long" or "short." From Heinemann (1984).

the subject will resample, and eventually guess if repeated sampling fails to yield stimulus information.

(2) *Changes in* d' *with training.* We now consider how our model deals with changes in sensitivity that cannot be attributed to decreases in the proportion of trials on which the subject guesses. Fig. 6.8 shows the effects of increasing the number of effective records available in the sample on estimates of *d'*. In this simulation, the LTM was filled with records of sensations induced by two stimuli. Simulations for two stimuli separated by one standard unit (dashed curve) and two stimuli separated by two standard units (solid curve) are shown. As sample size increases, the value of *d'* estimated from the choice proportions approaches that defined by the normal-normal equal-variance SDT model. For the dashed curve, this is a *d'* value of 1.0; for the solid curve, this is a value of 2.0. Our simulations show that, in the two-choice situation, the difference between the values yielded by our model and SDT becomes negligible for sample sizes of 32 or larger. The reason that our model becomes equivalent to the SDT model for large sample sizes is that, for the conditions under consideration here, the numerous distributions associated with the same response may be represented by a single distribution with a mean equal to the mean of the individual means and a variance equal to the mean of the variances. For practical purposes then, the samples retrieved from memory on different trials may be regarded as identical when the number of records in each sample is very large.

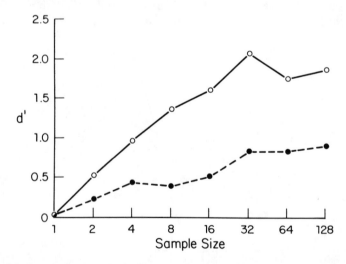

FIG. 6.8 Outcome of a simulation showing the effects of sample size on the value of *d'* estimated from the data of the theoretical "pigeon." The assumed difference between the sensory effects induced by the stimuli presented for discrimination was two standard units in one simulation (solid curve) and one standard unit in the other (broken curve).

It was pointed out earlier that the improvement in choice accuracy with training observed by Heinemann and Avin (1973) cannot be attributed completely to decreased guessing. According to our model, the changes in d' that occur during training to discriminate or identify stimuli result from a gradual increase in the size of the effective sample, that is, the number of retrieved records that carry stimulus information. Early in training there are very few such records in the average sample. As training progresses, records in LTM containing only response information are replaced by records containing stimulus information as well. Thus, training increases the size of the sample on which decisions are based.

(3) *The range effect and limits on information transmitted.* We turn now to a theoretical account of the limit on transmitted information that Miller (1956) referred to as *channel capacity.* If two stimuli are sufficiently different from each other, few errors of identification will occur. However, as the number of stimuli presented for identification is increased, the same two stimuli are represented, on the average, by fewer records in each sample retrieved from LTM. This circumstance will cause the number of identification errors to increase. For illustrative purposes let us assume that, on each trial of an absolute identification experiment, a sample of eight records is drawn randomly from the LTM. As noted in a previous section, if the sample does not contain at least one informative record, a new sample will be retrieved, and this process may be repeated several times. However, the decision made is determined by the information contained in a single sample. Thus, a response that is not represented on any record in the sample cannot be made. In a two-choice situation there will be, on the average, four records that provide stimulus information for each of the two responses. If four responses are possible then each response will be represented by only two records, on the average. In a situation in which eight stimuli are to be identified, each response will be represented, on the average, by only a single record. As the number of responses increases, the amount of stimulus information relevant to each response decreases. In addition, it becomes increasingly likely that the correct response will not be represented at all in the sample. In that case, increasing the separation between adjacent stimuli cannot produce any increase in accuracy. Errors will occur as a result of lack of sufficient information regarding all response alternatives. Thus, the limited number of records available when the decision is made seems to be the factor responsible for the range effect as well as the limit on the number of stimuli that can be identified with complete accuracy.

The three theoretical curves shown in Fig. 6.5 differ only in the value assumed for the size of the sample, θ: 6 for the pigeons, 10 for the monkeys, 16 for the humans. These values are crude approximations based on simplifying assumptions, primarily the assumptions that increased training or increased stimulus range would not improve performance.

(4) The edge effect. We have also attempted to account for the enhanced

resolution of stimulus differences near the ends of the stimulus range, the edge effect. Our simulations show that sensitivity would be highest at the ends of the stimulus range if the subject were to base its decisions solely on samples that contain at least one record representing each of the end stimuli and the rewarded responses. The subject could implement such a procedure by resampling on each trial until this condition is met. It is not clear what mechanism could lead to the systematic resampling needed to account for the edge effect. One possibility we are exploring has as its starting point the fact that the stimuli at the end of the range have a privileged position in that they can be confused only with stimuli to one side of the continuum. This asymmetry may result in more resampling when end stimuli are presented for identification.

This asymmetry is also responsible for the greater number of correct identifications of the end stimuli. The percentages of correct responses attained in absolute identification tasks are generally highest for the end stimuli. According to our model, this results in better representation of the end stimuli in the sample, and thus greater accuracy in identification. Simulations, however, have shown that without resampling the magnitude of this effect is not great enough to account for the edge effect.

While both humans and monkeys trained on a nine-choice absolute identification task show an edge effect, it is not clear whether the same mechanisms are responsible. It is possible that humans' sampling strategies are less random than those of monkeys or pigeons, as suggested by the anchor model proposed by Braida et al. (1984).

CONCLUSION

Our model of memory and decision processes originated from an attempt to apply SDT to data obtained from pigeons. As has been shown, the behavior of pigeons and monkeys, as well as of humans, deviates from that of the ideal statistical decision maker described by the most common version of SDT. We propose here that most of the observed deviations follow readily from the assumption that the subjects' decisions are based on a relatively small amount of information retrieved from LTM.

ACKNOWLEDGMENTS

The research reported here was supported by NSF Grant Number BNS–79241070, NIMH Grant Numbers MH18246 and MH40712 and PSC–CUNY Grant Nos. 14002 and 11510E and by computing resources provided by the City University of New York, University Computer Center. We thank Neil A. Macmillan and Hiroshi Yamashita for helpful comments on an earlier draft of this chapter.

REFERENCES

Berliner, J. E., Braida, L. D., & Durlach, N. I. (1977). Intensity perception: VII. Further data on roving-level discrimination and the resolution and bias edge effects. *Journal of the Acoustical Society of America, 61,* 1577–1585.

Berliner, J. E., Durlach, N. I., & Braida, L. D. (1978). Intensity perception: IX. Effect of a fixed standard on resolution in identification. *Journal of the Acoustical Society of America, 64,* 687–689.

Blough, P. M., & Blough, D. S. (1989). Visual effects of opiates in pigeons: II. Contrast sensitivity to sinewave gratings. *Psychopharmacology, 97,* 85–88.

Braida, L. D., & Durlach, N. I. (1972). Intensity perception: II. Resolution in one-interval paradigms. *Journal of the Acoustical Society of America, 51,* 483–502.

Braida, L. D., Durlach, N. I., Lim, J. S., Berliner, J. E., Rabinowitz, W. M., & Purks, S. R. (1984). Intensity perception: XIII. Perceptual anchor model of context coding. *Journal of the Acoustical Society of America, 76,* 722–731.

Chase, S. (1983). Pigeons and the magical number seven. In M. L. Commons, R. J. Herrnstein, & A. R. Wagner (Eds.), *Quantitative analyses of behavior: Discrimination processes* (vol. 4, pp. 37–57). Cambridge, MA: Ballinger.

Chase, S., Bugnacki, P., Braida, L., & Durlach, N. (1983). Intensity perception: XII. Effect of presentation probability on absolute identification. *Journal of the Acoustical Society of America, 73,* 279–284.

Chase, S., & Heinemann, E. G. (1972). Choices based on redundant information: An analysis of two-dimensional stimulus control. *Journal of Experimental Psychology, 92,* 161–175.

Chase, S., Murofushi, K., & Asano, T. (1985). *Memory limitations on absolute identification by monkeys and humans.* Presented at the annual meeting of the Psychonomic Society, Boston.

Church, R., & Gibbon, J. (1983). Temporal generalization. *Journal of Experimental Psychology: Animal Behavior Processes, 8,* 165–186.

Durlach, N. I., & Braida, L. D. (1969). Intensity perception: I. Preliminary theory of intensity resolution. *Journal of the Acoustical Society of America, 46,* 372–383.

Eriksen, C. W., & Hake, H. W. (1957). Anchor effects in absolute judgments. *Journal of Experimental Psychology, 53,* 132–138.

Ernst, A. J., Engberg, L., & Thomas, D. R. (1971). On the form of stimulus generalization curves for visual intensity. *Journal of the Experimental Analysis of Behavior, 16,* 177–180.

Heinemann, E. G. (1983a). A memory model for decision processes in pigeons. In M. L. Commons, R. J. Herrnstein, & A. R. Wagner (Eds.), *Quantitative analyses of behavior: Discrimination Processes* (vol. 4, pp. 3–19). Cambridge, MA: Ballinger.

Heinemann, E. G. (1983b). The presolution period and the detection of statistical associations. In M. L. Commons, R. J. Herrnstein, & A. R. Wagner (Eds.), *Quantitative analyses of behavior: Discrimination processes* (vol. 4, pp. 21–35). Cambridge, MA: Ballinger.

Heinemann, E. G. (1984). A model for temporal discrimination and generalization. In J. Gibbon & L. Allan (Eds.), *Annals of the New York Academy of Science* (Vol. 423): Timing and time perception (pp. 361–371). New York: New York Academy of Sciences.

Heinemann, E. G., & Avin, E. (1973). On the development of stimulus control. *Journal of the Experimental Analysis of Behavior, 20,* 183–195.

Heinemann, E. G., Avin, E., Sullivan, M. A., & Chase, S. (1969). An analysis of stimulus generalization with a psychophysical method. *Journal of Experimental Psychology, 80,* 215–224.

Heinemann, E. G., & Chase, S. (1975). Stimulus generalization. In W. K. Estes (Ed.), *Handbook of learning and cognitive processes* (vol. 2, pp. 305–349). Hillsdale, NJ: Lawrence Erlbaum Associates.

Heinemann, E. G., & Chase, S. (1989). A quantitative model for pattern recognition. In M. L. Commons, R. J. Herrnstein, S. Kosslyn, & D. Mumford (Eds.), *Quantitative analyses of behavior: Computational and clinical approaches to pattern recognition and concept formation* (vol. 9, pp. 109–126). Hillsdale, NJ: Lawrence Erlbaum Associates.

Lawrence, C. (1973). Generalization along the dimension of sound intensity in pigeons. *Animal Learning and Behavior, 1,* 60–64.

Miller, G. A. (1956). The magical number seven, plus or minus two: Some limits on our capacity for processing information. *Psychological Review, 63,* 81–97.

Pollack, I. (1952). The information of elementary auditory displays. *Journal of the Acoustical Society of America, 24,* 745–749.

Siegel, S. F., & Church, R. M. (1984). In J. Gibbon & L. Allan (Eds.), *Annals of the New York Academy of Science: Timing and time perception* (Vol. 423, pp. 643–645). New York Academy of Sciences.

Swets, J. A., & Sewall, S. T. (1963). Invariance of signal detectability over stages of practice and levels of motivation. *Journal of Experimental Psychology, 66,* 120–126.

Swets, J. A., Tanner, W. P., & Birdsall, T. G. (1961). Decision processes in perception. *Psychological Review, 68,* 301–340.

Wald, A. (1947). *Sequential analysis.* New York: Dover.

Weber, D. L., Green, D. M., & Luce, R. D. (1977). Effects of practice and distribution of auditory signals on absolute identification. *Perception and Psychophysics, 22,* 223–231.

7

How Each Reinforcer Contributes to Value: "Noise" Must Reduce Reinforcer Value Hyperbolically

Michael L. Commons
Harvard Medical School

Michael Woodford
University of Chicago Business School

Edward J. Trudeau
Harvard University

Empirical evidence has shown that the effectiveness of a reinforcer is related to the delay between reinforcer and response (e.g., for pigeons, see Chung & Herrnstein, 1967; Mazur, 1987). For people the finding of a similar function shows that the effectiveness of a stimulus is related to the delay between its presentation and the time at which it is to be recalled (for people, see Ebbinghaus, 1885). This decrease in effectiveness of an event over time has come to be known as the recency effect (e.g., Glanzer & Cunitz, 1966; Madigan, 1971; Murdock, 1962; Sternberg, 1966; Woodword, 1970). That reinforcer effectiveness over time may be represented as an exponential decay was not an unreasonable hypothesis, and has been suggested previously (e.g., Commons, 1981, and White & McKenzie, 1982, in animal psychology; Muth, 1960, in forecasting theory; Wickelgren, 1974, in human psychology). Yet previous data suggest that this relation is hyperbolic (Commons, Woodford, & Ducheny, 1982; McCarthy's data as analyzed in McCarthy & White, 1987). Theoretical considerations from a number of sources suggest that the decay of value is best represented by a hyperbolic model (Ainslie, 1975; Davison & Tustin, 1978; Fantino, 1981; Fantino, Abarca, & Dunn, 1987; Mazur, 1987).

The reduction in reinforcer effectiveness implicit in the hyperbolic model may be due to the imperfections of memory and the confusion caused by intervening events. From a signal-detection perspective, intervening events function as noise under this supposition, obscuring previous events. If reinforcer effectiveness decreases hyperbolically, then the decrease will be rapid at first and fall more slowly as time progresses, though perhaps never reaching zero. It will be shown that the relationship between reinforcer

139

effectiveness and reinforcer delay is predicted by a *hyperbolic model* derived using *statistical decision theory* (Raiffa, 1968; Raiffa & Schlaifer, 1961) and the additive noise assumption in Woodford's *additive noise model* (Commons, Woodford, & Ducheny, 1982), which is based on signal-detection theory (Egan, 1975).

THE EFFECTS OF DELAY BETWEEN ANTECEDENT REINFORCERS AND SUBSEQUENT RESPONSES

In order to assess the effect of delay between antecedent reinforcers and responses that follow them, discrimination procedures have been devised and utilized (e.g., Commons, 1979, 1981; Commons, Woodford, & Ducheny, 1982; Mandell, 1981, 1984). The reinforcement schedules used as stimuli in discrimination studies have been samples from a variety of schedules (Commons & Nevin, 1981). Mandell used rich and lean VI schedules in which the pattern and spacing of reinforcers on each trial was not measured; Commons (1979, 1981) used samples from a rich or a lean T-schedule that resembled random-interval (RI) schedules. Here, the derivations here will be carried out for a general form of Commons's (1981) procedure.

A number of questions about the nature of decrementation and the basic processes that cause decrementation have arisen. These questions will be addressed by examining decrementation functions. A theoretical basis that accounts for the hyperbolic decreases in perceived reinforcement value and in reinforcement effectiveness has not been set forth. Here, the form will be demonstrated theoretically, but not empirically, to be hyperbolic.

The purpose of this chapter is to show how the additive-noise account, which is consistent with delay data, leads to a hyperbolic decrementation function. Woodford constructed this account (see Commons, Woodford, & Ducheny, 1982) to explain the results obtained from preference- and discrimination-trial experiments. The *additive noise model* might fairly be called one of the simplest of the many models proposed thus far in that it makes only a few assumptions.

The first assumption is that each and every reinforcer obtained affects choice. The effect may be small to the point of vanishing if the time between the reinforcer and the response is very large. Second, the effects of each reinforcer are added to the effects of the other reinforcers (Commons, Woodford, & Ducheny, 1982; Mazur, 1987). Third, noise that occurs randomly during the delay between a response and a reinforcer decreases the effectiveness of that reinforcer in controlling that response. The noise randomly distorts the subject's memory of reinforcers, each distortion being statistically independent of previous distortions. These are reasonable assumptions because they are consistent with a number of traditional theories of memory mechanisms (Baddeley & Hitch, 1974; Ebbinghaus, 1885; Underwood, 1948a).

The additive noise model applies to both preference and discrimination situations. Decrementation in the discriminative and the preference situations is most likely symmetrical. Many of the laws describing one will hold for the other (Williams, 1982). The amount of conditioning is equal to a function of the product of the value remembered about the reinforcer "R" and value remembered about the reinforced response "S^{R+}" (Dickinson, 1980; Hall & Pearce, 1982; Kaye & Hall, 1982; Williams, 1982). As far as the memory effect on conditioning is concerned, the two situations are symmetrical if the combining of the remembered magnitudes of the two events that influence conditioning is commutative: a*b = b*a. In the discriminative case, the remembered magnitude of the two events that influence conditioning is the value remembered about R times the value remembered about S^{R+}. In the preference case the remembered magnitudes of the two events that influence conditioning is the value remembered about S^{R+} times the value remembered about R.[1] The effect would be symmetrical because the discriminative case is simply the reverse of the preference case. Hence, showing why the decrementation function is hyperbolic for either situation shows it for the other. The effect of a reinforcer is decremented as a hyperbolic function of the time between the making of the choice and the onset of a reinforcer in preference situations, and the time between the onset of a reinforcer and the making of a choice in discrimination situations. In this chapter the additive noise model will be constructed for discrimination situations.

PROCEDURE

Analogue of Procedure Used in Discrimination-of-reinforcement-density Experiments

The experimental task is like the task of discriminating from which of two randomly chosen urns, one representing a rich reinforcement schedule and

---

[1]Presumably the conditioning or the establishment of control depends on the first event being available for pairing, that is, remembered long enough to interact with the second. If memory were perfect, the initial value of an event would be maintained at the time of a second event. With noise, the initial value would move toward the mean of all possible initial values. Let us say the first event has either a value of 1 or -1, and the second event a value of 1. If the combining were multiplicative, there would be conditioning in either case, 1 × 1 = 1, −1 × 1 = −1. With noise, if initially the value of the first event was 1 it would be less than 1 when the second event occurred. If it was −1, then when the second event occurred, it would be more than −1. If there were total forgetting, the first event would be 0 whether it were 1 or −1 initially. Hence there would be no conditioning, 0 × 1 = 0. In the preference situation, the first event is the response and the second is the reinforcer. In the discrimination situation the order of the events are reversed.

one a lean reinforcement schedule, a sample is drawn. In the experiment, the sample is a period from a reinforcement schedule. In the analogue, the two urns or schedules contain different proportions of reinforcing and nonreinforcing balls. The rich urn, in which the probability of reinforcement is .6, has six reinforcing balls and four nonreinforcing balls. Conversely, the lean urn has four reinforcing balls and six nonreinforcing balls. During each stimulus period the subject is allowed n draws with replacement from an unknown urn, where n equals some number from 6 to 18. After the nth draw a choice period follows. During this period the subject indicates whether the sampled urn was the rich or the lean reinforcement one.

Method

The central purpose of this experiment is to provide a framework for the development of the additive noise model. Three versions of the experiment are used to characterize the role that time plays between a reinforcer and a choice. Qualitative tests on data that Commons (1981) previously collected show whether the pigeons' discrimination of reinforcement density is sensitive to time, relative time, or to the number of events between the reinforcer and the choice.

In Commons's 1981 study, four pigeons were each run in one 256-trial session per day. The experiment utilized a standard Skinner-box pigeon panel with three keys. Each trial consisted of a stimulus period followed by a choice period as shown in the bottom of Fig. 7.1.

The stimuli to be discriminated consisted of samples randomly drawn from one of two modified T-schedules (Schoenfeld & Cole, 1972) each composed of four cycles (Commons, 1979, 1981). On each trial, a substimulus sample from one of the two T-schedules was presented during the stimulus period. Each substimulus sample consisted of four equal-duration cycles. As shown at the top of Fig. 7.1, the cycles were numbered so that cycle C_4 in the stimulus period occurred at the beginning of the stimulus period and was furthest, temporally, from the choice period. Conversely, cycle C_1 occurred at the end of the stimulus period and was immediately followed by the choice period. Thus, a four-cycle trial would be numbered: $C_4 \, C_3 \, C_2 \, C_1 \rightarrow$ choice period.

At the beginning of each stimulus period, the center key was white. The first center-key peck turned off that key's light for that cycle. On each cycle, a center-key peck was ($v_i = 1$) or was not ($v_i = 0$) reinforced immediately. A reinforcer was one 20-mg pigeon pellet from an illuminated hopper. On the rich reinforcement schedule, the first center-key peck in each cycle was reinforced with a probability of .75. On the lean schedule the probability of reinforcement for the first peck in each cycle was .25.

Fig. 7.1 A stimulus example from a discrimination trial shown (*top left*) by means of a state diagram for a sample from a 3-s cycle schedule to illustrate what may happen if center-key pecks occur (and do not occur) when reinforcement has been programmed (or not). In reality this would be very unusual because there is a cycle without a peck occurring in it. Contingencies during an entire trial are shown (*bottom left*). The stimulus period contains substimuli of the form shown in the top left part. The choice period, which immediately follows the stimulus period, contains a single reinforcer for correct choice or extinction for incorrect ones. There is no intertrial interval.

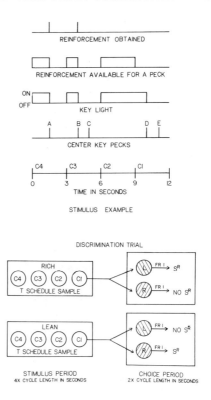

Rich and lean schedules were delivered with a probability of .50. In any given cycle, the first peck was reinforced with the same probability as the first peck on the rest of the cycles on that trial, $p(S^{R+}|R_c)$ having the value of either .25 for the entire trial or .75 for the entire trial. None of the center-key pecks that occurred subsequent to the first during any given cycle was reinforced.

As shown at the bottom of Fig. 7.1, after the last stimulus cycle of a given trial the choice period began. The center key was darkened and the two side keys were transilluminated, the left key with a red light, the right one with a green light. In the choice period the subject had twice the cycle length to identify the preceding stimulus period as consisting of either a sample from the rich reinforcement schedule or the lean reinforcement schedule. The first side-key peck, whether correct or not, darkened both keys, and no further pecks were counted. The rich schedule was indicated by making a left-key response, the lean schedule by a right-key response.

When a substimulus sampled from the rich schedule was presented on the center key, the first left-key peck was reinforced with a 96-mg pellet (a hit or "left-correct"). A right was not reinforced (a miss or "right-error"). When a substimulus from the lean schedule was presented on the center key, the first right-key peck was reinforced (a correct rejection or "right-correct"). A left was not reinforced (a false alarm or "left-error").

Although reinforcement probability for the first peck in any given cycle was neither one nor zero, each first center-key peck in a cycle was either reinforced or not. Therefore, for a given trial, a reinforcement pattern can be written with a *1* representing one earned reinforcer and a *0* representing no earned reinforcers for a given cycle. An obtained reinforcement pattern for a trial might be *1110* → choice. These patterns generally represent both "obtained" reinforcement and "scheduled" reinforcement [2] since subjects almost always respond at least once during each cycle (Commons, 1979). The binary pattern of scheduled reinforcement that is delivered is called the sampled substimulus or just substimulus. Here there were $2^4 = 16$ different substimulus samples, comprising every possible combination of reinforcement over the four cycles.

Three different standard cycle lengths were used: 2 s, 3 s, and 4 s ($t = 2$, 3, 4). A standard t-value remained constant across trials until the pigeon's performance stabilized so that p(L) did not vary more than $+0.1$ from session to session. In daily sessions the standard cycle length was of base length (i.e., t multiplied by 1) on 224 trials, doubled (t multiplied by 2) on 16 probe trials, and tripled (t multiplied by 3) on another 16 probe trials. The probe trials were randomly distributed throughout a session.

The frequencies with which substimuli for standard and probe trials with 0, 1, 2, 3, or 4 reinforcers came from the rich schedule and from the lean schedule are shown in Fig. 7.2. Any substimulus could come from either the rich or lean schedule. All that differed was the frequency with which they did so. The modal number of reinforcers was three reinforcers per trial for the rich schedule, and one for the lean schedule.

The Additive Noise Model:
Derivation of a Simple Form

A model for the process by which reinforcers lose control over responses is introduced and illustrated with the four-cycle data. The general additive noise model developed here shows that a hyperbolic function must describe the decrease in value of reinforcement the further reinforcement occurs from the behavior that it controls, given some assumptions about the effect of noise on memory for reinforcement. To illustrate how the additive noise model may be applied in one experimental situation, three versions of it will be shown to distinguish qualitatively between the effects of programming a given temporal-length base cycle for a number of sessions and changing

---

[2]Only one reinforcement schedule of all the possible schedules did not appear in any trial due to the nature of the program used.

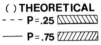

( ) THEORETICAL
- - - P = .25
—— P = .75

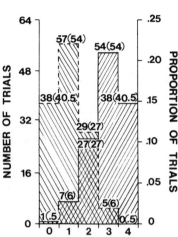

Fig. 7.2 The distribution of reinforcement for the first center-key peck ($S^{R+}|C$) for 4-cycle (*left*) are shown. The number of center-key pecks and proportion of trials on which reinforcement occurs in a sample is shown for the rich (positive-slope hatching) and lean (negative-slope hatching) schedules. The respective $p(S^{R+}|C)$ are 0.75 and 0.25. Theoretical values represent predicted outcomes based on the binomial distribution with $n = 4$ and the respective p given previously.

NUMBER OF CENTER KEY PECK REINFORCEMENT OPPORTUNITIES PER TRIAL

them momentarily on probe trials. The data will not be used to show whether the decrementation function is hyperbolic. Again, the remembered value could depend on: (a) the time between a reinforcer and choice, (b) the relative time between those events, or (c) the number of intervening cycles.

The simplest overall model of forgetting assumes that the *signal* stays constant while the amount of *noise* increases linearly with time. This is similar to the interference theories in human learning and cognition (e.g., Baddeley & Hitch, 1974; Barnes & Underwood, 1959; Ebbinghaus, 1885; Melton & Irwin, 1940; Underwood, 1948a, 1948b, 1957), as well as Grossberg's (1978) theory of scaled short term memory. The overall model assumes that at the time of reinforcement the perceived value of the reinforcement in a sample is a random variable. What is discriminated about overall reinforcement density depends on what is remembered about what happened on each cycle. Perceived value of a substimulus is a random variable because the noise added to the memory of each reinforcer makes the discrimination of that reinforcement event imperfect. The noise affects the memory of whether or not a reinforcer occurred on a particular cycle. With each cycle that occurs thereafter, another random noise component is added to the previous memory of that reinforcement. The random noise terms are independent of the initial random noise. Hence, the events on the previous cycle are remembered as follows:

C_4	C_3	C_2	C_1	$\rightarrow$	choice
1 (M1)	1 (M2)	1 (M3)	0 (M4)		
$M_1 + n_1$	$M_1 + n_1 + n_2$	$M_1 + n_1 + n_2 + n_3$	$M_1 + n_1 + n_2 + n_3 + n_4$		
	$M_2 + n_2$	$M_2 + n_2 + n_3$	$M_2 + n_2 + n_3 + n_4$		
		$M_3 + n_3$	$M_3 + n_3 + n_4$		
			$M_4 + n_4$		

M_1 is the memory of whether or not there was a reinforcer on cycle i and n_i represents the noise on cycle i. Let y_i be the amount of reinforcement in cycle c_i, as remembered by the organism at the time of choice. Then $y_4 = M1 + n1 + n2 + n3 + n4$ and $y_3 = M2 + n2 + n3 + n4$, and so on. Assume that y_i is a normally distributed random variable with variance σ^2_i and mean μ_i in the case that $vi = 1$ and mean $-\mu_i$ in the case that $v_i = 0$. Given two normal distributions of reinforcement density with mean μ_n and μ_{sn}, then according to Egan (1975), the z_{sn} – score for the sn distribution is

$$z_{s\,n} = \frac{c - \mu_{sn}}{\sigma_{sn}}, \tag{1}$$

and the z_n – score for the n distribution is

$$z_n = \frac{c - \mu_n}{\sigma_n}, \tag{2}$$

where c is the cutoff or criterion value along the x-axis for both distributions (not to be confused with c_i, which represents cycle i). The criterion value is that value along the decision axis above which a signal is present and below which no signal is present. The measure of overlap between the two distributions is denoted as d' and is equivalent to

$$d' = z_n - z_{sn} = \frac{\mu_{sn} - \mu_n}{\sigma_{sn}}. \tag{3}$$

Therefore, assuming that the two means are additive inverses involves no loss of generality, and only the difference $d' = [\mu_i - (-\mu_i)]/\sigma_i$ turns out to have observable significance. Here, the term μ_i represents the mean of the μ_{sn} distribution, or the distribution with reinforcement, and the term $-\mu_i$ is equivalent to the μ_n distribution, or the distribution without reinforcement. σ_i is the variance of the both distributions, as both are assumed to be normally distributed y_i curves. The sensitivity, d', is the standard psychophysical index of discriminability (Green & Swets, 1966), and here measures the discriminability of a reinforcer on cycle c_i. That index does not generally refer to a sequence of stimuli occurring over a period of time, however (Nevin, 1969, 1981).

Representing Perceived Value

The most elemental form of analysis of the discrimination data examines the choices that an organism makes following a substimulus presentation. The *bias* value represents the tendency to indicate that the substimulus comes from the rich schedule. Why examine bias and not simply discriminability? The reason is that there is no way to figure out discriminability on an individual substimulus. A hit is correctly indicating rich when the rich schedule is presented. But the rich schedule consists of a distribution of all the substimuli, not just one of them. Therefore, there is no way to construct a hit or false alarm rate for individual substimuli. However, there is a very easy way to construct the proportion of left-key responses, p(L), out of the total responses for each substimulus. That is why we are examining bias and not discriminability. There is, however, a relationship between the bias and discriminability at the overall level (Commons, 1981).

A left-key peck to a substimulus is the decision that indicates that the substimulus is rich. Although only a single left- or right-key peck can occur on each dichotomous choice trial, $p(L|S_n)$ indicates the proportion of times the pigeon indicates that the sample was from the rich schedule.[3] The proportion (relative frequency) of a left-key peck in response to the given substimulus is:

$$p(L|S_n) = (L|S_n)/(L|S_n + R|S_n). \tag{4}$$

This proportion is called the bias for a given substimulus sample, S_n, in signal-detection theory (Commons, 1979, 1981). That proportion also indicates the perceived richness of the sample in the following sense. Because the bias proportion is estimated by probability, it can be linearized by a probit transformation, $z^{-1}p(L)$, as shown in Commons (1981). The value, $z^{-1}p(L)$, the inverse-probability (probit) transform of bias, is the *perceived value*, V_{sn}, of the substimulus schedule sample. This probit transformation makes linear a plot of value versus number of reinforcers in a sample (Commons, 1981). Perceived value is just the sum of the decremented values of each reinforcer. A difference exists between this probabilistic estimate and the perceived outcome because sometimes the pigeon would make a choice before having responded to every cycle. For example, on a schedule of 0001, the pigeon might respond after the second or third cycle and never get the reinforcer on the last cycle.

Linear regressions of perceived value were carried out to see what the contributions were of a reinforcer on a cycle. The coefficients, a_i, which

---

[3]This proportion is simplified to p(L).

represent the contributions, were estimated using the following multivariate equation:

$$V_{sn} = V_{sn} (L, R) = z^{-1}p(L|S_n) = \sum_{i=1}^{n} a_i v_i .$$ (5)

The value-weights, a_i, are applied to the reinforcer-occurrence variable v_i. The reinforcer-occurrence variable $v_i = 1$ when a reinforcer did occur and $v_i = 0$ when a reinforcer did not occur on the instance i time periods before choice where a reinforcer might be programmed. An a_i coefficient reflects the value of a reinforcer at the time of choice when it occurred i time periods before the choice. This is because it represents the contribution of the presence of a reinforcer on cycle$_i$ to the prediction that the probability of the choice was 1. The probability of a left choice should be 1 if the stimulus was rich (0 is the value for a lean choice).

Insensitivity–The δ Measure

Here we will introduce a new variable, δ_i, which we will call the *inverse of sensitivity* to the signal "reinforcement." It will be represented by the numerical value of $4/(d')^2$ (Egan, 1975; Green & Swets, 1966; Nevin, 1969, 1981). This inverse of sensitivity is introduced so that the form of the following equations is simplified.[4] The general form of the following equations are shown in the appendix and the cases described by the experiment are shown here. The probability density function (PDF) of the amount of reinforcement remembered on a cycle, y_i, in the case of the rich schedule, $S_r : v_i = 1$ with probability 3/4 and $v_i = 0$ with probability 1/4, is:

$$f(y_i) = \frac{3}{4} \frac{1}{\sqrt{2\pi}\,\sigma_i} \cdot e^{\frac{-(y_i - \mu_i)^2}{2\sigma^2_i}}$$

$$+ \frac{1}{4} \frac{1}{\sqrt{2\pi}\,\sigma_i} \cdot e^{\frac{-(y_i + \mu_i)^2}{2\sigma^2_i}} .$$

Here, reinforcement on the rich key comes with probability 3/4, so the normal distribution for reinforcement on the rich key has a coefficient of 3/4, and nonreinforcement only occurs with probability 1/4 so that is the coefficient of the other normal distribution. This probability density function, which is the expectation, is simply the weighted values of

---

[4]When variables are normally distributed, detectability of reinforcement density (Commons, 1979) is $d' = z^{-1}p(\text{Hit}) - z^{-1}p(\text{False Alarm}) = z^{-1}p(\text{Indicates Rich}|\text{Was Rich}) - z^{-1}p$ (Indicates Rich|Was Lean).

reinforcement or nonreinforcement. The expectation is simply the weighted values of getting reinforcement or nonreinforcement. The expected value of the random variable y_i on any given trial, and has the form:

$$\sum_{i=1}^{n} p_i v_i$$

where v_i is the value of the random variable on cycle i, p_i is the probability of that value occurring, and n is the number of cycles in the trial.

Assume that probabilistic responding is a result of the combination of signal and random noise in the perceptual and memory processing of reinforcers in the schedule sample. With reasonable amounts of noise, the perceived density will be higher when the actual mean density is higher (Commons, 1979).

As in the case of the rich schedule, in the case of the lean schedule, S_L: $v_i = 1$ with probability 1/4, $v_i = 0$ with probability 3/4, y_i will have density function:

$$f(y_i) = \frac{3}{4} \frac{1}{\sqrt{2\pi}\sigma_i} \cdot e^{\frac{-(y_i - \mu_i)^2}{2\sigma^2_i}}$$
$$+ \frac{1}{4} \frac{1}{\sqrt{2\pi}\sigma_i} \cdot e^{\frac{-(y_i + \mu_i)^2}{2\sigma^2_i}} .$$

If a bird chooses left or right so as to maximize the expected payoff, given the particular remembered values y_1, y_2, y_3, y_4, of the sequence of events v_1, v_2, v_3, v_4 in the scheduled sample, it will employ a likelihood ratio criterion. That is, it will peck left only when the ratio

$$\frac{EP(L|y_1, y_2, y_3, y_4)}{EP(R|y_1, y_2, y_3, y_4)} > 1.$$

Now,

$$\frac{EP(L|y_1, y_2, y_3, y_4)}{EP(R|y_1, y_2, y_3, y_4)} = \frac{U_L \, p(y_1, y_2, y_3, y_4)}{U_R \, p(y_1, y_2, y_3, y_4)} = \frac{U_L \pi_i f(y_i|S_R)}{U_R \pi_i f(y_i|S_R)}$$

Where U_L and U_R represent the utility values for the reinforcers received for a left or right key peck

$$= \frac{U_L}{U_R} \frac{\prod_{i=1}^{4} \left[\frac{3}{4} e^{\frac{-(y_i - \mu_i)^2}{2\sigma_i^2}} + \frac{1}{4} e^{\frac{-(y_i + \mu_i)^2}{2\sigma^2}}\right]}{\prod_{i=1}^{4} \left[\frac{1}{4} e^{\frac{-(y_i - \mu_i)^2}{2\sigma_i^2}} + \frac{3}{4} e^{\frac{-(y_i + \mu_i)^2}{2\sigma_i^2}}\right]},$$

Taking out the $II(1/4)$ from top and bottom and then expanding, yields

$$= \frac{U_L}{U_R} \prod_{i=1}^{4} \frac{3\,e^{\frac{-(y_i^2 - 2y_i\,\mu_i + \mu_i^2)}{2\sigma_i^2}} + e^{\frac{-(y_i^2 + 2y_i\mu_i + \mu_i^2)}{2\sigma^2}}}{e^{\frac{-(y_i^2 - 2y_i\mu_i + \mu_i^2)}{2\sigma_i^2}} + 3\,e^{\frac{-(y_i^2 + 2y_i\mu_i + \mu_i^2)}{2\sigma_i^2}}} \quad ,$$
$$-(y_i^2 + \mu_i^2)$$

Then the term, $e^{2\sigma^2}$ may be factored out and canceled top and bottom, and simultaneously dividing top and bottom by the term

$$e^{\frac{-(y_i\mu_i)}{2\sigma_i^2}} \quad \text{yields}$$

$$= \frac{U_L}{U_R} \prod_{i=1}^{4} \frac{3\,e^{\frac{(2y_i\mu_i)}{\sigma_i^2}} + 1}{3 + e^{\frac{(2y_i\mu_i)}{\sigma_i^2}}} \quad ,$$

The bird will peck left when this quantity is greater than 1. We see that this equation is a nonlinear condition on the y_i values. But in the case that the discrimination of the reinforcers is difficult (that is, all the δ_i are relatively large), and therefore $\mu_i << \sigma_i^2$ which would appear to be the case in this experiment, the following truncated Taylor series expansions of the exponential may be used as approximations:

$$\frac{3\,e^{\frac{(2y_i\mu_i)}{\sigma_i^2}} + 1}{3 + e^{\frac{(2y_i\mu_i)}{\sigma_i^2}}} \cong \frac{3\left[1 + \frac{2y_i\mu_i}{\sigma_i^2} + \frac{2y_i^2\mu_i^2}{\sigma_i^4}\right] + 1}{3 + \left[1 + \frac{2y_i\mu_i}{\sigma_i^2} + \frac{2y_i^2\mu_i^2}{\sigma_i^4}\right]} \quad ,$$

Dividing top and bottom by 4/3

$$\cong \frac{1 + \frac{3}{2}\frac{y_i\mu_i}{\sigma_i^2} + \frac{3}{2}\frac{y_i^2\mu_i^2}{\sigma_i^4}}{1 + \frac{1}{2}\frac{y_i\mu_i}{\sigma_i^2} + \frac{1}{2}\frac{y_i^2\mu_i^2}{\sigma_i^2}} \quad ,$$

Multiplying top and bottom by

$$\cong \left[1 + \frac{3}{2}\frac{y_i\mu_i}{\sigma_i^2} + \frac{3}{2}\frac{y_i^2\mu_i^2}{\sigma_i^2} \right]\left[1 - \frac{1}{2}\frac{y_i\mu_i}{\sigma_i^2} - \frac{1}{4}\frac{y_i^2\mu_i^2}{\sigma_i^2} \right]$$

yields

$$\cong 1 + \frac{y_i\mu_i}{\sigma_i^2} + \frac{1}{2}\frac{y_i^2\mu_i^2}{\sigma_i^2} \,, \tag{5a}$$

and finally

$$\cong e^{y_i\mu_i/\sigma_i^2}.$$

This is the formula for the four-cycle data collected by Commons (1981). A more generalized form of this equation is derived in the appendix, where a sample of n-cycles over any symmetrical reinforcement densities is analyzed as above.

So, for four-cycle data, the condition for the bird to peck left is

$$\frac{U_L}{U_R} \prod_{i=1}^{4} e^{\frac{y_i\mu_i}{\sigma_i^2}} > 1.$$

That is,

$$\prod_{i=1}^{4} e^{\frac{y_i\mu_i}{\sigma_i^2}} > \frac{U_R}{U_L}\,.$$

Taking the natural log of both sides gives

$$\sum_{i=1}^{4} \frac{y_i\mu_i}{\sigma_i^2} > \ln\frac{U_R}{U_L}\,.$$

Note that both linear and quadratic terms in each of the four Taylor expansions are kept, so that the result is correct up to terms of order $(1/\delta_i)^3$; when δ_i is very large, $(1/\delta_i)^3$ is very small. Furthermore, we only care about the validity of the approximation in the region where $EP(L)/EP(R) \cong 1$; that is, where

$$\sum_{i=1}^{4} (y_i\mu_i) / \sigma_i^2 \cong \ln(U_R/U_L),$$

which in the case of only moderate bias, will mean y_i values such that none of the $(y_i\mu_i)/\sigma_i^2 = y_i/\delta\mu_i$ is very large. The term on the left has been derived directly from the PDF given.

Here we have shown that the bird will peck left when

$$\sum_{i=1}^{4} \frac{y_i \mu_i}{\sigma_i^2} > \ln \frac{U_R}{U_L} ,$$

But the expression on the left, as a sum of normally distributed multivariate random variables, is itself normally distributed,

$$M_i = \sum_{i=1}^{4} \frac{(2v_i - 1)}{\delta_i} , \text{ which is the mean}$$

$$V_{S\,n} = \sum_{i=1}^{4} \frac{1}{\delta_i} , \text{ which is the variance}$$

and is conditional on the occurrence of the substimulus described by the v_i, since the conditional distribution of y_i is $N(\mu_i (2v_i - 1), \sigma_i^2)$. Therefore the probability of its being greater than $\ln (U_R/U_L)$, given the occurrence of that substimulus is given by

$$z_{p(L)} = \frac{M - \mu_i}{\sigma_i} = \frac{M - \ln(U_R/U_L)}{V_{sn}^{1/2}}$$

so that

$$z_{p(L)} = \sum_{i=1}^{4} a_i v_i + b ,$$

where

$$a_i = \frac{2}{\delta_i \left[\sum_{j=1}^{4} \frac{1}{\delta_j} \right]^{1/2}} \qquad (6)$$

The a_i coefficients can now be interpreted as indicating the rate at which discriminability of reinforcement declines with time. The value of δ_i (indistinguishability) was defined as $4/(d')^2$. The set of δ_i implied by a given set of a_i coefficients are easily reconstructed by inversion of Equation (6):

$$\sum_{i=1}^{4} a_i = \sum_{i=1}^{4} \frac{2}{\delta_i \left[\sum_{j=1}^{4} \frac{1}{\delta_j} \right]^{1/2}}$$

$$= \left[\sum_{i=1}^{4} \frac{1}{\delta_i} \right] \left[\frac{2}{\left[\sum_{j=1}^{4} \frac{1}{\delta_j} \right]^{1/2}} \right]$$

$$= 2 \left[\sum_{i=1}^{4} \frac{1}{\delta_i} \right]^{1/2} .$$

From Equation 6 we get

$$\delta_i = \frac{2}{a_i \left[\sum_{j=1}^{4} \frac{1}{\delta_i} \right]^{1/2}}$$

$$= \frac{4}{a_i \left[\sum_{j=1}^{4} a_j \right]}$$

The mean μ_i is the value of reinforcement remembered (i.e., perceived value) for a given cycle. Since the contributions of reinforcers will be added, the detectabilities should be in a form in which they add easily. By having the variance in the numerators, it will be possible to add the detectabilities, since the variance of the sum of independent variables equals the sum of the individual variances. The inverse of discriminability of reinforcement in cycle$_i$ is then measured by:

$$\delta_i = \frac{\sigma_i^2}{\mu_i^2} . \tag{7}$$

The parameter δ_0 is the inverse of sensitivity of reinforcement that occurs with no delay between reinforcement and choice. Note that when $\delta_i = 0$, variance is 0 and detection is perfect. Likewise, as δ_i gets larger, detection becomes poorer.

The simplest model of forgetting would be to assume that the *signal* stays constant while the amount of *noise* increases linearly with time. If it is assumed that the perceived value Y at the time of reinforcement is a random variable Y_0 (random because of imperfect discrimination of reinforcement even at that time), and that with each cycle that passes thereafter there is added another random noise component e (with the random noise terms independent of Y_0 and of each other, and all identically distributed), then the random variable Y_i, representing remembered values of reinforcement after i cycles have passed (in the case of the four-cycle experiment), can be written as

$$Y_i = Y_0 + \sum_{j=1}^{4} e_j \,.$$

Therefore,

$$E(Y_i) = E(Y_0) \,,$$

$$\text{var } (Y_i) = \text{var } (Y_0) + i * \text{var } (e) \,,$$

and

$$\delta_i = \frac{\text{var } (Y_i)}{E(Y_i)^2} = \frac{\text{var } (Y_0)}{E(Y_0)^2} + i * \frac{\text{var } (e)}{E(Y_0)^2} \,.$$

The discriminability measure δ_i, as a function of cycle number i, is therefore predicted to be a linear function. The first term in the last equation is replaced by its equivalent, δ_0; the second term by its equivalent, $i \, \gamma$:

$$\delta_i = \delta_0 + i \, \gamma \,.$$

As noise is linearly added to the initial inverse of discriminability, the variance goes up so δ_i increases. Hence, according to a simple additive model, the inverse of discriminability of reinforcement on cycle$_i$ is simply a function of the initial discriminability plus the product of τ, the rate at which noise is added between the reinforcer and choice, and γ, the rate of forgetting:

$$\delta_i = \delta_0 + \tau \, \gamma, \text{ for some } \delta_0 \text{ and } \gamma > 0. \tag{8}$$

How the General Additive Noise Model Predicts Perceived Reinforcement Value

The rate at which noise is added between the reinforcer and choice, τ, can be represented by the product of three terms: i, t^α, and s^β. The parameter i represents how far (in time periods) a possible reinforcer is away from choice. The value t is the length of the standard cycle and s is the probe multiplier ($s = 1$ for standard, $s = 2$ for double, $s = 3$ for triple). Note that the passage of time or elapsed time equals $i \, t \, s$. Three submodels, which are created by setting α, β, or both equal to 1 or 0, generate three notions of the rate of noise addition. If there is no effect of cycle length on perceived value, $\alpha = 0$. If there is no effect of probe multiplier on perceived value, $\beta = 0$. These submodels will be presented.

Each of the submodels is subsumed by the more general model:

$$\delta_i = \delta_0 + i\, t^\alpha s^\beta \gamma . \tag{9}$$

This equation might be used to estimate the four parameters: δ_i, α, β, γ by employing the data for all substimuli, all cycle lengths, and all probes, and special hypotheses (e.g., submodel 1 assumes $\alpha = \beta = 1$) subjected to a statistical hypothesis test (chi-square).

To show that value decreases as a hyperbolic function of i, the representation of value in the present experimental example is defined. As explained in Commons, Woodford, and Ducheny (1982) and here, the perceived reinforcement density, $V_{s\,n}$ of a sample, S_n, is a function of the δ's. That value is defined as the bias to indicate rich, $z^{-1}p(L)$. Again, it is assumed that the value of the entire substimulus is just the value of the sum of the contributions, $a_i v_i$, which is the effect of each reinforcer as remembered: Then the value of a sample as a function of δ_i is derived in the appendix. That derivation shows that the value of a sample should fit a hyperbolic model. The results are as follows:

$$V_{s_n} = z^{-1}p(L) = \sum_{i=1}^{4} a_i v_i , \tag{2, 10}$$

where

$$a_i = [\delta_i \left(\sum_{j=1}^{4} \frac{2}{\delta_j} \right)^{1/2}]^{-1} . \tag{11}$$

The value V_{s_n} in hyperbolic form is as shown:

$$z^{-1}p(L) = \sum_{i=1}^{4} \frac{c}{d + i} v_i , \tag{12}$$

where

$$c = \frac{\left[t^\alpha s^\beta \gamma \right]^{-1}}{\left[\sum_{j=1}^{4} \frac{1}{\delta + jt^\alpha s^\beta \gamma} \right]^{1/2}} , \tag{13}$$

$$d = \frac{\delta_0}{\alpha\,\beta} \cdot \tag{14}$$
$$\quad\ \ t\, s\, \gamma$$

Equation 12 shows that the equation for reinforcer value has a hyperbolic form. The parameter i represents how far (in cycles) a possible reinforcer is away from choice. Equations 12, 13 and 14 give the predicted effects of varying t and s on the parameters of the hyperbolic model. There are several plausible hypotheses about how the rate of forgetting (γ) varies as the length of the cycles varies. The submodels are presented next.

Submodel 1 (Time)

It might be supposed that the rate at which noise is added to the memory of a reinforcer depends solely on the passage of time, rather than on intervening events or a combination of events and time. In this case sensitivity on cycle$_i$ would be

$$\delta_i = \delta_0 + i\,t\,s\,\gamma. \tag{15}$$

The value t = length of the standard cycle and s = probe multiplier (s = 1 for standard, s = 2 for double, s = 3 for triple). Again, elapsed time equals $i\,t\,s$. In Equation 15, δ_0 and γ should be the same for all cycle lengths and probes. Neither δ_0 nor γ is affected by time.

To see if submodel 1 fits the data, a linearization of bias measured by $z^{-1}p(L)$, which is the perceived value of the schedule sample, is examined as a function of time in Fig. 7.3.

If memory were perfect, then perceived value of the sample for all substimuli taken together would be zero, $z^{-1}p(L) = 0$. Any indiscriminate change from the average bias would either increase false alarms (indicating rich when it was in fact lean) or misses (indicating lean when it was rich). Decreases in $z^{-1}p(L)$, therefore, represent forgetting. As standard cycle length t increased, $i\,t\,s$ would increase and submodel 1 would predict a decrease in discriminability. This would appear as a decrease in $z^{-1}p(L)$. This decrease was not found in the data shown in the left column of panels in Fig. 7.3. Submodel 1 would predict that the substimuli with the shorter cycles (circles) should be better discriminated than the middle length cycles (triangles) and those in turn better than the long cycle length (squares). The base-length-cycle substimuli were all equally well discriminated, which does not support submodel 1.

Submodel 2 (Number of Intervening Cycles)

The contrary extreme hypothesis would be to suppose that the rate at which noise is added depends solely on the number of subsequently occurring events between the reinforcer in question and choice, and not on the amount of time that elapsed. The number of cycles (number of events

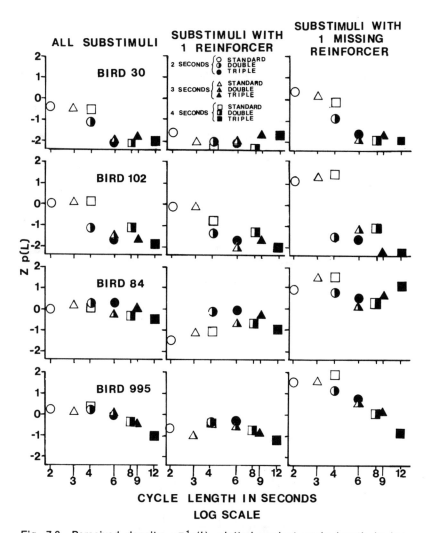

Fig. 7.3   Perceived density, $z^{-1}p(L)$, plotted against cycle length in log seconds. The left-hand column shows the effect of cycle length on the perceived density of all substimuli considered together. This is the macrolevel relation. At the molar level, Columns 2 and 3 show the relation between perceived density and cycle length for substimuli with one reinforcer and substimuli with three reinforcers (one missing reinforcer).

to store) is all that matters. Here those intervening events are the cycles with possible reinforcers in them. In that case it would be expected that:

$$\delta_i = \delta_0 + i\,\gamma. \tag{16}$$

In this submodel, δ_0 and γ values should be the same for all cycle lengths and probes. This means each a_i is identical to the corresponding a_i although the base-cycle length or probe multiplier differs. The only dimension that pigeons should be sensitive to is number of reinforcers.

In Fig. 7.3, for substimuli with one missing reinforcer, submodel 2 predicts that there would be no forgetting and $z^{-1}p(L)$ would remain constant. As shown in the right -most column, there was forgetting for all the pigeons; $z^{-1}p(L)$ did not remain constant. All the standard length substimuli were remembered better than the equivalent length doubles.

If submodel 2 were correct, time in the form of base cycle length or probe doubling or tripling should make no difference. In Fig. 7.4, this would mean that all the slopes would be the same for all cycle lengths and all probes. If the slopes differed it would reflect differential sensitivity. Again, the steeper the slope the more sensitive to the number of reinforcers. The slopes get flatter for double- and triple-length cycles, which is inconsistent with submodel 2.

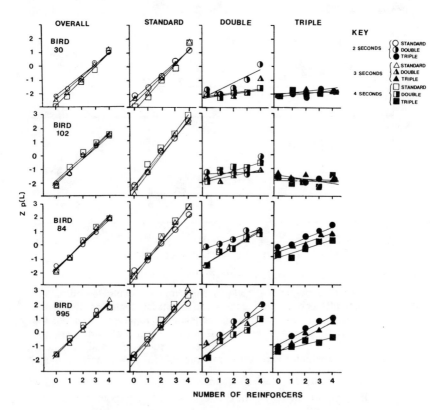

Fig. 7.4 Perceived density, $z^{-1}p(L)$, shown as a function of actual density (the number of reinforcers in a substimulus). This molar relation is shown for all trials together (Column 1), for trials with standard cycle length (Column 2), for probe trials where the standard length was doubled (Column 3) and tripled (Column 4).

Submodel 3 (Relative Time)

An intermediate submodel assumes that the rate at which the remembered value of a reinforcement decreases is adjusted according to the average rate at which events occur in a particular experimental situation. Hence it is not how much time has passed that causes the decrease in value, but simply length of time relative to the average time between events in the particular environment. According to this hypothesis, a change in the length of the standard cycle would have no effect, but the inclusion of a probe substimulus when the organism has calibrated its rate of memory decay to a different rate of occurrence of events will affect the size of the a_i. This is a finite storage capacity model given that probe stimuli are interpreted as a larger number of events:

x - - x - - - x x   events

. . . .   points at which reinforcers could occur.

The pigeon expects events at all the points and so allocates memory space to each. This submodel is especially consistent with submodel 3a, a generalization of submodel 3 that contains parameters for bias. It is presented in the appendix. The pigeon remembers events at the standard-cycle frequency. Remembering all the nonevents (in case of a probe) as events of nonreinforcement causes the bias. In this case one would expect:

$$\delta_i = \delta_0 + i\, s\, \gamma. \tag{17}$$

The value of $i\, s$ increases with increased probe multipliers or with cycles further from choice. Note that in the left panels of Fig. 7.3 the three left-most points do not show much change for $z^{-1}p(L)$ for all substimuli taken together, consistent with the predictions of submodel 3. That is, the perceived value of reinforcement did not change for the 2, 3, and 4 second base cycle lengths. The very problems that submodel 1 and submodel 2 had are solved by submodel 3. The effects of both probes and time are predicted. For instance, the 4-s standard, shown in the right column, is always above the 2-s double probe.

Submodel 3 was generally supported by the data shown in Fig. 7.4. For this submodel, if the probe multiplier s increased, all the δ_i's should increase. Increased δ_i's would indicate decreased sensitivity—the slope of V_{sn} versus number of reinforcers should decrease. In Fig. 7.4, for all pigeons, the slopes for the standard base cycle length are similar. As the probe cycle-length multiplier increased, the slope decreased as submodel 3 predicts. The data points for trials with standard cycle lengths fell on top of each other for all four birds. These points began to diverge for trials of double standard length (i.e., as s increased, base trial length made a greater difference in slope), and diverged even more for trials of triple standard length in the cases of Pigeons 84 and 995. This is all consistent with submodel 3; an increase in s should cause a greater divergence in slope as base cycle length increases because δ_0 increases as base cycle length increases, and therefore δ_i does as well. But this increase is linear, the sum of increased s γ and δ_0, and thus divergence should be linear as well. For pigeons 84 and 995, this assumption is supported.

The exceptions to submodel 3 can be seen in the *Triple* column of Fig. 7.4. Pigeons 30 and 102 show extreme bias: Their responses to probes are severely biased in favor of the lean reinforcer. Note that none of these submodels predicts the value of a bias term for the entire hyperbolic model. Hence, birds that react to the probe trials in a severely biased fashion cannot be used to distinguish any of these hypotheses. An alternative explanation exists, however, for the data that indicate bias as shown for the pigeon 30 and 102 in the top middle panels of Fig. 7.4.

Fully General Model with Parameters for Bias, Models 1a, 2a, 3a

Pigeons 30 and 102 exhibited extreme bias for going to the right for triples as shown in Fig. 7.4. This is consistent with submodel 3a, a generalization of submodel 3 that adds terms to estimate this form of bias. A fully general model with the parameter s for this form of right bias is shown in the appendix. If this bias parameter, s, is small in submodel 3a, then the tendency to choose left would increase. If it is exactly 1, then submodel 3a reduces to just submodel 3. If s is very large then the value of a substimulus is markedly decreased, resulting in a strong right bias. This is just what was found as shown in the top middle panels of Fig 7.4. There is no general theoretical basis at this time for expecting such right bias, other than the possibility that all events outside a time period fixed by the length of the cycles ($2 \times 4 = 8$ s, $3 \times 4 = 12$ s, $4 \times 4 = 16$ s) are totally ignored. If these events are ignored, then subjects act as if they had zero value. Another possibility is that longer probe cycles result in memory of a large number of nonreinforcements (without truncation of time period over which memory occurs).

CONCLUSION

It was shown analytically that the time window must be a hyperbolic function of value versus some measure of time. The major assumption made was that noise interfering with the effectiveness of reinforcement is added in a linear fashion.

Applying the general additive noise model to the results from Commons (1981) showed that the decrementation function is not a simple function of simple time. The effectiveness of reinforcement decreased as a function of a form of time. This form of time progressed along the relative rate dimension; thus time progressed relative to the rate of baseline reinforcement. Three submodels and a set of variants were qualitatively tested. The experimental requirement was for the pigeons to detect the richness of the sample. Therefore, the number of reinforcers in the sample determined which choice would be most likely to be reinforced. The best decision rule required sensitivity only to number of reinforcers. Out of the possible four reinforcers, if there were zero or one reinforcers the best choice would be to indicate lean; if there were three or four reinforcers the best choice would be rich. Other decision rules could mean that the pigeons are less sensitive in some way since they would not exhibit an exclusive preference. Mazur (1984, 1987) leaves time in one schedule constant while varying delay in another. Until background rate of reinforcement is varied, the role of context per se in the choice situations consisting of a single or a few reinforcers will not be clear. From the perspective of melioration theory (Herrnstein, 1982; Herrnstein & Vaughan, 1980) and our own acquisition theory (Commons, Woodford, Boitano, Ducheny, & Peck, 1982) the background rate of reinforcement as well as its variability should be important as we have found here.

Qualitative fits of submodels of the general additive noise model showed that neither simple time nor the number of reinforcements (i.e., the number of cycles with reinforcement) accounted for the findings. A test of the third submodel suggested that a parameter for overall bias independent of experimental conditions should be included. The decrease in reinforcement value was sensitive to changes in reinforcement rate with respect to background rate and not with respect to number of reinforcements or time. The general additive noise model can be used in preference studies since the model was formulated in terms of "time" between a response and a reinforcing schedule component. The schedules modeled here are general in form, since they are T-schedules that resemble random interval schedules. As Schoenfeld and Cole (1972) have shown, T-schedules with certain parameter selections behave like interval schedules. From the assumption that noise is linearly added between reinforcement and choice, hyperbolic decrementation functions were analytically derived and then illustrated.

APPENDIX

The value of a substimulus, V_{sn}, is the bias to indicate that a substimulus is rich, $z^{-1}p(L)$. That value is directly related to δ_i. Again, it is assumed that the value of the entire substimulus is just the value of the sum of the contributions, $a_i v_i$, which is the effect of each reinforcer as remembered. This derivation gives the predicted effects of varying t and s on the parameters of the hyperbolic model. The second important result of the derivation is that our use of the additive noise model yields a value of a sample that fits a hyperbolic model.

$$V_{s_n} = z^{-1}p(L) = \sum_{i=1}^{4} a_i v_i , \qquad (2, 10)$$

where

$$a_i = \frac{2}{\delta_i \left[\sum\limits_{j=1}^{4} \dfrac{1}{\delta_j} \right]^{1/2}} . \qquad (11)$$

Fully General Submodel: Submodel 3a

By Equation 13, which states that $\delta_i = \delta_0 + i\, t^\alpha s^\beta \gamma$, and Equation 2, 10, and 11,

$$v_{s_n} = 2\sum_{i=1}^{4} [\, (\delta_0 + i\, t^\alpha s^\beta \gamma) \, [\sum_{j=1}^{4} \frac{1}{\delta_j}]^{1/2}]^{-1} v_i \qquad (18)$$

$$= 2\sum_{i=1}^{4} [\, (t^\alpha s^\beta \gamma)\frac{(\delta_0 + i)}{t^\alpha s^\beta \gamma} \, [\sum_{j=1}^{4} \frac{1}{\delta_i}]^{1/2}]^{-1} v_i$$

$$= \frac{2\sum\limits_{i=1}^{4} [\, (t^\alpha s^\beta \gamma) \, [\sum\limits_{j=1}^{4} \frac{1}{\delta_j}] \,]^{1/2} v_i^{-1}}{\dfrac{\delta_0}{t^\alpha s^\beta \gamma} + i} . \qquad (20)$$

Equation 21, which is derived from Equation 20, shows that the decrementation function is hyperbolic in form:

$$z^{-1}p(L) = \sum_{i=1}^{4} \frac{c}{d + i} v_i , \qquad (12, 21)$$

where

$$c = [(t^\alpha s^\beta \gamma) [\sum_{j=1}^{4} \frac{2}{\delta_j}]^{1/2}]^{-1} , \qquad (13,22)$$

$$d = \frac{\delta_0}{t^\alpha s^\beta \gamma} . \qquad (14,23)$$

Generalizing to *n* Cycles and any Symmetrical Reinforcement Densities

The models in the text are generated for four-cycle data only. Fully generalized derivations of the Probability Density Function (PDF) and δ_i for n cycles are as follows:

For the rich schedule where a left response indicates reinforcement the probability density function has the form

$$f(y_i) = p(R|S_R)\frac{1}{2\Pi\,\sigma_i} \cdot e^{\frac{-(yi - \mu_i)^2}{2\sigma_i^2}} + p(N|S_R)\frac{1}{2\Pi\,\sigma_i} \cdot e^{\frac{(y_i + \mu_i)^2}{2\sigma_i^2}} .$$

Likewise, for the lean schedule where reinforcement is delivered on the right response, the probability density function has the form

$$f(y_i) = p(R|S_L)\frac{1}{2\Pi\,\sigma_i} \cdot e^{\frac{-(yi - \mu_i)^2}{2\sigma_i^2}} + p(N|S_L)\frac{1}{2\Pi\,\sigma_i} \cdot e^{\frac{-(y_i + \mu_i)^2}{2\sigma_i^2}}.$$

Where $p(R|S_n)$ is the probability of reinforcement on the given substimulus, (i.e., $v_i = 1$) and $p(N|S_n)$ the probability of no reinforcement on the substimulus. The condition for the bird to peck left

$$\frac{EP(L|y_1, y_2, y_3, y_4 \cdots y_n)}{EP(R|y_1, y_2, y_3, y_4 \cdots y_n)} > 1 ,$$

$$\frac{EP(L|y_1, y_2, y_3, y_4 \cdots y_n)}{EP(R|y_1, y_2, y_3, y_4 \cdots y_n)} = \frac{U_L}{U_R} \frac{p(y_1, y_2, y_3, y_4 \cdots y_n)}{p(y_1, y_2, y_3, y_4, \cdots y_n)}$$

$$= \frac{U_L \Pi_i f(y_i|S_R)}{U_R \Pi_i f(y_i|S_R)} ,$$

$$= \frac{U_L}{U_R} \frac{\prod\limits_{i=1}^{n} \left(p(R|S_R) \, e^{\frac{-(y_i - \mu_i)^2}{2\sigma_i^2}} + p(N|S_R) \, e^{\frac{-(y_i + \mu_i)^2}{2\sigma_i^2}} \right)}{\prod\limits_{i=1}^{n} \left(p(R|S_L) \, e^{\frac{-(y_i - \mu_i)^2}{2\sigma_i^2}} + p(N|S_L) \, e^{\frac{-(y_i + \mu_i)^2}{2\sigma_i^2}} \right)} \, .$$

Factoring and expanding, as shown, yields

$$= \frac{U_L}{U_R} \prod\limits_{i=1}^{n} \frac{p(R|S_R) \, e^{\frac{-(y_i^2 - 2y_i\mu_i + \mu_i^2)}{2\sigma_i^2}} + p(N|S_R) \, e^{\frac{-(y_i^2 + 2y_i\mu_i + \mu_i^2)}{2\sigma_i^2}}}{p(R|S_L) \, e^{\frac{-(y_i^2 - 2y_i\mu_i + \mu_i^2)}{2\sigma_i^2}} + p(N|S_L) \, e^{\frac{-(y_i^2 + 2y_i\mu_i + \mu_i^2)}{2\sigma_i^2}}} \, .$$

Factoring and dividing again, as shown, yields

$$= \frac{U_L}{U_R} \prod\limits_{i=1}^{n} \frac{p(R|S_R) \, e^{\frac{(2y_i\mu_i)}{\sigma_i^2}} \, p(N|S_R)}{p(N|S_L) + p(R|S_L) \, e^{\frac{(2y_i\mu_i)}{\sigma_i^2}}} \, .$$

For the next part of this discussion, it is sufficient to work with only the function within the iterative multiplication. The function in this product is approximated by the Taylor expansion

$$\cong \frac{p(R|S_R) \left[1 + \frac{2y_i\mu_i}{\sigma_i^2} + \frac{2y_i^2\mu_i^2}{\sigma_i^4} \right] + p(N|S_R)}{p(N|S_L) + p(R|S_L) \left[1 + \frac{2y_i\mu_i}{\sigma_i^2} + \frac{2y^2\mu_i^2}{\sigma_i^4} \right]} \, ,$$

and, since this case is symmetrical, expanded to

$$\frac{1 + \frac{p(R|S_R)2y_i\mu_i}{\sigma_i^2} + \frac{p(R|S_R)2y_i^2\mu_i^2}{\sigma_i^4}}{1 + \frac{p(N|S_L)2y_i\mu_i}{\sigma_i^2} + \frac{p(N|S_L)2y_i^2\mu_i^2}{\sigma_i^4}} \, .$$

Multiply top and bottom by

$$\left[1 - \frac{p(R|S_L)2y_i\mu_i}{\sigma_i^2} - \frac{p(R|S_L) \, (1 - p(R|S_L)) \, 2y_i^2\mu_i^2}{\sigma_i^2} \right]$$

and drop all but linear and quadratic terms. The denominator thereby approximates 1 and we are left with the product of the numerator and our polynomial:

$$\left[1 + \frac{p(R|S_R)2y_i\mu_i}{\sigma_i^2} + \frac{p(R|S_R)2y_i^2\mu_i^2}{\sigma_i^4} \right]$$

$$\left[1 - \frac{p(R|S_L)2y_i\mu_i}{\sigma_i^2} - \frac{p(R|S_L)\,(1 - 2p(R|S_L)\,)2y_i^2\mu_i^2}{\sigma_i^4} \right]$$

ACKNOWLEDGMENTS

This work has a long history that would have been terminated except for the inspiration and encouragement of Edmund Fantino. On two occasions Fantino and Ben Williams, along with their students, listened to presentations of our ideas in their formative stages. Parts of this chapter were also reported at the Symposium on Quantitative Analyses of Behavior at Harvard in a paper entitled "The Effects of Delay and Intervening Events" (1982). That paper's authors were Michael L. Commons and Michael Woodford. The data appeared in Commons (1981). Data acquisition was carried out with the support of Richard J. Herrnstein, and with the assistance of Brian Cabral, Wilson R. Fong, and Joseph P. McNamara. Fong assisted with the data analyses. The computer analysis was performed at the Northeastern University academic computer center. The first author served as lecturer in Foundation of Education and in Psychology. William Minty of the Harvard University Drafting Department and Rebecca M. Young drew the graphs.

The extensive editorial help was provided by Michael Davison and John Anthony Nevin, the co-editors. In addition, Leonard S. Miller made extensive substantive suggestions for explicating the theory. William Vaughan, Jr., and Charlotte Mandell commented on the manuscript. Brian Cabral wrote some of the introductory material. Rebecca M. Young, Patrice M. Miller, L. Brockman, and Stanley J. Morse edited the manuscript for style. The research and analysis were supported by grants from the Dare Association, Inc., and NIHM 15494 to Harvard University, Richard J. Herrnstein, principal investigator, and from the Dare Association, Inc., to the first author; and a MacArthur Foundation Award and a National Science Foundation Fellowship to the second author.

REFERENCES

Ainslie, G. W. (1975). Specious reward: A behavioral theory of impulsiveness and impulse control. *Psychological Bulletin, 82,* 463–496.

Baddeley, A. D., & Hitch, G. (1974). Working memory. In G. H. Bower (Ed.), *Psychology of Learning and Motivation, 8,* 47–90.

Barnes, J.M., & Underwood, B. J. (1959). "Fate" in first-list associations in transfer theory. *Journal of Experimental Psychology, 58,* 97-105.

Chung, S., & Herrnstein, R. J. (1967). Choice and delay of reinforcement. *Journal of the Experimental Analysis of Behavior, 32,* 101-120.

Commons, M. L. (1979). Decision rules and signal detectability in a reinforcement density discrimination. *Journal of the Experimental Analysis of Behavior, 32,* 67-74.

Commons, M. L. (1981). How reinforcement density is discriminated and scaled. In M. L. Commons & J. A. Nevin (Eds.), *Quantitative analyses of behavior: Vol. 1. Discriminative properties of reinforcement schedules* (pp. 51-85). Cambridge, MA: Ballinger.

Commons, M. L., & Nevin, J. A. (Eds.). (1981). *Quantitative analyses of behavior: Vol. 1. Discriminative properties of reinforcement schedules.* Cambridge, MA: Ballinger.

Commons, M. L., Woodford, M., Boitano, G. A., Ducheny, J. R., & Peck, J. R. (1982). Acquisition of preference during shifts between terminal links in concurrent chain schedules. In M. L. Commons, R. J. Herrnstein, & A. R. Wagner (Eds.), *Quantitative analyses of behavior: Vol. 3. Acquisition* (pp. 391-426). Cambridge, MA: Ballinger.

Commons, M. L., Woodford, M., & Ducheny, J. R. (1982). How reinforcers are aggregated in reinforcement-density discrimination and preference experiments. In M. L. Commons, R. J. Herrnstein, & H. Rachlin (Eds.), *Quantitative analyses of behavior: Vol. 2. Matching and maximizing accounts* (pp. 25-78). Cambridge, MA: Ballinger.

Davison, M. C., & Tustin, R. D. (1978). The relation between generalized matching law and signal detection theory. *Journal of the Experimental Analysis of Behavior, 29,* 331-336.

Dickinson, A. (1980). *Contemporary animal learning theory.* Cambridge, England: Cambridge University Press.

Ebbinghaus, H. (1885). *Memory: A contribution to experimental psychology* (H. A. Ruger & C. E. Bussenius, Trans., 1913). New York: Teachers College, Columbia University.

Egan, J. P. (1975). *Signal detection theory and ROC analysis.* New York: Academic Press.

Fantino, E. J. (1981). Contiguity, response strength, and the delay-reduction hypothesis. In P. Harzem & M. H. Zeiler (Eds.), *Advances in analysis of behavior: Vol 2. Predictability, correlation, and contiguity* (pp. 169-201). Chichester, England: Wiley.

Fantino, E. J., Abarca, N., & Dunn, R. M. (1987). The delay-reduction hypothesis: Extensions to foraging and three-alternative choice. In M. L. Commons, J. E. Mazur, J. A. Nevin, & H. Rachlin (Eds.), *Quantitative analyses of behavior: Vol. 5. The effect of delay and of intervening events on reinforcement value.* Hillsdale. NJ: Lawrence Erlbaum Associates.

Glanzer, M., & Cunitz, A. R. (1966). Two storage mechanisms in free recall. *Journal of Verbal Learning and Verbal Behavior, 5,* 351-360.

Green, D. M., & Swets, J. A. (1966). *Signal detection theory and ROC analysis.* New York: Academic Press.

Grossberg, S. (1978). Theory of human memory: Self organization and performance of sensory motor codes, maps and plans. In R. Rosen & F. Snell (Eds.), *Progress in theoretical biology, Vol. 5.* (pp. 233-374). New York: Academic Press.

Hall, G., & Pearce, J. M. (1982). Changes in stimulus associability during conditioning: Implications for theories of acquisition. In M. L. Commons, R. J. Herrnstein, & A. R. Wagner (Eds.), *Quantitative analyses of behavior: Vol. 3. Acquisition* (pp. 221-240). Cambridge MA: Ballinger.

Herrnstein, R. J. (1982). Melioration as behavioral dynamism. In M. L. Commons, R. J. Herrnstein, & H. Rachlin (Eds.), *Quantitative analyses of behavior: Vol. 2. Matching and maximizing accounts* (pp. 433-458). Cambridge, MA: Ballinger.

Herrnstein, R. J., & Vaughan, W., Jr. (1980). Melioration and behavioral allocation. In J. E. R. Staddon (Ed.), *Limits to action: The allocation of individual behavior* (pp. 143-176). New York: Academic Press.

Madigan, S. A. (1971). Modality and recall order interactions in short-term memory for serial order. *Journal of Experimental Psychology, 87,* 294–296.

Mandell, C. (1981). A psychophysical analysis of time-based schedules of reinforcement. In M. L. Commons & J. A. Nevin (Eds.), *Quantitative analyses of behavior: Vol. 1. Discriminative properties of reinforcement schedules* (pp. 31–50). Cambridge, MA: Ballinger.

Mandell, C. (1984). Discriminability of frequency of food or stimulus presentations in variable-time schedules. *Journal of the Experimental Analysis of Behavior, 42,* 291–303.

Mazur, J. E. (1984). Tests of an equivalence rule for fixed and variable reinforcer delays. *Journal of Experimental Psychology: Animal Behavior Processes, 10,* 426–436.

Mazur, J. E. (1987). An adjusting procedure for studying delayed reinforcement. In M. L. Commons, J. E. Mazur, J. A. Nevin, & H. Rachlin (Eds.), *Quantitative analyses of behavior: Vol. 5. The effect of delay and of intervening events on reinforcement value.* Hillsdale, NJ: Lawrence Erlbaum Associates.

McCarthy, D.C., & White, K. G. (1987). Behavioral models of delayed detection and their application to the study of memory. *Quantitative analyses of behavior: Vol. 5. The effect of delay and of intervening events on reinforcement value.* Hillsdale, NJ: Lawrence Erlbaum Associates.

Melton, A. W., & Irwin, J. M. (1940). The influence and degree of interpolated learning on retroactive inhibition and the overt transfer of specific responses. *American Journal of Psychology, 53,* 173–203.

Murdock, B. B., Jr. (1962). The serial position effect of free recall. *Journal of Experimental Psychology, 64,* 482–488.

Muth, J. F. (1960). Optimal properties of exponentially weighted forecasts. *Journal of the American Statistical Association, 55,* 299–306.

Nevin, J. A. (1969). Signal detection theory and operant behavior [Review of D. M. Green & J. A. Swets, *Signal detection theory and psychophysics*]. *Journal of the Experimental Analysis of Behavior, 12,* 475–480.

Nevin, J. A. (1981). Psychophysics and reinforcement schedules: An integration. In M. L. Commons & J. A. Nevin (Eds.), *Quantitative analyses of behavior: Vol. 1. Discriminative properties of reinforcement schedules* (pp. 3–27). Cambridge, MA: Ballinger.

Pearce, J. M., Kaye, H., & Hall, G. (1982). Predictive accuracy and stimulus associability: Development of a model for Pavlovian learning. In M. L. Commons, R. J. Herrnstein, & A. R. Wagner (Eds.), *Quantitative analyses of behavior: Vol. 3. Acquistion* (pp. 241–256). Cambridge, MA: Ballinger.

Raiffa, H. (1968). *Decision analysis: Introductory lectures on choices under uncertainty.* Reading, MA: Addison–Wesley.

Raiffa, H., & Schlaifer, R. O. (1961). *Applied statistical decision theory.* Boston: Division of Research, Harvard Business School.

Schoenfeld, W. N., & Cole, B. K. (1972). *Stimulus schedules: The t-tau systems.* New York: Harper & Row.

Sternberg, S. (1966). High-speed scanning in human memory. *Science, 153,* 652–654.

Underwood, B. J. (1948a). Retroactive and proactive inhibition after five and forty-eight hours. *Journal of Experimental Psychology, 38,* 29–38.

Underwood, B. J. (1948b). "Spontaneous recovery" of verbal associations. *Journal of Experimental Psychology, 38,* 429–439.

Underwood, B. J. (1957). Interference and forgetting. *Psychological Review, 64,* 49–60.

White, K. G., & McKenzie, J. (1982). Delayed stimulus control: Recall for single and relational stimuli. *Journal of the Experimental Analysis of Behavior, 38,* 305–312.

Wickelgren, W. A. (1974). Strength/resistance theory of the dynamics of memory storage. In D. H. Krantz, R. C. Atkinson, R. D. Luce, & P. Supper (Eds.), *Contemporary developments in mathematical psychology: Learning, memory and thinking.* San Francisco: Freeman.

Williams, B. (1982). Blocking the response-reinforcer association. In M. L. Commons, R. J. Herrnstein, & A. R. Wagner (Eds.), *Quantitative analyses of behavior: Vol. 3. Acquisition* (pp. 427–448). Cambridge, MA: Ballinger.

Woodword, A. E. (1970). Continuity between serial memory and serial learning. *Journal of Experimental Psychology, 85,* 90–94.

Signal Detection and Matching: Analyzing Choice on Concurrent Schedules

8

A. W. Logue
State University of New York at Stony Brook

Monica L. Rodriguez
Columbia University

The matching law (Herrnstein, 1961, 1970) and signal-detection theory (Green & Swets, 1966) both provide quantitative methods for analyzing choice. Comparisons of the similarities and differences between these two methods can indicate how each may best be used and can also improve our understanding of both methods and of choice in general. The two experiments reported here compare these two approaches empirically. First, however, it will be useful to outline briefly some of the purposes and procedures of each approach.

The usual signal-detection procedure employs discrete trials. One of two explicit stimuli (signal plus noise or noise alone) is presented at the start of each trial. The subject's task is to make one of two responses indicating which stimulus was presented. A payoff, a punisher, and/or feedback is ordinarily then presented, the trial ends, and after an intertrial interval, a new trial begins. This procedure results in four possible types of response (see Fig. 8.1). Substituting payoffs for each of the four classes of response in Fig. 8.1 yields a payoff matrix.

The purpose of signal-detection theory has been to provide independent measures of the effects on responding of (a) outcomes, and (b) the discrimination of the explicit stimuli. According to traditional signal-detection theory, "bias" will ideally be affected only by motivational factors (e.g., the relative values in the cells of the payoff matrix), whereas "sensitivity" will ideally be affected only by manipulations of the physical character of the signal and of the noise (Green & Swets, 1966; Nevin, 1981; Swets, Tanner, & Birdsall, 1961). When the values of the payoff matrix have been varied, bias, not sensitivity, has indeed usually been affected

RESPONSE

	SIGNAL	NOISE
SIGNAL	HIT (correct detection)	MISS (error)
NOISE	FALSE ALARM (error)	CORRECT REJECTION

STIMULUS

FIG. 8.1   Classification of responses in a signal-detection experiment.

(Davenport, 1968, 1969; Hobson, 1978; Hume & Irwin, 1974; Nevin, 1967; Stubbs, 1968, 1976; Wright; 1972, Wright & Nevin, 1974; but for a contrary example, see McCarthy & Davison, 1984). However, contrary to traditional signal-detection theory, reinforcing errors (i.e., reinforcement for false alarms and misses, which are no longer strictly errors as these responses do result in some reinforcement) affects sensitivity, not just bias (Davison & McCarthy, 1980; McCarthy & Davison, 1981; Nevin, 1970; Nevin, Olson, Mandell, & Yarensky, 1975; for detection models of choice that better maintain the independence between bias and sensitivity see, e.g., Alsop, this volume; Davison & Jenkins, 1985; Davison & Tustin, 1978; McCarthy, 1983; McCarthy & Davison, 1981).

Experiments on reinforcer choice within a matching law paradigm typically use continuous, rather than trial, procedures. Generally, two concurrent variable-interval (VI) schedules program reinforcement for responses on two levers or two keys. In these experiments subjects must discriminate the differences between the reinforcer rates programmed by the concurrent VI schedules along with the source of the reinforcers delivered by the individual VI schedules (e.g., whether left or right lever presses are reinforced by a given VI schedule). The distribution of responses across the two alternatives reflects both of these types of discrimination. When subjects distribute their responses in proportion to the distribution of reinforcers, they are said to match (de Villiers, 1977).

In matching law experiments, response distribution is often affected by factors other than the actual reinforcer distribution. The terms "response bias" and "discriminability" can be used to classify these factors (see also Baum, 1974). Response bias would occur if, for instance, one lever were harder to push than another due either to differences in the levers or to a physical asymmetry in the animal. Discriminability reflects factors that scale the perceived differences between the two concurrent schedules of reinforcement, making these differences seem smaller or larger. For example, if a rat is being reinforced from a single food source for responses on two adjacent, identical levers, the differential consequences for responding on the two levers might not seem so marked (see Miller, Saunders, & Bourland, 1980).

Response bias and discriminability within the matching law are expressed as follows:

$$\frac{B_1}{B_2} = k \left(\frac{R_1}{R_2}\right)^a, \tag{1}$$

where B_1 and B_2 represent responses on two alternatives; R_1 and R_2, reinforcers obtained by responses on the two alternatives; k, response bias; and a, discriminability (Baum, 1974). If k is greater than 1.0, there is response bias for the first alternative; if k is less than 1.0, there is response bias for the second alternative. If a is less than 1.0, there is undermatching (low discriminability); if greater than 1.0, overmatching (high discriminability). Note that the matching law's measure of discriminability, a, is affected by variations in both types of discrimination described: reinforcer rate and reinforcer source. However, in the matching law paradigm, presentations of the stimuli, the VI schedules, are not explicit as are the presentation of the stimuli in the signal-detection paradigm.

The matching law and signal-detection paradigms have much in common. Aside from certain basic procedural similarities, such as the collection of steady-state data from a small number of subjects (see Nevin, 1969b, for a summary), both paradigms record response distributions following variations in stimuli and outcomes. Both attempt to measure the influence of these factors, with the matching law using discriminability and response bias, and signal detection using sensitivity and bias, respectively. However, because no explicit stimuli are presented in the matching law paradigm, Fig.8.1 is collapsed so that there is only one column and only two types of response: signal and noise (left and right) responses. Both of these types of response are used in calculating a and k; therefore the matching law's measures of discriminability and response bias cannot be independent (Staddon, 1978). The value of a measures the rate of change in the tendency to make one response or another as the VI schedules are changed. The value of k measures whatever constant tendency there is to make one or the other response. In the signal-detection paradigm, which uses the four types of responses diagrammed in Fig. 8.1, sensitivity is measured by comparing hits with false alarms, and bias is measured by comparing hits and false alarms with misses and correct rejections (see Fig. 8.1). Although signal-detection's and the matching law's actual measures of the effects of varying stimuli and outcomes are not the same, the two theories are closely related.

It is possible to design a procedure similar enough to both the standard matching law and signal-detection paradigms so that the data could reasonably be analyzed according to the standard methods of each paradigm. Signal-detection theory does not require that there be only one response per trial, as long as the discrimination involved prior to responding is clear (Green & Swets, 1966, p. 11). This suggests the possibility of using a signal-detection trials procedure with an explicit discrimination but with more than one response permitted per trial and with reinforcers programmed according to schedules, similar to a matching law experiment. There have been previous signal-detection experiments in which the prior explicit discrimination was between a pair of schedules (e.g., Lattal, 1979; Mandell, 1981; Rilling & McDiarmid, 1965), and in which signal detection was examined in a free-operant setting (e.g., Davison, McCarthy, & Jensen, 1985; McCarthy, Davison, & Jenkins, 1982). There have also been previous matching law experiments in which discrete trials were used (e.g., Nevin, 1969a; Shimp, 1966).

The following two experiments adopted this strategy. In both experiments, the subjects were first required to discriminate between explicit stimuli. One reinforcement schedule programmed reinforcers for correct responses (hits and correct rejections), and another schedule programmed (usually fewer) reinforcers for "errors" (false alarms and misses). In both experiments, the reinforcement schedule for errors was varied.

In a matching law analysis of such a design, the two types of responses measured would be correct and incorrect responses, instead of the usual left and right responses. Because subjects must first discriminate the explicit stimuli that are presented, in addition to the reinforcement schedules and the sources of the reinforcers, the extent of a subject's discrimination between the explicit stimuli would determine a limit for a. Variations in the reinforcement schedules for correct and incorrect responses should affect the distribution of correct and incorrect responses but not discriminability of reinforcement or response bias. A signal-detection analysis also predicts that changing the reinforcer distribution should produce changes in response distribution. In addition, to the extent that errors are reinforced, previous research predicts, contrary to traditional signal-detection theory, that sensitivity should decrease.

In Experiment 1 (Logue, 1983), concurrent VI schedules of reinforcement were used. In Experiment 2, concurrent variable-ratio (VR) schedules were used. These two types of schedules were chosen because they are the types used most frequently in matching law experiments. In addition, concurrent VR schedules have been shown to tend to generate responses that are largely distributed on the alternative delivering reinforcers according to the smaller VR schedule (Herrnstein & Loveland, 1975), rather than being a linear function of the relative reinforcer rate, as is obtained and is predicted by the matching law for concurrent VI schedules (de Villiers, 1977). Therefore, it was predicted that reinforcement for errors would have less effect on signal detection's measure of sensitivity in Experiment 2 than in Experiment 1, and that the matching law would fit the data in Experiment 1 better than the data in Experiment 2.

Thus the present experiments had several objectives. First, they examined matching in two experiments in which subjects had to make an explicit discrimination between presented stimuli before discriminating reinforcer rate and the source of reinforcement. Second, the experiments examined signal detection in situations in which responding is measured in a free-operant setting. Third, these two experiments compared performance on VI and VR schedules using both matching law and signal-detection analyses. For both experiments, and for both the matching law and the signal-detection analyses, the effects of varying relative reinforcer rate was of specific concern.

METHOD

Subjects

Experiment 1. Four adult White Carneau pigeons, numbered 1, 2, 3, and 4, served in this experiment. They were maintained at 80% of their free-feeding weights. All of these pigeons had previously participated in a variety of operant conditioning experiments, but none of these experiments had employed a signal-detection paradigm nor ratio schedules of reinforcement.

Experiment 2. Four adult White Carneau pigeons, numbered 32, 33, 35, and 36, served in this experiment. They were maintained at 80% of their free-feeding weights. All of these pigeons were experimentally naïve at the start of the experiment. Prior to participating in the actual experiment which will be described, all were initially trained to peck using an autoshaping procedure (automatic pairing of key light and food hopper presentations, which elicits key pecking).

Apparatus

Experiment 1. The experimental chamber, one side of a partitioned ice chest, was 37.5 cm long, 30 cm wide, and 30 cm high. Two response keys were mounted in the partition wall of the chamber. The keys were 12 cm apart, and each required a minimum force of .12 N to operate. Each key could be transilluminated by two 6-W green lights and two 6-W red lights. A food hopper below the keys provided access to mixed grain. Two 6-W white lights were located above a Plexiglas panel in the ceiling of the chamber. A Sonalert was situated just above the hopper mechanism behind the partition and outside of the chamber. A speaker, also located behind the partition, produced continuous white noise that helped mask extraneous sounds. An air blower provided ventilation. A PDP–8 computer in another room controlled the stimuli and recorded responses using a SKED program.

Experiment 2. The apparatus used in Experiment 2 was similar to that used in Experiment 1 with the following exceptions. The experimental chamber was constructed of Plexiglas and aluminum, and was 32 cm long, 32 cm wide, and 30 cm high. Each key required a minimum force of .17 N to operate. The Sonalert was situated on the top, front, center of the chamber ceiling. The chamber was placed inside a sound-attenuating box. This box contained an air blower for ventilation that also helped to mask extraneous sounds. A SUPERSKED program was used.

Procedure

Noncorrection procedures were used. The pigeons first participated in several months of training sessions in which they learned to peck a red key after presentation of a 2-s tone and a green key after presentation of a 10-s tone. At first only the "correct" key was illuminated after each tone presentation and each correct response was followed by reinforcement. Next both keys were lit, one red and one green, and finally reinforcement programming for pecks on the correct key was changed to either a VI (Experiment 1) or a VR (Experiment 2) schedule.

During the actual experiment each session began with illumination of the white overhead lights. These lights remained on throughout the session. Five s after the start of a session a trial began and the Sonalert emitted a tone. A probability generator set at .5 determined whether a short (2-s) or a long (10-s) tone was emitted. Immediately after the tone terminated, both keys were transilluminated, one key with red light and the other key with green light. They remained illuminated until a reinforcer was received. Key color was determined nonsystematically for each trial in order to prevent position biases. Pecks on either lit key were followed by a feedback click. Pecks on the red key following a short tone or the green key following a long tone, "correct" pecks, were reinforced with 2.5-s access to food according to a VI (Experiment 1) or a VR (Experiment 2) schedule. Pecks on the red key following a long tone or the green key following a short tone, "incorrect" pecks, were reinforced with 2.5-s access to a leaner VI (Experiment 1) or VR (Experiment 2) schedule or were not reinforced at all. The schedules for correct and incorrect pecks operated independently. Both the VI and the VR schedules were constructed according to the distribution given by Fleshler and Hoffman (1962). The VI timers in Experiment 1 operated only while the key lights were on.

A 1-s changeover delay (COD) was in effect; 1 s had to elapse after a changeover response from a red to a green key or vice versa, or after the first response during a trial, before a subsequent key peck could deliver a reinforcer. The purpose of the COD was to decrease the probability of reinforcement of sequences of responses involving both keys. Such reinforcement can decrease choice discrimination as indicated by undermatching (de Villiers, 1977), and would probably also result in a lower value of signal detection's measure of sensitivity, although there has not yet been any research directed specifically at this issue.

A trial terminated with food delivery. After a 5-s intertrial interval, the Sonalert came on and another trial began. Sessions ended after 50 trials. Sessions were conducted 5 to 6 days per week.

Conditions were changed when all of the pigeons in an experiment simultaneously satisfied a stability criterion. This criterion specified a minimum of 10 sessions in a condition. In addition, in at least the last 5 consecutive sessions, the percentage of correct responses for each pigeon had to be neither higher nor lower than the percentage of correct responses in all previous sessions within that condition. In Experiment 1, Pigeon 4 did not appear to acquire a good discrimination (only 61% correct responses in the first condition compared with a mean of 73% for the other three pigeons), and was therefore dropped from the experiment. The particular schedules used and the number of sessions that each condition was in effect are shown in Table 8.1.

RESULTS

Overall Performance

Data were analyzed using the results of the last five sessions from each condition, these being stable data as defined by the stability criterion. Data were recorded separately for the time that the key lights came on until the first changeover response (or the time until the end of a trial if there were no changeover responses in a trial) and over the whole session's time that the key lights were on.

Table 8.2 presents the values of three overall measures of the pigeons' performance in Experiments 1 and 2. Pigeons in Experiment 1 made about the same number of responses per reinforcer as in Experiment 2. This is not surprising because the VR schedules in Experiment 2 were chosen specifically so as to make the number of responses per reinforcer approximately equivalent for both experiments. The time that the key lights were on (the

TABLE 8.1
Summary of Experimental Conditions

Condition Number	Schedule for Correct Responses	Schedule for Incorrect Responses	Number of Sessions
	Experiment 1 (VI schedules in seconds)		
1	5	EXT	22
2	5	120.0	40
3	5	60.0	37
4	5	30.0	26
5	5	15.0	22
6	5	7.5	14
7	5	5.0	15
8	5	7.5	18
9	5	15.0	19
10	5	30.0	16
11	5	60.0	17
	Experiment 2 (VR schedules)		
1	5	EXT	54
2	5	75	44
3	5	50	46
4	5	35	43
5	5	20	16
6	5	10	32
7	5	5	53
8	5	10	13
9	5	20	44
10	5	35	34
11	5	50	36
12	5	75	26
13	5	EXT	31

mean choice time per trial), and the mean time per trial until the first changeover response (or until the end of a choice period if there was no changeover response on that trial) appear to be shorter in Experiment 2, suggesting that, although the pigeons made about the same number of responses in order to receive their reinforcers in Experiment 2 as in Experiment 1, the pigeons in Experiment 2 responded at a higher rate. Such results would be consistent with previous comparisons of responding on VI and VR schedules (Reynolds, 1968, Chap. 6). However, these differences between the two experiments, in terms of the time that the key lights were on and the time until the first changeover response, were not statistically significant here ($t(5) = +2.46$ and $t(5) = +2.13$, respectively, $p > .05$ in each case).

Fig. 8.2 presents the percentage of correct responses and the percentage of responses on the red key as a function of condition, separately for Experiments 1 and 2. For both experiments the pigeons tended to respond

TABLE 8.2
Comparisons of Overall Performance in Experiment 1 and Experiment 2

Measure	Experiment 1 (VI, n = 33) Mean(SE)	Experiment 2 (VR, n = 52) Mean(SE)
Responses per reinforcer	9.2(0.3)	8.9(0.1)
Time key lights on (s per trial)	5.0(0.2)	3.3(0.2)
Time until first changeover or until end of trial if no changeovers (s per trial)	4.3(0.2)	2.9(0.2)

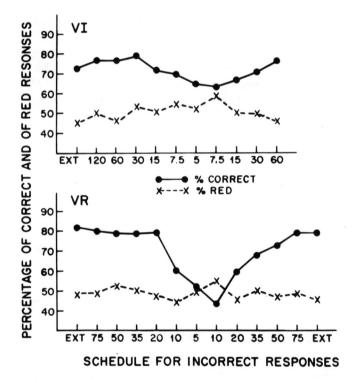

SCHEDULE FOR INCORRECT RESPONSES

FIG. 8.2 The percentage of correct-key responses and red-key responses as a function of the conditions in both Experiment 1 (VI schedules) and Experiment 2 (VR schedules). The conditions are presented in the order in which they were conducted, beginning with the left-most condition. The data shown are means over all of the pigeons in a given experiment.

about 50% of the time on the red key. In other words, they did not demonstrate a key-color bias. On the other hand, the percentage of correct responses tended to be lower when the schedule of reinforcement for incorrect responses was more similar to the schedule of reinforcement for correct responses (the data from each of the two experiments show a significant quadratic trend; for Experiment 1, excluding the extinction and the VI 120-s conditions, $t(7) = +3.35$, $.01 < p < .02$; for Experiment 2, excluding the extinction conditions, $t(9) = +3.64$, $.005 < p < .01$). Both experiments show this pattern; however, the percentage of correct responses was initially higher and decreased to a lower value for the pigeons in Experiment 2 (VR schedules) than for the pigeons in Experiment 1 (VI schedules).

Signal Detection

Fig. 8.3 shows the classification of responses for the signal-detection analysis in the present experiments. To determine the values of sensitivity and bias according to traditional signal-detection theory, the nonparametric methods of Grier (1971) were used (for other researchers who have used these methods see, for example, Lattal, 1979; Nevin et al., 1975; Stubbs, 1976; Wright & Nevin, 1974). The computational formulas used for calculating Grier's (1971) nonparametric indexes of sensitivity (*A′*) and bias (*B″*) were as follows:

$$A' = \frac{3 + d + \dfrac{c(d - 1)}{(1 - c)} - \dfrac{c}{d}}{4},$$

where c = p(false alarm) = false alarms/(false alarms + correct rejections); and d = p(hit) = hits/(hits + misses);

STIMULUS		RESPONSE: RED PECK	RESPONSE: GREEN PECK
	SHORT TONE	HIT red/short	MISS green/short
	LONG TONE	FALSE ALARM red/long	CORRECT REJECTION green/long

FIG. 8.3 Classification of responses for the signal-detection analysis in the present experiments.

$$B'' = \frac{y - x}{x} 100, \text{ if } d > 1.0 - c,$$

and

$$B'' = \frac{y - x}{y} 100, \text{ if } d < 1.0 - c,$$

where $x = c/d$, and $y = (1-d)/(1-c)$, and c and d are as described. In the present experiments Grier's index of sensitivity, A', represents subjects' sensitivity between the long and short tones. Grier's index of bias, B'', represents subjects' bias to make a response on the red (short-tone correct) or the green (long-tone correct) keys.

Fig. 8.4 plots A' as a function of the condition, separately for Experiment

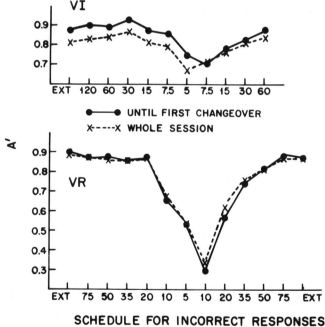

SCHEDULE FOR INCORRECT RESPONSES

FIG.8.4 Signal-detection sensitivity, A', as a function of the conditions in both Experiment 1(VI schedules) and Experiment 2 (VR schedules). The data shown are means over all of the pigeons in a given experiment. The values of A' are calculated using both data collected during all of the time that the key lights were on during the sessions, as well as data collected only while the key lights were on prior to the first changeover response (or until the end of a trial if there were no changeover responses on that trial).

1 (VI schedules) and Experiment 2 (VR schedules). The data shown are means over all of the pigeons in an experiment. Data from all of the time that the key lights were on during the sessions, as well as data collected only while the key lights were on prior to the first changeover response (or until the end of a trial if there were no changeover responses on that trial), are shown. Note, for both experiments, that the closer the reinforcement schedule for incorrect responses was to the schedule for correct responses, the lower was the value of A'. This decrease is more marked for Experiment 2 (VR schedules). The data from both experiments tend to show quadratic trends; and in most cases these trends are significant: for Experiment 1 whole-session data, excluding the extinction and the VI 120-s conditions, $t(7) = +7.84, p < .002$; for Experiment 1 until the first changeover data, excluding the extinction and the VI 120-s conditions, $t(7) = +2.07, .05 < p < .1$; for Experiment 2 whole-session data, excluding the extinction conditions, $t(9) = +4.79, p < .002$; for Experiment 2 until the first changeover data, excluding the extinction conditions, $t(9) = +3.00, .01 < p < .02$. For Experiment 1 only, the values of A' were consistently higher for data collected until the first changeover than for data collected over the entire time that the key lights were on during a session.

Fig. 8.5 plots Grier's index of bias, B'', as a function of condition separately for Experiment 1 (VI schedules) and Experiment 2 (VR schedules). As in Fig. 8.4, the data shown are means over all of the pigeons in the experiment. Also as in Fig. 8.4, data from all of the time that the key lights were on during sessions, as well as data collected only while the key lights were on prior to the first changeover response, are shown. There were no systematic changes in the values of B'' across the conditions of Experiment 2. However, the data for Experiment 1 (excluding the extinction and VI 120-s conditions) show significant quadratic trends [for whole-session data, $t(7) = +3.23, .01 < p < .02$; for until the first changeover data, $t(7) = +2.07, .05 < p < .1$].

Matching Law

The data were also analyzed according to Baum's (1974) generalized matching law so that response bias and under- or overmatching could be assessed. The logarithm of Equation 1,

$$\log(B_1/B_2) = a \log(R_1/R_2) + \log k, \tag{2}$$

is an equation for a straight line. Therefore data were fit to the matching law by plotting reinforcer and behavior ratios in log–log coordinates and determining the best-fitting line by the method of least squares. Data from

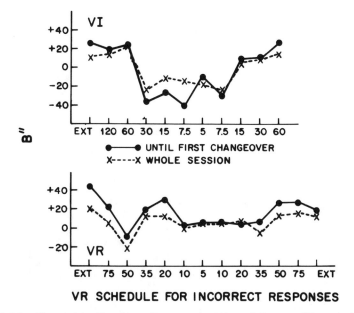

FIG.8.5 Signal-detection bias, B'', as a function of the conditions in both Experiment 1(VI schedules) and Experiment 2 (VR schedules). The data shown are means over all of the pigeons in a given experiment. The values of B'' are calculated using both data collected during all of the time that the key lights were on during the sessions, as well as data collected only while the key lights were on prior to the first changeover response (or until the end of a trial if there were no changeover responses on that trial).

the first two conditions of Experiment 1 were not used to calculate the best-fitting lines because Fig. 8.1 and the signal-detection analyses suggested that the pigeons were still learning the discrimination during that time period. In addition, data from the first and last conditions of Experiment 2 were not used to calculate the best-fitting lines because for these conditions $R_1/R_2 = R_1/0$, and Equation 2 cannot be used with such ratios. In all cases the subscript 1 in Equation 2 referred to the response alternative designated as correct for the signal-detection analysis, and the subscript 2 to the response alternative designated as incorrect for the signal-detection analysis.

Figs. 8.6 and 8.7 show, for Experiment 2, the ratio of correct responses plotted as a function of the ratio of reinforcers (for comparable graphs of the data in Experiment 1, see Logue, 1983). The data are shown separately for each pigeon, and for the whole session and until the first changeover data. Data are not shown for the conditions in which there was no reinforcement for errors. The values of a and k (the slopes and intercepts, see Equations 1 and 2) and the percentage of variance accounted for by the best-

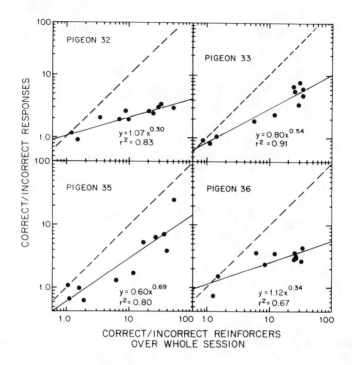

FIG. 8.6 Correct (smaller VR schedule) divided by incorrect (larger VR schedule) pecks as a function of correct divided by incorrect obtained reinforcers, on logarithmic coordinates using whole-session data from Experiment 2. The best fitting (solid) lines, calculated by the method of least squares, are shown in each graph along with the equations for these lines (on linear coordinates) and the percentage of variance accounted for by each regression (r^2). The data from the conditions in which there was no reinforcement for errors are not shown and were not used in calculating the best-fitting lines. The dashed lines represent matching directly to reinforcement, $y = 1.0x^{1.0}$.

fitting lines (r^2) are given in each graph. Note that only one of the eight values of r^2 is below .80; in other words, the generalized matching law fits the data fairly well despite the use of concurrent VR schedules, which usually generate exclusive responding to the alternative delivering responses according to the smaller VR schedule, not the linear functions shown in Figs. 8.6 and 8.7 (see Herrnstein & Loveland, 1975). Note also that the data in Figs. 8.6 and 8.7, as was found in Logue (1983), do appear to follow straight, and not curved lines, indicating that the slopes and intercepts relating adjacent pairs of points in these figures do not change.

Table 8.3 compares the mean matching law parameters obtained in both experiments. Each mean value of a is significantly less than 1.0 [$t(2) < -4.5, p < .05$, for Experiment 1; $t(3) < -5.7, p < .05$, for Experiment

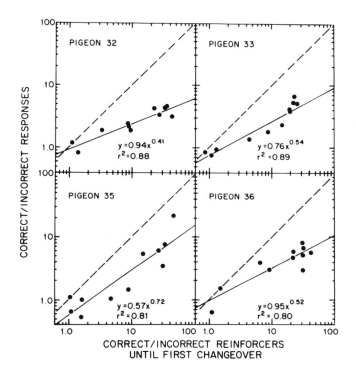

FIG. 8.7 Correct (smaller VR schedule) divided by incorrect (larger VR schedule) pecks as a function of correct divided by incorrect obtained reinforcers, on logarithmic coordinates using until-first-changeover data from Experiment 2. The best-fitting (solid) lines, calculated by the method of least squares, are shown in each graph along with the equations for these lines (on linear coordinates) and the percentage of variance accounted for by each regression (r^2). The data from the conditions in which there was no reinforcement for errors are not shown and were not used in calculating the best-fitting lines. The dashed lines represent matching directly to reinforcement, $y = 1.0 \times^{1.0}$.

2], but no mean value of k is significantly different from 1.0. In other words, there was significant undermatching in each experiment, but there was no significant bias to respond on either the key associated with the correct reinforcement schedule or the key associated with the incorrect reinforcement schedule. There are no significant differences between the values of a obtained in Experiments 1 and 2 or between any of the matching law parameters compared using whole-session or until the first changeover data, either in Experiment 1 or Experiment 2. On the other hand, the values of k were significantly higher for the VI schedules (Experiment 1) than the VR schedules (Experiment 2), and this was so for both whole-session data [$t(5) = +2.87, p < .05$] and until-first-changeover data [$t(5) = +3.54, p$

TABLE 8.3
Mean Matching Law Parameters

Experiment	a M(SE)	k M(SE)	r^2 M(SE)	n
1 (whole session)	0.3(0.2)	1.7(0.3)	0.6(0.3)	3
1 (until 1st CO)	0.5(0.1)	1.5(0.2)	0.7(0.1)	3
2 (whole session)	0.5(0.1)	0.9(0.1)	0.8(0.04)	4
2 (until 1st CO)	0.6(0.1)	0.8(0.1)	0.8(0.02)	4

$< .05$]. In other words, there was a significantly greater tendency for the pigeons in Experiment 1 (VI schedules) to respond on the key associated with the correct reinforcement schedule.

DISCUSSION

Some aspects of the pigeons' performance in the two experiments were consistent with typical VR and VI performance. Response rates were higher on the VR schedules. In addition, response distribution was more extreme on the VR schedules, resulting in higher percentages of correct responses and values of signal detection's measure of sensitivity, A'. However, at least one aspect of the pigeons' performance was not consistent with typical VR and VI performance. Despite the use of VR schedules in Experiment 2, the matching law still fit the data from that experiment fairly well. In other words, response distribution was not as extreme as has been found in other experiments using concurrent VR schedules (e.g., Herrnstein & Loveland, 1975).

There were many similarities in performance across the two experiments. For both concurrent VI (Experiment 1) and concurrent VR (Experiment 2) schedules, the percentage of correct responses as well as signal detection's measure of sensitivity, A', decreased as the schedule of reinforcement for incorrect responses became more similar to the schedule of reinforcement for correct responses. In both experiments, relative responding plotted as a function of relative reinforcement appeared to form a linear function, thus indicating that the matching law's measures of response bias and discriminability did not change as a function of the changes in relative reinforcement. Further, in both experiments, using a matching law analysis, there was no significant bias to respond on either the alternative reinforcing correct responses or the alternative reinforcing incorrect responses, but there was significant undermatching. In other words, relative responding was significantly closer to indifference than was relative reinforcement for correct and incorrect responses. This finding is consistent with previous experiments indicating that undermatching occurs when a difficult discrimination (in this case between two tone durations) is necessary to determine which responses are reinforced by a particular schedule (Bourland & Miller, 1981; Miller et al., 1980; Vaughan & Herrnstein, 1987; White, Pipe, & McLean, 1983). Finally, neither the values of the matching law's parameters for response bias, k, nor for discriminability, a, differed when comparisons were made between data collected only until the first changeover response (or until the end of a trial if there was no changeover response on that trial) and data collected over the whole session's time that the key lights were on.

All of these similarities between performance in the two experiments, as well as the fact that the matching law fit the data well from both experiments, are probably due to the duration discrimination at the beginning of each trial. This discrimination would have made it more difficult for the pigeons to discriminate which of the alternatives reinforced responses according to the richer VI schedule or the smaller VR schedule (the schedule for correct responses) in Experiments 1 and 2, respectively (see Baum, 1974; Davison & McCarthy, 1988; Davison & Tustin, 1978; McCarthy & Davison, 1979, for discussions of similar points). The essential difference between concurrent VI and concurrent VR schedule responding is that, in terms of overall reinforcement rate, with VI schedules there is some advantage to at least occasionally responding on each alternative, whereas with concurrent VR schedules there is never an advantage to responding on any but the alternative reinforcing responses according to the smaller VR schedule (Davison & McCarthy, 1988; Herrnstein & Loveland, 1975). Therefore responding tends to be more extreme on concurrent VR schedules. However, this can only occur if the subjects are able to discriminate which alternative is which, and that may have been difficult in the present experiments due to the use of the prior tone duration discrimination (Logue, 1983).

There were three major differences in VI and VR performance in the present experiments. First, the matching law's values of response bias, k, were significantly higher for Experiment 1 when VI schedules were used. The pigeons in Experiment 1 were significantly more likely to show a bias for the key reinforcing correct responses than were the pigeons in Experiment 2 (when VR schedules were used). This is a new finding and it is not clear what aspects of the feedback functions of VI and VR schedules might result in such differences in behavior maintained by the two types of schedules.

Second, signal detection's measure of sensitivity, A', was consistently larger for data collected until the first changeover response in Experiment 1 (VI schedules), but not in Experiment 2 (VR schedules). This finding was probably due to a memory effect present in Experiment 1 but not Experiment 2. In Experiment 1, over all trials there was a mean of 4.3 s until the first changeover response, and a mean of 5.0 s until the start of a reinforcer. By the end of a trial the pigeons could have forgotten which tone duration had been presented at the beginning of that trial, thus resulting in lower values of A'. Such a finding is consistent with many previous experiments that have found that discrimination decreases as time increases since the stimuli to be discriminated have been presented (e.g., Chatlosh & Wasserman, 1987; Harnett, McCarthy, & Davison, 1984; McCarthy & Davison, 1986; McCarthy et al., 1982; McCarthy & White, 1987; Nevin & MacWilliams, 1983; White, 1985). On the other hand, in Experiment 2, over all trials the mean time until the start of a reinforcer was only 3.3 s, less than the mean time until the first changeover response in Experiment 1. Therefore, if the explanation concerning the data from Experiment 1 is correct, there would have been insufficient trial length for a memory effect to have occurred in Experiment 2.

Third, in Experiment 1 (VI schedules), but not in Experiment 2 (VR schedules), signal detection's measure of response bias, B'', decreased as the reinforcement schedule for incorrect responses approached that for correct responses. Recall that in the present experiments B'' measures subjects' bias to respond on the red (short-tone correct) or the green (long-tone correct) keys. Therefore this finding in Experiment 1 simply represents changes in key-color bias. Signal-detection theory makes no predictions with regard to key-color bias. Given this fact, and the fact that B'' changed reliably only in Experiment 1, it is possible that this finding is a Type I error.

Within the context provided by the two experiments reported here, it is possible to point out some similarities and differences between the parameters for each model (for signal-detection theory: bias, B'', and sensitivity, A'; for the matching law: response bias, k, and discriminability, a). A' represents a subject's sensitivity between the short and long tones. On the other hand, a represents the rate of change in a subject's tendency to make a correct response or an incorrect response as the reinforcement schedules are changed. B'' represents the tendency of a subject to emit a signal (red-key) response or a noise (green-key) response. In contrast, k represents a subject's response bias for the alternative with the schedule of reinforcement for correct responses, as opposed to the alternative with the schedule of reinforcement for incorrect responses. Because signal detection's two measures and the matching law's two measures have different definitions, it is not surprising that they can be affected differently by the manipulations in the present experiments. For example, compare the effects on the values of A' and a of increasing reinforcement for errors. A' decreases as reinforcement for errors increases. This occurs because, in a signal-detection analysis, correct and incorrect responses are defined by the presence and absence of reinforcers. As this distinction breaks down, the actual discrimination between the two types of tones becomes less important, in effect resulting in a decrease in sensitivity. When errors are reinforced, maintaining a high A' actually reduces reinforcement if VI schedules are in effect. This is not, however, true if VR schedules are being used, at least until the point at which reinforcement for errors equals reinforcement for correct responses. It is therefore not surprising that A' decreased at a faster rate in Experiment 2 (VR schedules) than Experiment 1 (VI schedules). On the other hand, a did not change as reinforcement for errors changed. There was no change because a is essentially a scaling parameter that takes the ratio between the rates of reinforcement for correct and incorrect responses and scales this ratio; responses match this scaled ratio.

SUMMARY

Table 8.4 summarizes the major effects on the signal-detection and matching law parameters observed given the manipulations in the present two experiments. Reinforcement for errors resulted in changes in behavior that were predicted by the matching law, but not by traditional signal-detection theory. The present experiments, Experiment 1 using concurrent VI schedules of reinforcement and Experiment 2 using concurrent VR schedules of reinforcement, demonstrated that signal detection's measure of sensitivity, A', decreased as reinforcement for errors was increased. This finding is consistent with previous results (Nevin, 1970; Nevin et al., 1975); the present experiments extend this finding to free-operant schedules of

TABLE 8.4
Summary of Effects on Signal-Detection and Matching Law Parameters

Experimental Manipulation	Signal Detection		Matching Law	
	Sensitivity A'	Bias B''	Discriminability a	Response Bias k
Experiment 1 (VI)				
Increased relative reinforcement for incorrect responses	decreased	decreased	no change	no change
Prior to first changeover	increased	no change	no change	no change
Experiment 2 (VR)				
Increased relative reinforcement for incorrect responses	decreased	no change	no change	no change
Prior to first changeover	no change	no change	no change	no change

reinforcement. In addition, the present experiments extend the ability of the matching law to describe choice data to experiments involving discrete trials and an explicit discrimination at the beginning of each trial. The difficulty of this prior discrimination can apparently have strong effects on the distribution of responding. The two parameters of discrimination and bias for each of the two models examined here, signal-detection theory (A' and B'') and the matching law (a and k), were affected to some extent similarly and to some extent differently by the reinforcement for errors in the present experiments. Signal-detection theory is superior to the matching law for quickly demonstrating changes in discrimination, because only two conditions are necessary in order to see a change in A', signal detection's measure of sensitivity. In contrast, to observe changes in discrimination with the matching law, enough conditions are needed to calculate two linear functions, so that two values of a, the matching law's measure of discriminability, can be determined and compared. On the other hand, the matching law is superior to signal-detection theory for demonstrating changes in behavior due to changes in payoffs because in a matching law analysis, only the response distribution will change; however, in signal-detection analysis, both A' and B'', signal detection's measure of bias, can change. In conclusion, signal-detection theory and the matching law are two somewhat different ways of looking at similar problems of choice behavior. Both are useful in particular contexts.

ACKNOWLEDGMENTS

Preparation of this research was supported by NSF Grant BNS–8416302, A. W. Logue, Principal Investigator. We gratefully acknowledge the assistance of J. Barlow, A. Chavarro, G. King, E. Paquette, T. Pena, S. Salomaa, M. Smith, and V. Upham in conducting the experiments reported here, and of L. Bonvino in performing the data analyses for Experiment 2.

REFERENCES

Baum, W. M. (1974). On two types of deviation from the matching law: Bias and undermatching. *Journal of the Experimental Analysis of Behavior, 22,* 231–242.

Bourland, G., & Miller, J. T. (1981). The role of discriminative stimuli in concurrent performances. *Journal of the Experimental Analysis of Behavior, 36,* 231–239.

Chatlosh, D. L., & Wasserman, E. A. (1987). Delayed temporal discrimination in pigeons: A comparison of two procedures. *Journal of the Experimental Analysis of Behavior, 47,* 299–309.

Davenport, W. G. (1968). Auditory vigilance: The effects of costs and values on signals. *Australian Journal of Psychology, 20,* 213–218.

Davenport, W. G. (1969). Vibrotactile vigilance: The effects of costs and values on signals. *Perception and Psychophysics, 5,* 25–28.

Davison, M., & Jenkins, P. E. (1985). Stimulus discriminability, contingency discriminability, and schedule performance. *Animal Learning & Behavior, 13,* 77-84.

Davison, M., & McCarthy, D. (1980). Reinforcement for errors in a signal-detection procedure. *Journal of the Experimental Analysis of Behavior, 34,* 35-47.

Davison, M., & McCarthy, D. (1988). *The matching law: A research review.* Hillsdale, NJ: Lawrence Erlbaum Associates.

Davison, M., McCarthy, D., & Jensen, C. (1985). Component probability and component reinforcer rate as biasers of free-operant detection. *Journal of the Experimental Analysis of Behavior, 44,* 103-120.

Davison, M. C., & Tustin, R. D. (1978). The relation between the generalized matching law and signal-detection theory. *Journal of the Experimental Analysis of Behavior, 29,* 331-336.

de Villiers, P. (1977). Choice in concurrent schedules and a quantitative formulation of the law of effect. In W. K. Honig & J. E. R. Staddon (Eds.), *Handbook of operant behavior* (pp. 233-287). Englewood Cliffs, NJ: Prentice-Hall.

Fleshler, M., & Hoffman, H. S. (1962). A progression for generating variable-interval schedules. *Journal of the Experimental Analysis of Behavior, 5,* 529-530.

Green, D. M., & Swets, J. A. (1966). *Signal detection theory and psychophysics.* New York: Wiley. (reprinted by Robert E. Krieger, 1974)

Grier, J. B. (1971). Nonparametric indexes for sensitivity and bias: Computing formulas. *Psychological Bulletin, 75,* 424-429.

Harnett, P., McCarthy, D., & Davison, M. (1984). Delayed signal detection, differential reinforcement, and short-term memory in the pigeon. *Journal of the Experimental Analysis of Behavior, 42,* 87-111.

Herrnstein, R. J. (1961). Relative and absolute strength of response as a function of frequency of reinforcement. *Journal of the Experimental Analysis of Behavior, 4,* 267-272.

Herrnstein, R. J. (1970). On the law of effect. *Journal of the Experimental Analysis of Behavior, 13,* 243-266.

Herrnstein, R. J., & Loveland, D. H. (1975). Maximizing and matching on concurrent ratio schedules. *Journal of the Experimental Analysis of Behavior, 24,* 107-116.

Hobson, S. L. (1978). Discriminability of fixed-ratio schedules for pigeons: Effects of payoff values. *Journal of the Experimental Analysis of Behavior, 30,* 69-81.

Hume, A. L., & Irwin, R. J. (1974). Bias functions and operating characteristics of rats discriminating auditory stimuli. *Journal of the Experimental Analysis of Behavior, 21,* 285-295.

Lattal, K. A. (1979). Reinforcement contingencies as discriminative stimuli: II. Effects of changes in stimulus probability. *Journal of the Experimental Analysis of Behavior, 31,* 15-22.

Logue, A. W. (1983). Signal detection and matching: Analyzing choice on concurrent variable-interval schedules. *Journal of the Experimental Analysis of Behavior, 39,* 107-127.

Mandell, C. (1981). A psychophysical analysis of time-based schedules of reinforcement. *Quantitative Analyses of Behavior: Discriminative Properties of Reinforcement Schedules, 1,* 31-50.

McCarthy, D. (1983). Measures of response bias at minimum-detectable luminance levels in the pigeon. *Journal of the Experimental Analysis of Behavior, 39,* 87-106.

McCarthy, D., & Davison, M. (1979). Signal probability, reinforcement and signal detection. *Journal of the Experimental Analysis of Behavior, 32,* 373-386.

McCarthy, D., & Davison, M. (1981). Matching and signal detection. *Quantitative Analyses of Behavior: Discriminative Properties of Reinforcement Schedules, 1,* 393-417.

McCarthy, D., & Davison, M. (1984). Isobias and allobias functions in animal psychophysics. *Journal of Experimental Psychology: Animal Behavior Processes, 10,* 390-409.

McCarthy, D., & Davison, M. (1986). Delayed reinforcement and delayed choice in symbolic matching to sample: Effects on stimulus discriminability. *Journal of the Experimental Analysis of Behavior, 46,* 293–303.

McCarthy, D., Davison, M., & Jenkins, P. E. (1982). Stimulus discriminability in free-operant and discrete-trial detection procedures. *Journal of the Experimental Analysis of Behavior, 37,* 199–215.

McCarthy, D., & White, K. G. (1987). Behavioral models of delayed detection and their application to the study of memory. *Quantitative Analyses of Behavior: The Effect of Delay and of Intervening Events on Reinforcement, 5,* 29–54.

Miller, J. T., Saunders, S. S., & Bourland, G. (1980). The role of stimulus disparity in concurrently available reinforcement schedules. *Animal Learning and Behavior, 8,* 635–641.

Nevin, J. A. (1967). Effects of reinforcement scheduling on simultaneous discrimination performance. *Journal of the Experimental Analysis of Behavior, 10,* 251–260.

Nevin, J. A. (1969a). Interval reinforcement of choice behavior in discrete trials. *Journal of the Experimental Analysis of Behavior, 12,* 875–885.

Nevin, J. A. (1969b). Signal detection theory and operant behavior [A review of David M. Green and John A. Swets' *Signal detection theory and psychophysics*]. *Journal of the Experimental Analysis of Behavior, 12,* 474–480.

Nevin, J. A. (1970). On differential stimulation and differential reinforcement. In W. C. Stebbins (Ed.), *Animal psychophysics* (pp. 401–423). New York: Appleton–Century–Crofts.

Nevin, J. A. (1981). Psychophysics and reinforcement effects of schedules: An integration. *Quantitative Analyses of Behavior: Discriminative Properties of Reinforcement Schedules, 1,* 3–27.

Nevin, J. A., & MacWilliams, S. (1983). Ratio reinforcement of signal detection. *Behaviour Analysis Letters, 3,* 317–324.

Nevin, J. A., Olson, K., Mandell, C., & Yarensky, P. (1975). Differential reinforcement and signal detection. *Journal of the Experimental Analysis of Behavior, 24,* 355–367.

Reynolds, G. S. (1968). *A primer of operant conditioning.* Atlanta: Scott, Foresman.

Rilling, M., & McDiarmid, C. (1965). Signal detection in fixed-ratio schedules. *Science, 148,* 526–527.

Shimp, C. P. (1966). Probabilistically reinforced choice behavior in pigeons. *Journal of the Experimental Analysis of Behavior, 9,* 443–455.

Staddon, J. E. R. (1978). Theory of behavioral power functions. *Psychological Review, 85,* 305–320.

Stubbs, A. (1968). The discrimination of stimulus duration by pigeons. *Journal of the Experimental Analysis of Behavior, 11,* 223–238.

Stubbs, D. A. (1976). Response bias and the discrimination of stimulus duration. *Journal of the Experimental Analysis of Behavior, 25,* 243–250.

Swets, J. A., Tanner, W. P., & Birdsall, T. G. (1961). Decision processes in perception. *Psychological Review, 68,* 301–340.

Vaughan, W., & Herrnstein, R. J. (1987). Choosing among natural stimuli. *Journal of the Experimental Analysis of Behavior, 47,* 5–16.

White, K. G. (1985). Characteristics of forgetting functions in delayed matching to sample. *Journal of the Experimental Analysis of Behavior, 44,* 15–34.

White, K. G., Pipe, M.-E., & McLean, A. P. (1983). Dimensional stimulus control of multiple schedule performance. *Behaviour Analysis Letters, 3,* 51–57.

Wright, A. A. (1972). Psychometric and psychophysical hue discrimination functions for the pigeon. *Vision Research, 12,* 1447–1464.

Wright, A. A., & Nevin, J. A. (1974). Signal detection methods for measurement of utility in animals. *Journal of the Experimental Analysis of Behavior, 21,* 373–380.

9

A Detection and Decision Process Model of Matching to Sample

Anthony A. Wright
University of Texas Health Science Center,
Graduate School of Biomedical Sciences

The topic of this chapter is matching to sample by pigeons and the decision processes that pigeons make when they are choosing between the comparison stimuli. Since the topic of this volume is signal-detection theory (SDT), I should mention at the outset that the model presented in this chapter shares with signal-detection theory a similar detection framework, but the decision aspects and their consequences are quite different.

Matching to sample is a favorite paradigm with which to study animal learning and memory. The diagram in Fig. 9.1 is a schematic of the matching-to-sample procedure. In the first panel (9.1a) the pigeon pecks a sample stimulus (e.g., red) which is the shape of a vertical bar, recessed behind a clear pecking key. The sample goes off, and two comparison stimuli appear behind similar pecking keys on either side of the center sample (panel 9.1b). In this example the matching comparison is on the left and the nonmatching one on the right. In the second panel, the pigeon pecks the matching comparison stimulus and is rewarded with mixed grain.

The focus of this chapter is on the pigeon's decision processes that precede and include the comparison choice. Let us consider several possibilities of how subjects could, in general, go about making this choice. One possibility is that after observing the sample stimulus (making their observing response to it), pigeons could stand back and observe both comparison stimuli simultaneously so that the match, or closest match, is obvious, and then make a decision. But it will be shown that pigeons do not do this. Another possibility is that pigeons could first look at each comparison stimulus individually, and then choose one of them, the one that most closely matches the sample stimulus. But it will be shown that

Fig. 9.1 First panel: A drawing of a pigeon pecking a center key behind which is displayed a sample stimulus. Second panel: drawing of a pigeon pecking the left key, behind which is displayed the comparison stimulus which matches the sample in the top panel.

Fig. 9.1b

pigeons do not do this either. A third possibility is that pigeons could observe one of the comparison stimuli. If the comparison matches the sample, then the pigeon chooses it, but if the comparison does not match, then the pigeon automatically chooses the other comparison stimulus. According to this rule or strategy, the pigeon does not really have to evaluate the second comparison stimulus because if the first does not match then the second must match — by default. This was the strategy that Roberts and Grant (1978) proposed that pigeons were using in the matching-to-sample task. But it will be shown that pigeons do not do this either. Thus, three rules or decision strategies have been so far mentioned. They are all reasonable strategies for performing the matching-to-sample task, but it will be shown here that they do not engage in any of these three strategies, and instead employ an altogether different strategy.

By way of illustrating the actual strategy that pigeons do use in performing the matching-to-sample task, I will describe how I came about discovering this strategy. The term strategy will be used here in a way similar to its usage in the human problem-solving literature (e.g., Newell & Simon, 1972). In very general terms, it refers to one of several ways to go about performing a task, whether or not it leads to the optimal solution or, indeed, to any solution at all. According to this very general definition, one can think of many trivial examples of strategies (e.g., position preference), but these are readily discernible from ones that are of more psychological interest.

HISTORICAL DEVELOPMENT

The discovery of the pigeons' decision strategies began with three pigeons working in a delayed matching-to-sample task. During the delay interval, the pigeons would peck or "drum" on the stimulus panel. For example, one pigeon pecked on the stimulus panel next to the sample key when the delay interval began. As the delay progressed, this pigeon pecked its way down the stimulus panel to a point close to the grain hopper opening, then moved up again, and was in the vicinity of the right-side key as the delay interval expired. This stereotyped behavior was reminiscent of the mediational behavior reported by D. Blough (1959) for pigeons in a delayed matching task. It appeared possible that, in this case, too, the way in which this pigeon pecked the stimulus panel (rhythm, location, etc.) might be a memory code to mediate the delay interval. So we put a microphone behind the stimulus panel to record when, and how hard, the pigeons pecked the stimulus panel.

We also observed the pigeons as they performed the task. One of the difficulties in observing them was that trials were conducted in darkness, for psychophysical reasons unrelated to this research. So, to observe them, we borrowed a pair of infrared "sniper scope" goggles that were designed for military night surveillance. I removed the exhaust fan from the rear of the chamber to provide an opening large enough to observe them. The screen in front of the fan was left in place, which provided some minimal barrier between the pigeon and experimenter, and probably reduced disruption that might have otherwise occurred. Unfortunately, the analysis of the pigeons' "stimulus panel" pecking behavior during the delay interval revealed nothing systematic related to the different samples and delay interval mediation.

What we did discover, however, was the way in which the pigeons observed the comparison stimuli before making a choice response. They would look at one stimulus, occasionally switch over and look at the other one, sometimes switch back to the first, and even switch back to the second. We recorded and analyzed all of these looking movements and eventual choices, and paired them with the stimuli on the trials. We discovered that the chances that they would choose a particular comparison stimulus was the same whether it was the first time that it was observed, the second time, or indeed the nth time. We worked out virtually the complete mathematics of the pigeon's comparison stimulus choice process before it was pointed out to me that we had rediscovered the Markov process; that is, the transition probabilities (choosing a comparison stimulus or switching to observe the other comparison stimulus) were the same, independent of whether it was the first, second, or third time that a particular comparison stimulus was observed. Said otherwise, the transition probabilities were path-independent. What I will describe in this chapter are results from matching to sample, modeled according to this Markov choice process.

I would like to emphasize that I came to the mathematical model inductively, by observing the responses and building the formal mathematical structure from the behavior. This is very different from what typically is done. Usually the process is deductive, beginning with a complete and formal mathematical model. Concerning the model itself, the results and the model presented in this chapter are not dependent on hypothetical constructs, which typically is the case with models and theories, including Markov process models. By contrast, the model presented in this chapter is based on the looking movements and switching movements by the pigeons, which are observable, recordable responses. These responses are not the ones typically recorded, but nevertheless are objective responses.

One of the things that made this analysis possible was the particular stimulus display in my experimental chamber. The stimuli were recessed behind the clear-glass pecking keys. The pigeon cannot see a stimulus until it moves almost in front of the pecking key, and this movement by the pigeon makes each "look" by the pigeon obvious to the experimenter.

An Example of the Pigeon's 'Looking' and 'Switching' Behavior

The sequence of pictures shown in Figs. 9.2a and 9.2b is from a delayed matching-to-sample trial. The pictures are photographs of a videotape (stop-action video recorder) displayed on a TV screen, and approximately every fourth frame is shown. At the beginning of the picture sequence the delay interval has just expired, and the comparison stimuli have just been displayed. In the first picture, the pigeon is observing the left comparison stimulus. By the third picture, the pigeon is beginning to switch over to observe the right-side stimulus. By the ninth picture, the pigeon is beginning to switch back to reobserve the left-side stimulus, and is observing this stimulus in the beginning of Fig. 9.2b. The pigeon then switches back to reobserve the right-side stimulus. It pecks the key in the eighth picture of

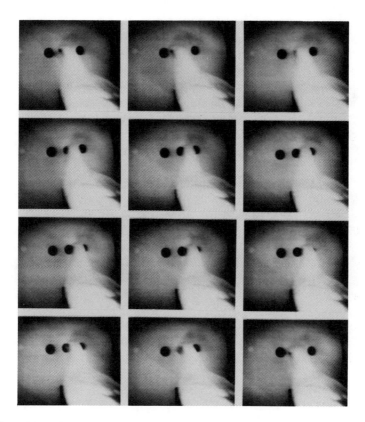

Fig. 9.2a Sequence of pictures from a videotape of a delayed matching-to-sample trial showing the behavior of a pigeon after the comparison stimuli are displayed. The pigeon inspects the left stimulus, then switches over to inspect the right one, and then switches back to inspect again the left one.

Fig. 9.2b (notice the grain hopper light in the ninth picture), and is eating in the final picture.

The trials are scored individually in terms of which comparison (matching or nonmatching) was first observed, the number of switches made, and the comparison chosen or pecked. The relative frequency of these responses is then used to derive two model parameters and to test how well the model fits the obtained results. A schematic of the mechanics of this model are shown in Fig. 9.3.

MODEL DESCRIPTION

Fig. 9.3 shows a red-sample trial; green-sample trials would be similar, but with the "reds" and "greens" reversed. Human color names are used only to

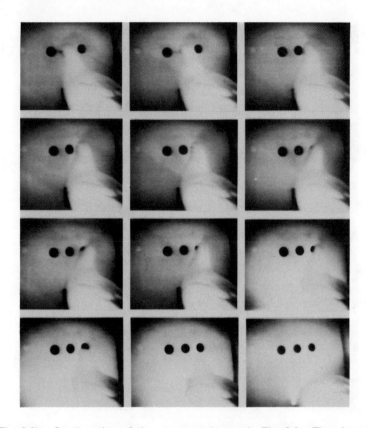

Fig. 9.2b   Continuation of the sequence begun in Fig. 9.2a. The pigeon is inspecting the left stimulus for the second time, rejects it as the match to the sample, switches over to inspect the right one again, pecks it, and receives access to grain via the lighted grain hopper opening.

facilitate a description of the model. The pigeon's hues are different from the human's hues (Wright, 1972, 1974, 1979; Wright & Cumming, 1971). The pigeon's hues and its hue scale has been determined so that separations in nanometers (physical units) can be adjusted (Wright, 1978) to produce equal discriminability steps (psychological units). The abscissa of Fig. 9.3 (top) is labeled "Stimulus Effects Scale of Hue." This is the psychological (hue) scale. It represents variability of the color sensation upon repeated presentations of the same physical stimulus (wavelength). The values of this scale, and the form of the distributions, are not critical to the research presented in this chapter. Emphasis will be on the proportion of the distributions *transacted* by the criterion line. The probability density, which is the ordinate of the graph, can be thought of as relative frequency. The red

RED–SAMPLE TRIALS

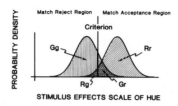

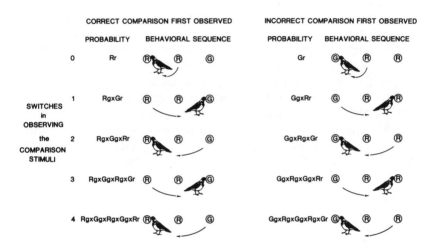

Fig. 9.3   Diagram depicting the movements and behavior of the pigeons as they choose between the comparison stimuli. This behavior is modeled by a multiplication of probabilities. The probabilities are related to the variance of the sensory experiences, and a choice criterion shown in the top of the figure. The probabilities reflect the pigeons' acceptance rate (Rr) of the correct comparison (the red comparison because in this case it is a red sample trial), rejection rate (Rg) of the correct comparison, acceptance rate (Gr) of the incorrect comparison, and rejection rate (Gg) of the incorrect comparison. The behavior is divided into two different groups: those where the correct comparison is first observed, and those where the incorrect comparison is first observed. The probabilities and frequencies of the different possibilities are computed with the experimentally determined Rr and Gr values.

comparison stimulus (represented by the right-hand distribution) excites a hue sensation most frequently at the point of the distribution peak, but there is variability in the hue sensation produced upon successive repetitions of the same wavelength. The nonmatching comparison stimulus (green, in this example) has its peak of hue sensation to the left of the red comparison, and a similar distribution or variability in hue sensation. The distributions overlap. The subject criterion is set according to a particular hue sensation, so that any stimulus which is as red or redder than this criterion will be accepted as a match on this red sample trial.

The acceptance/rejection probabilities are graphically depicted as the distribution proportions. The Rr part of the distribution represents the proportion of time that the red stimulus (R) will be perceived (r) as red. When it is perceived as such it will be accepted as a match. Thus, there is a region of stimulus effects called the match-acceptance region which lies to the right of the criterion line. When the stimulus produces a hue sensation that is to the left of the criterion ("greener" than the criterion sensation), then the pigeon will reject that comparison as a match and switch over to the other comparison stimulus. There will, of course, be mistakes. At times even the incorrect green comparison will be accepted (Gr) as as a match. This type of error is identical to the SDT false alarm. Most of the time, however, the green comparison will be correctly rejected (Gg) as the sample match. A comparison stimulus that is not accepted as a match is, by definition, rejected and the pigeon switches over to consider the other comparison stimulus. Errors will also occur occasionally to the correct comparison stimulus. The correct comparison will occasionally be perceived as too "green" (g) to qualify as a match, and be incorrectly rejected (Rg). This type of error is similar to an SDT false negative, but there are some important differences in consequences following this error type.

The lower part of Fig. 9.3 shows a series of possible outcomes when the pigeon is choosing between the correct "red" comparison and the incorrect "green" comparison. When the correct comparison is first observed (left), it is chosen (pecked) Rr percent of the time. For example, let us say that, in this situation, this stimulus qualifies as a match and is chosen 80% of the time (see left-hand column). The other 20% of the time the pigeon rejects it (Rg) and switches over to observe the other comparison, the incorrect one in this example. Furthermore, let us say, that the incorrect comparison is accepted as the match 30% of the time (or is correctly rejected 70% of the time). Thus, the chances that the incorrect comparison will be chosen after first observing and rejecting the correct comparison is Rg $\times$ Gr = 0.2 $\times$ 0.3, or 0.06. However, if the pigeon correctly rejects the incorrect comparison, then it will switch back to the correct one. The correct one may then be chosen. The chances of it being chosen under these circumstances are Rg $\times$ Gg $\times$ Rr = 0.2 $\times$ 0.7 $\times$ 0.8, or 0.112. If the correct one is rejected for the second time and the incorrect one then chosen upon its re-observation, the probability of such a sequence of events would be Rg $\times$ Gg $\times$ Rg $\times$ Gr = 0.2 $\times$ 0.7 $\times$ 0.2 $\times$ 0.3, or 0.008. The final example in the left hand part of Fig. 9.3 is where the pigeon rejects the incorrect one for the second time and returns and finally accepts the correct one, or Rg $\times$ Gg $\times$ Rg $\times$ Gg $\times$ Rr =

0.2 $\times 0.7$ $\times 0.2$ $\times 0.7$ $\times 0.8$, or 0.016. Similar logic would hold for computations where the incorrect comparison is first observed (right-hand column). For all of these behavior sequences (right and left columns), there are two parameters to be estimated since Rr + Rg = 1.0 and Gr + Gg = 1.0. The acceptance rates when each are first observed were the two parameters used to model the data presented in this chapter.

Asymmetry of Error Types

False negatives are errors of falsely rejecting the correct comparison stimulus, but they are errors of an unusual variety. False negatives are really more suspended judgments than errors in the true sense of the word. From a decision standpoint, a false negative is an error, but from the matching-to-sample standpoint it is not an error. The pigeon still has a chance to be correct. The trial is not over until a choice is made; one or the other comparison must be pecked and accepted as a match. For example, consider the behavioral sequence depicted in the third row of the left-hand column. The subject could incorrectly reject the correct comparison (Rg), switch over and correctly reject the incorrect comparison (Gg), and switch back to the originally observed comparison, the correct one, and still be correct on that trial if it then accepted it (Rr) as the match. Now, if the criterion moves over to the right, that is, if the match-acceptance region narrows and the subject becomes more strict in what it accepts as a match, the Gr rate will be reduced. These Gr decisions are the incorrect choices or false alarms, which are the actual errors from the matching-to-sample standpoint. As in SDT, one trades off one error type for another. Thus, the other error type depicted by the Rg area in Fig. 9.3 will increase, but as was mentioned, these are not matching-to-sample errors. These latter errors are switching errors. So we can think of movement of the criterion as a change in the bias. The measure of detectability is the same as it is in signal-detection theory—the distance between the peaks of the two distributions.

The next two sections are examples from two different paradigms, scored and analyzed according to the MTS Markov model. The first example is from delayed matching to sample, where pigeons employed a Markov decision process throughout the range of delays, from short ones where performance was very good, to long ones where near-chance performance was approached. The second example is from simultaneous matching to sample, where pigeons employed a Markov decision process throughout the discriminability range, from large stimulus separations where performance was very good to small stimulus separations where near chance performance was approached.

DELAYED MATCHING TO SAMPLE
AND INCREASING DELAY

Apparatus and Procedure

The apparatus and procedures are only briefly described (see Wright &
Sands, 1981, for a more complete description). A diagram of the apparatus
is shown in Fig. 9.4. Wavelengths and intensities were precisely controlled,
and adjusted for the spectral sensitivity and hue discriminability of the
pigeon. The essential apparatus details were that the vertical monochromatic "bars" (2.68 mm × 5.88 mm) were recessed 42.7 mm behind
color-clear glass pecking keys so that the pigeon had to move in front of
each pecking key in order to see the stimulus behind it. Trials were
conducted in darkness, requiring an infrared light source and infrared video
camera to record the pigeon's looking and switching responses.

A standard three-key, delayed, matching-to-sample procedure was used.
A trial began when the house light was turned off and the sample stimulus
displayed. There was a 4-s fixed-interval requirement, after which the next
peck turned off the sample and initiated the delay. Following the delay, the
comparison stimuli (behind the side keys) were displayed. A peck to the
matching comparison stimulus resulted in approximately 3-s access to
mixed grain. Following reward, or a peck to the nonmatching comparison,
a 6-s intertrial interval began with the house light on. There were 176 trials
conducted daily with the same delay throughout. The two stimuli were
621.9 nm and 567.5 nm, and the sequence of trial types varied daily. Delay
testing began at the training delays (5 s for p5144, 6.4 s for P4263) and was
progressively increased by 28% to 22-s delay. This involved six delay

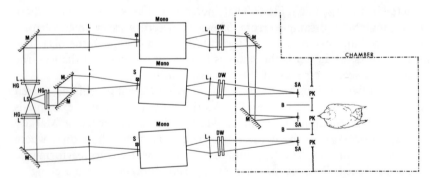

Fig. 9.4 Diagram of optical system to produce three vertical bars of
monochromatic light whose wavelength and intensity are separately
controlled: LS = xenon arc light source; HG = heat absorbing glass; L
= lens; M = mirror; S = shutter; Mono = monochromator; DW = density
wedge; B= baffle; SA = stimulus aperture; PK = pecking key; SP =
stimulus panel.

increases for P5144 and five for P4263. Typically, four consecutive sessions were conducted at each delay with the first session designated as warm-up, and performance was averaged over the last three.

Results

The top panels of Fig. 9.5 show performance and model for one of the subjects, P4263. The top panel shows results for a 6.4-s delay, this subject's training delay. The second panel shows results from a much longer

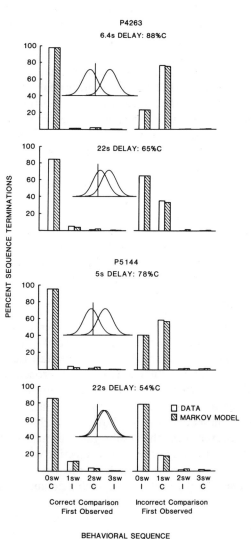

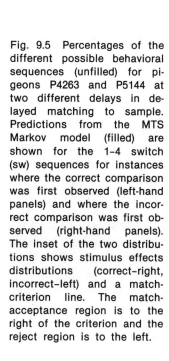

Fig. 9.5 Percentages of the different possible behavioral sequences (unfilled) for pigeons P4263 and P5144 at two different delays in delayed matching to sample. Predictions from the MTS Markov model (filled) are shown for the 1–4 switch (sw) sequences for instances where the correct comparison was first observed (left-hand panels) and where the incorrect comparison was first observed (right-hand panels). The inset of the two distributions shows stimulus effects distributions (correct–right, incorrect–left) and a match-criterion line. The match-acceptance region is to the right of the criterion and the reject region is to the left.

delay, 22 s. In each panel, the left-hand set of four histogram pairs is for the behavior sequence when the subject first observed the correct comparison, and the right-hand set for the sequences when the subject first observed the incorrect comparison. Considering the left-hand set, the subject was correct when it chose the first observed comparison stimulus, and did so a large proportion of the time. The subject was incorrect when it chose the comparison stimulus following the first switch, correct after the second switch, incorrect after the third, and so on. The "C" and "I" below the histogram pairs refers to whether the subject was correct and incorrect respectively. The insets in each panel show the distributions of stimulus effects and the subject's criterion (according to the zero-switch performance parameters) in the same manner as those shown in Fig. 9.3.

As the delay became longer, the transition probability of accepting the incorrect stimulus as a match increased (e.g., first histogram pair of the right-hand set). This transition probability increase is reflected in the inset diagram by the much larger proportion of the area for the incorrect stimulus being to the right of the criterion line. There was, of course, a concomitant decrease in the one-switch rate, choosing the correct comparison in this case. Now turning our attention to the left-hand set of histograms, there was a slight decrement in the zero-switch rate (.979 vs. .943), but not as substantial a decrease as one might expect. The reason that the zero-switch rate did not decrease more was that the criterion (bias) changed very little. (The distributions are drawn so that the right-hand distributions for the correct comparisons are vertically aligned, and one can "sight" along the page and notice even slight changes in criterion relative to the correct comparison distribution.) The vast majority of change due to the longer delay was a discriminability change.

The zero-switch results are used as parameters to model the results when the subject rejected the first observed comparison and switched to the alternative comparison. These data serve as tests of the matching-to-sample Markov model. The left-hand part of Table 9.1 shows deviations from the Markov process for P4263 and the statistical results of Fmax tests (Bower, 1959). None of the Dmax values approaches significance. The p values are all greater than .99. Thus, the decision strategy used by this pigeon appears to be a Markov decision strategy; said otherwise, one cannot reject the hypothesis that it is Markovian. In addition to providing tests of the MTS Markov model, the results for the three-switch and four-switch cases are important in that they allow rejection of possible strategies such as "choose the alternative by default if the first is rejected," as was proposed by Roberts and Grant (1978). Such a default strategy would allow only a single switch, at most.

The lower panels of Fig. 9.5 show performance from another pigeon, P5144, in the delayed matching-to-sample experiment. This pigeon was

TABLE 9.1
Goodness of Fit Tests (Kolmogorov–Smirnov) for P4263 and P5144 in Delayed
Matching to Sample at Different Delays

	P4263				P5144			
	Correct Comparison First Observed		Incorrect Comparison First Observed		Correct Comparison First Observed		Incorrect Comparison First Observed	
Switches	Data	Model	Data	Model	Data	Model	Data	Model
	6.4s Delay				5s Delay			
0	.979	.979	.232	.232	.955	.955	.404	.404
1	.984	.984	1.000	.984*	.988	.973*	.987	.973*
2	1.000	1.000	1.000	.988	.999	.998	.995	.984
3	1.000	1.000	1.000	1.000	1.000	1.000	1.000	1.000
dmax	.0		.016		.015		.014	
N	188		164		269		240	
	22s Delay				22s Delay			
0	.943	.943	.648	.648	.856	.856	.791	.791
1	.994	.980*	1.000	.980*	.967	.970	.977	.970*
2	1.000	1.000	1.000	.993	1.000	.996*	.989	.994
3	1.000	1.000	1.000	1.000	1.000	1.000	1.000	1.000
dmax	.014		.020		.004		.007	
N	176		176		90		86	

Note. The asterisk denotes maximum difference (dmax) between predicted and
obtained. None of the p values is significant; all are > .99.

not as accurate as the previous subject, and the training delay was slightly
shorter (5.0 s, as opposed to 6.4 s). At the long delay of 22 s, performance
was near chance level, as shown by almost complete overlap of the
distributions. Like the previously discussed subject, this subject showed
that as the delay was extended, performance deteriorated because of a
discriminability change, with a much greater proportion of the incorrect
comparison distribution extending into the match acceptance region. There
was very little criterion change. The two variables, discriminability (distribution separation) and bias (criterion), are really quite independent, and it
will be shown later in this article that bias can, in theory, compensate for
decreasing discriminability by raising overall performance. The right-hand
part of Table 9.1 shows the values and Dmax tests for P5144, and here, too,
this subject was shown to be using a Markov decision strategy.

SIMULTANEOUS MATCHING TO SAMPLE AND DECREASING DISCRIMINABILITY

In this section some examples are presented from an experiment where the
discriminability (wavelength separation) between the correct comparison

(and sample) and incorrect comparison was manipulated in a simultaneous matching-to-sample experiment. These examples demonstrate that pigeons in simultaneous matching employed a Markov decision strategy, as did pigeons in delayed matching. Furthermore, it will be shown that pigeons employed a Markov decision strategy throughout their performance range from near-perfect performance to near-chance level performance.

The apparatus and procedure were very similar to those used in the previous experiment on delayed matching, except that the sample stimuli were present during the entire trial. Correct choices were reinforced only 30% of the time (random determination), and the reinforcement time was adjusted for the subjects individually: 4 s for 381 and 2.2 s for 378. The two wavelengths used each session were selected to be from either side of the pigeon's 600-nm hue boundary (see Wright, 1972, 1974). At the beginning of the experiment, the stimuli were easy for the pigeons to discriminate. The stimuli were then gradually made more difficult to discriminate by reducing the wavelength spacing. Typically, several days of training were conducted with the new spacing until performance stabilized, and then two consecutive sessions were observed and scored.

Figure 9.6 shows performance of Pigeon P378. The wavelength difference is labeled at the top of each of the three panels along with the overall percentage of correct performances for those session averages. A difference of 10.2 nm produced 88% correct performance, a difference of 5.1 nm produced 75% correct performance and a difference of 4.3 nm produced only 56% correct performance (near-chance performance). Consider the right-hand parts of each panel first. As the stimuli were made more similar, the error rate of accepting the first observed comparison, the incorrect one, increased considerably. As in the previous experiment on delayed matching, there was very little change in the criterion with respect to the distribution of stimulus effects for the correct comparison, and consequently the zero-switch rate for the correct comparison first observed (left-most histogram pair) changed little. One can sight along from the bottom of Fig. 9.6 and see only the slightest movement of the criterion line to the right as performance takes more than a 30% drop. The histograms show that the Markov model fits the data well, and the statistical tests are shown in the left-hand part of Table 9.2.

Figure 9.6b shows performance from the other subject, P381. These results and conclusions are virtually identical to those for P378, except that this subject did not discriminate the wavelengths as well as P378, and required a somewhat larger separation between the correct and incorrect comparison wavelengths to produce the same performance level. The fit to the Markov model is equally good and the value and statistics are shown in the right-hand part of Table 9.2.

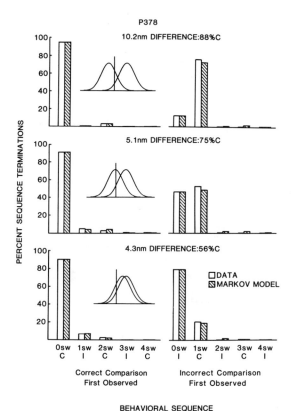

Fig. 9.6 Percentages of the different behavioral sequences (unfilled) for Pigeons P378 and P381 (Fig. 9.6b) at three levels of discrimination difficulty in simultaneous matching to sample. Each panel is headed by the wavelength difference and performance level. Predictions from the Markov model (filled) are shown for the 1–4 switch (sw) sequences for instances where the correct comparison was first observed (left-hand panels) and where the incorrect comparison was first observed (right-hand panels). The inset of the two distributions shows stimulus effects distributions (correct–right, incorrect–left) and a match-criterion line. The match-acceptance region is to the right of the criterion and the reject region is to the left.

Both experiments show a good fit to the Markov model; the p values are all greater than .99 for all of the results from both experiments. In some cases (e.g., left halves of the six panels in Fig. 9.6), the parameter estimate absorbs most of the behavior, but in other cases (e.g., the right halves of the two upper panels in Fig. 9.6) the parameter estimate absorbs only a small part of the total behavior. As previously mentioned, even the small percentages for some of the greater number of switches have important implications for the decision strategies employed by the subject (see

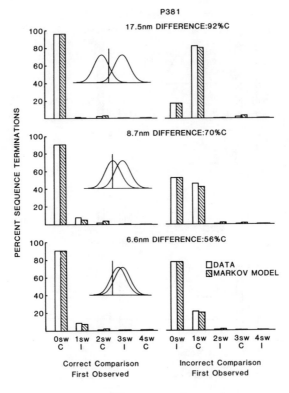

Fig. 9.6b

discussion to follow). Distinguishing among such strategies can have important implications for the ultimate performance obtainable in these decision situations.

LEARNING, ACQUISITION, AND PRESOLUTION PERIOD

The foregoing examples demonstrated that pigeons employed a Markov decision process for both delayed and simultaneous matching to sample over a substantial performance range. In both of these experiments, the performance was modeled when it had stabilized and was at steady state. But what about learning? Can this analysis and accompanying model be used in a way that might determine how learning itself actually occurs?

Acquisition Resulting
from a Discriminability Change

One possibility is that learning by experimentally naïve subjects would look like the reverse of the performances shown in Fig 9.6. That is, the

TABLE 9.2
Goodness of Fit Tests (Kolmogorov–Smirnov) for P378 and P381 in Simultaneous Matching to Sample for Different Wavelength (nm) Separations

| | P378 | | | | P381 | | | |
| | Correct Comparison First Observed | | Incorrect Comparison First Observed | | Correct Comparison First Observed | | Incorrect Comparison First Observed | |
Switches	Data	Model	Data	Model	Data	Model	Data	Model
	10.2 nm Difference				17.5 nm Difference			
0	.956	.956	.226	.226	.960	.960	.169	.169
1	.967	.966*	.993	.965*	.971	.967	.989	.967*
2	1.000	.999	.993	.973	.994	.999*	.989	.973
3	1.000	.999	.999	.998	.994	.999	1.000	1.000
4	1.000	1.000	1.000	1.000	1.000	1.000	1.000	1.000
$d$max		.001		.028		.005		.022
N		180		159		175		172
	5.1 nm Difference				8.7 nm Difference			
0	.909	.909	.467	.467	.904	.904	.532	.532
1	.960	.951*	.994	.952*	.983	.955*	.994	.955*
2	.988	.995	.994	.975	1.000	.996	1.000	.979
3	.994	.997	1.000	.999	1.000	.999	1.000	.998
4	1.000	.999	1.000	1.000	1.000	1.000	1.000	1.000
$d$max		.009		.042		.028		.039
N		176		165		177		172
	4.3 nm Difference				6.6 nm Difference			
0	.907	.907	.791	.791	.906	.906	.778	.778
1	.979	.981*	.995	.981*	.994	.979*	.994	.979*
2	1.000	1.000	1.000	.996	1.000	.998	1.000	.995
3	1.000	1.000	1.000	1.000	1.000	1.000	1.000	1.000
4	1.000	1.000	1.000	1.000	1.000	1.000	1.000	1.000
$d$max		.002		.014		.015		.015
N		332		358		341		352

Note. The asterisk denotes maximum difference ($d$max) between predicted and obtained. None of the p values is significant; all are $> .99$.

distributions would be completely overlapped before any learning has occurred as it was in the bottom panels of Fig. 9.6. Then, as learning occurs, these distributions would pull apart as they do when going from the bottom to the top panels. In its strong form, this discriminability change would completely account for learning, and the criterion would remain fixed, relative to the correct comparison distribution.

The top panel of Fig. 9.7 shows this possibility, graphically. All of these distribution pairs shown at the top of this panel have the same position of the criterion line relative to the distribution for the correct comparison. The distribution for the incorrect comparison pulls away (to the left) from the distribution for the correct comparison (and criterion line). Hence, it is called the "discrimination model of acquisition." Shown in this panel are the

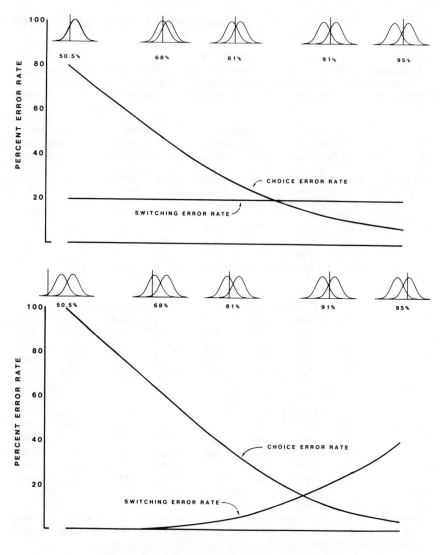

Fig. 9.7 Hypothetical learning (successive sessions) according to a discrimination model of learning in the upper panel and a bias/criterion model of learning in the lower panel. In the upper panel, the distributions of stimulus effects (top of panel) show the distribution for the incorrect comparison stimulus (left distribution) separate from the criterion line which is fixed relative to the distribution for the correct comparison stimulus. In the lower panel, the distributions of stimulus effects show the criterion line moving to the right across the fixed pair of distributions with successive sessions. The functions show the changes in the two types of errors: choosing the incorrect comparison (choice errors) and rejecting the correct comparison (switching errors).

rates of the two types of errors: choice errors where the incorrect comparison is accepted as a match (virtually identical to SDT false alarms or Type II errors where a false null hypothesis is accepted that the comparison and sample are not different), and switching errors where the correct comparison is incorrectly rejected as a match (similar, but not identical, to false negatives or Type I errors). As acquisition begins, the choice error rate is high. As acquisition progresses, the distributions pull apart, and the choice error rate goes down. Notice that, according to this model, the switching error rate should remain constant throughout acquisition.

Acquisition Resulting from Bias/Criterion Changes

Another possibility to account for acquisition is that the subject would begin acquisition with an extremely lax criterion, located far to left of both stimulus-effects distributions. Under this condition, any comparison would qualify as a match. Pigeons typically check one particular side first each trial; some go left and some go right. Since everything qualifies as a match, a complete position preference would be produced. This possibility is appealing because it accounts for the complete position preferences often observed during MTS acquisition without correction procedures. It also bears upon the old issue of continuity vs. noncontinuity. The subject can be "learning" something by beginning to move its criterion before these criterion movements materially affect performance. Performance would still be at chance level because the criterion is too lax to exclude as a match any of the encounters with the incorrect comparison. As the subject begins to acquire the discrimination, the criterion line begins to move to the right. As it moves to the right, the subject will occasionally reject the incorrect stimulus, and switch over to the other comparison stimulus. As the criterion continues to move to the right, the incorrect comparison will be rejected with greater frequency. In its pure form, this possibility is the "bias model of acquisition."

The bottom panel of Fig. 9.7 graphically shows this possibility. The distributions at the top of the panel show what is happening at different stages in acquisition. (Each distribution pair has been positioned on the panel so that the point on the panel depicted by the distribution pair coincides with the criterion line.) The spacing between the two distributions of each pair is identical. The only difference is the positioning of the criterion line. The criterion line begins to the far left of the distributions, so far to the left that performance (50.5%) is, for all practical purposes, at chance level. As the criterion moves to the right performance rises: 68%, 81%, 91%, 95%, as shown under each distribution pair. This bias conceptualization of acquisition predicts that there should be a regular rise in the switching error rate, along with a concomitant drop in the choice error rate as the discrimination is acquired.

Of course, combinations of the two possibilities, bias and discrimination, are possible where the criterion line moves to the right, while at the same time the distributions pull apart. But what is important here is to identify the two extreme cases as pure examples of these separate processes. This is where the MTS Markov presented in this chapter, and signal-detection theory are most valuable (cf. Bower, 1959; Heyman, 1979; Jeffress, 1964, 1967; Siegel, 1969; Wright & Sands, 1981). They provide a standard against which results can be evaluated.

Acquisition of 2-Alternative Matching to Sample

In order to provide a test of which of these two processes underlies the learning of a discrimination, pigeons were trained in two alternative matching to sample. The apparatus and procedures were similar to those previously described for the simultaneous matching experiments, except that the two wavelengths were 621.9 nm and 584.1 nm, there were 100 trials per session, the intertrial interval was 15 s, and reinforcement (3 s) was given for each correct choice. Key-peck shaping consisted of rewarding successive approximations to center-key pecks with these wavelengths on the center key, followed by 5 continuous reinforcements (crfs) for pecks to each wavelength presented individually on each key, and then repeated for a total 10 crfs per wavelength. Throughout acquisition the pigeons' looking responses, switches, and key pecks were tape-recorded and analyzed.

Individual results are presented in Fig. 9.8 for these three experimentally naïve subjects in this experiment. At the beginning of acquisition (percent correct about 50%), the choice error rates were about 80% and declined as acquisition occurs. None of the subjects showed any apparent trend toward a rising switching error rate as acquisition progressed.

This lack of a rise in the switching error rate is best shown in the lower-right panel of Fig. 9.8, which is a composite of the data from all three subjects. The regression line fit to the switching error data actually has a slight negative slope. Thus, the data strongly support the "discrimination model of acquisition." Recall that the discrimination model (Fig. 9.7, upper panel) predicts that the switching error rate should be constant, and the choice error rate should begin at about 80% and decline with acquisition. This prediction almost perfectly describes the results from the experiment. On the other hand, the bias model of acquisition (Fig 9.7, lower panel) predicts that the switching error rate should begin at zero and rise with acquisition, and the choice error rate should begin at about 100% and fall with acquisition. Clearly, the bias model of acquisition is not supported by

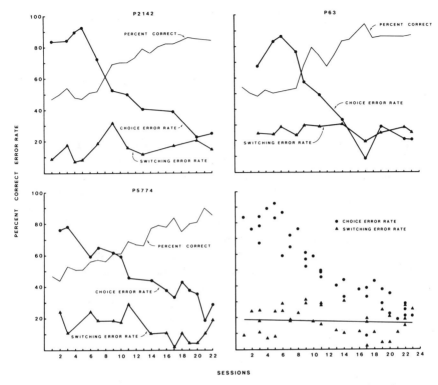

Fig. 9.8 Acquisition of two-alternative matching to sample by three individual pigeons along with their composite data in the lower right panel (the least-squares regression line for the switching error rate is given by: Y = 20.1 − .2 X). The broken line function for the individual subjects shows overall accuracy (percentage correct). The two other functions show changes in the two error types (see Fig 9.7).

these data. Seldom do data support one alternative as strongly as these data support the discrimination model of learning and acquisition. I would not want to claim that all learning is via the discrimination model of learning. Indeed, at the time of writing this chapter, I am just completing some MTS acquisition studies with three wavelengths instead of two as in this experiment. MTS acquisition with three wavelengths (each from a different pigeon hue) is much more difficult and protracted (about 100 sessions) than with two wavelengths (about 22 sessions). Some of the preliminary evidence from this three-alternative MTS experiment looks like the bias model may play a role. The strategy embodied in the discrimination model might function best in situations where the discrimination is comparatively easy. In more difficult situations the strategy embodied in the bias model might make the rules of the task more obvious to the subject and hence easier to learn.

THE MTS MARKOV MODEL COMPARED
WITH SDT MODELS

In this section the performance strategy of the MTS Markov model will be compared with two different strategies, both of which were mentioned at the beginning of this chapter. These two strategies are the ones inherently bound to the two most common signal-detection theory paradigms: Yes/No and Two-Alternative Forced Choice (2AFC).

By way of example, the upper panel of Fig. 9.9 describes a hypothetical MTS situation where the wavelength separation gives a constant index of discriminability of 2.0 (d' = 2.0). The pairs of distributions at the top of this panel are all separated by the same distance (in accordance with d' = 2.0), but the difference among them is the position of the criterion line. Going from right to left, for example, the criterion moves to the right, producing an increasingly strict match criterion; that is, fewer sensations produced by the stimuli will qualify as a match. This match criterion proportion (shown at the arrow head) is the same as the Hit rate from signal-detection theory, and is the scale for the abscissa.

One of the possible strategies of matching to sample that was first mentioned at the beginning of this chapter was the strategy of looking at both stimuli and then making a choice. Under this strategy, both comparison stimuli are always observed, once and only once, before making a choice. This is the strategy inherent in the two-alternative, forced-choice SDT paradigm. Typically there are two listening intervals (stimulus observation intervals). The first stimulus observation period is presented and the subject computes a likelihood ratio; for example, then the second is presented and the subject computes another likelihood ratio, and then (during the response interval) the subject makes a choice and chooses the one with the largest likelihood ratio. Another strategy mentioned at the beginning of the chapter (and also one which pigeons do not use) was the strategy of accepting the first observed comparison stimulus (the Y response) if it matches the sample, but automatically choosing the second if the first does not match (the N response). Thus, this latter strategy is that of the Yes/No SDT paradigm. Performance from the Yes/No strategy is shown in the lower function of Fig. 9.9. Moving from right to left, performance first rises and then falls. The same basic form of the function is shown by the 2AFC strategy or model; 2AFC is related to Yes/No by the square root of two (Green & Swets, 1966).

By contrast, Fig. 9.9 shows that performance produced by the MTS Markov strategy continues to increase, rather than decrease as do those from the 2AFC or Yes/No strategies. The reason that performance continues to increase under the MTS Markov strategy has to do with the different consequences of the two types of errors. In the SDT paradigms the

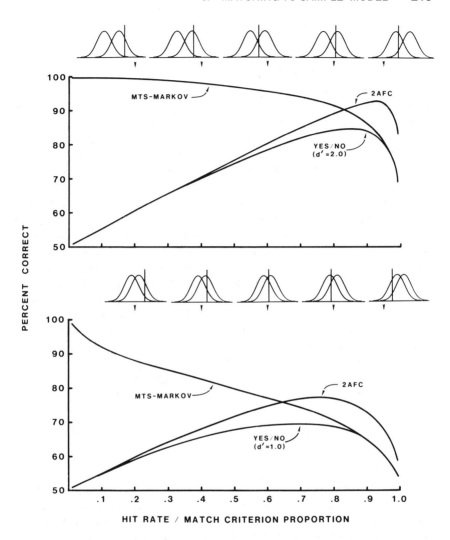

Fig. 9.9   Calculated performances according to three different strategies: the MTS Markov strategy, the strategy according to a two-alternative, forced-choice paradigm, and the strategy according to a Yes/No signal detection paradigm. The Hit rate or match-criterion proportion is plotted along the abscissa. Performances are from a moderately easy discrimination ($d' = 1.0$) in the upper panel and from a somewhat more difficult discrimination ($d' = 2.0$) in the lower panel.

two error types (false alarms, false negatives) have the same consequence: They terminate the trial with an incorrect response. In the MTS Markov model only choice errors are similar to the errors of the SDT paradigms; switching errors are different. As the match criterion moves to the right (moving from right to left in the upper panel of Fig 9.9), the false alarm rate decreases. This is the choice error rate of Fig. 9.8, and is the fatal error with respect to matching to sample — choosing the incorrect comparison and terminating the trial. With this change in bias, the false negative rate increases; this is the switching error rate of Fig. 9.8. But these errors are switches. They are not errors from the standpoint of matching to sample; they are not choice responses; they do not terminate the MTS trial. By moving the criterion so that the subject is more strict on what it will accept as a match, a huge increment in performance is possible relative to the alternative SDT strategies. This appears to be quite a remarkable conclusion.

The performance achievements possible are, in some ways, even more dramatic under slightly more difficult discriminations. The lower panel of Fig. 9.9 is similar to the upper one, except that the discrimination is more difficult: a $d' = 1.0$, instead of $d' = 2.0$. As before, performance under the 2AFC and Yes/No paradigms rises and then falls as one moves from right to left and the hit rate is diminished. By contrast, the MTS Markov model shows that as criterion for a match becomes stricter and the match acceptance region (proportion) diminishes, performance begins to rise, and, in the limit, this function points toward perfect performance. The performance difference possible according to the MTS Markov strategy is substantial. This is *The* decision strategy that the pigeons actually employ. It is not some hypothetical strategy. We actually observed them doing it. But as with most things, there is a price to pay for this increased performance.

The Price of Increased Accuracy

Reproduced in Fig. 9.10 is the same percentage correct function that was shown in the lower panel of Fig 9.9 ($d' = 1.0$). As percentage rises from successively greater restrictions of the match criterion, the number of switches also rises. Plotted on the right-hand side of Fig. 9.10 is the maximum expected number of switches of this number or more, on 1 trial of a 176-trial session. When the match criterion proportion falls below 0.2, the expected number of switches rises dramatically, and it quickly goes out of sight. In practice, pigeons operate with a match-criterion of about 0.75 to 1.0. They seem reluctant to operate in the region from 0.0 to 0.75, even though better performance could be achieved. But we can ask what it might take for any organism, a human for example, to operate in this region. We all probably have, at one time or another, operated within this region without even realizing its benefits. Some of the examples that come to mind are those for which the decision is really important, for example, making a career choice. One compares the alternatives, between say becoming a

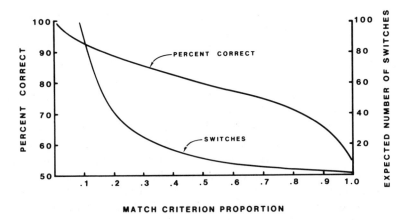

Fig. 9.10   The top function is from Fig. 9.9 at a discrimination difficulty of d' = 2.0. The bottom function shows how many switches between the comparison stimuli (right-hand ordinate) should be observed in a 176-trial session for the trial containing the most switches.

psychologist vs. a medical doctor, back and forth, not just over minutes or hours, but days and years, trying to make the right decision. By this process, one can conceivably operate over in the left-hand region of Fig. 9.10, and even in a tough situation achieve a high performance level. Another example, albeit somewhat less dramatic, is the decision of choosing a new car. It is a major purchase for most of us. One reads reports, drives the cars, compares the alternatives back and forth. You try to visualize first one alternative (e.g., BMW 3 series), and then another alternative (e.g., Acura/Honda Legend). One compares them on dimensions of performance, features, styling, reliability, and price. Comparing back and forth tends to distill quality differences, so that they can be weighed against any price differential. By comparing them back and forth (switching), frequently with no new information, a strong preference often emerges accompanied by the conviction (and frequent result) that it is the correct choice.

Further Comparisons with SDT Models

The ability to distinguish among different strategies highlights the importance of the "looking" responses by the pigeons being objective, observable responses and not intervening variables or hypothetical constructs. If they had been only hypothetical responses (e.g., Spence, 1960), then many of the distinctions which have been made among the different strategies would not have been possible.

The 2AFC SDT Strategy.   This is the strategy where the subject looks at both choices, once and only once, before making a choice of either. If the pigeons had engaged in such a strategy, then the pigeons would never choose the first observed comparison stimulus, and no responses would occur in the 0-SW categories. Clearly, this did not occur. The 0-SW categories often contain the majority of responses. Indeed, the 0-SW category for the correct comparison must be the largest category according to a Markov choice rule, and the data follow accordingly. It may appear, upon initial contact with the model proposed in this chapter, that switches in observing the comparison stimuli are analogous to Toman's vicarious-trial-and-error (VTE) of rats choosing an arm of a T-maze (e.g., Tolman, 1938). The similarity of the behavior itself is inescapable, but the manner in which it was incorporated into a theory of choice and decision processes is different from the way in which Tolman conceptualized it. Tolman hypothesized that the more the rat looked back and forth between the stimuli, the more information the rat accumulated about the stimuli. As more information was accumulated, it was more likely that the rat would make a choice. But as Still (1976) has pointed out, this means that the transition probabilities to the absorbing states (Rr and Gr of the example in Fig. 9.3) should increase as VTE increases and as the trial progresses. If this occurred then the results would violate the Markov process model. In a Markov process the transition probabilities remain constant. The transition probabilities for pigeons matching to sample do remain constant, and thus meet the requirements of a Markov process. Even for rats selecting between T-maze arms, they do not grow, although the rats' selection process apparently is not Markovian (Siegel, 1969; Still 1976).

Yes/No SDT Strategy.   This choice strategy is based on the knowledge that one of two comparison stimuli will always match the sample, and the assumption that if the first observed comparison does not match, then by default the other must match. This type of choice strategy has been hypothesized to account for rats' choices in a two-choice discrimination box (Pullen & Turney, 1977), rats' choices in a Lashley jumping-stand apparatus (Hall, 1973), and pigeons' choices in a matching-to-sample task (Roberts & Grant, 1978). As Roberts and Grant said, "the alternative key will be pecked automatically if the first is rejected as a match" (p. 80). This type of choice strategy is clearly not the one that pigeons use in the matching-to-sample task. If it were the one used, then there would be at most only one switch between the comparison stimuli. The pigeon should never switch back to reconsider the first comparison (which it rejected). But there are switches back to the first rejected comparison and even to the second, and so on. Indeed, there have been examples (not shown here) where each comparison was observed (and rejected) three and even four times before a choice was made. The ability to determine experimentally how many times the pigeons actually observe and reject each stimulus before making a choice response depends on having clearly defined "looking" movements by the pigeons. The stimuli recessed behind the pecking keys accomplished this, although the apparatus was not designed explicitly for this purpose. It is not clear, at this point in time, that modifications to the design would help, either in terms of making the "looking" responses more obvious or changing aspects of the Markov choice strategy in any interesting ways. Possibly physically separating the comparison stimuli would decrease switching between them because it would require more time and effort. But it would be more interesting from the standpoint of the Markov choice model to increase switching rather than decrease it. The comparison stimuli are already about as physically close as is possible.

MTS Markov Model Compared with Other Behavioral Markov Models

The majority of Markov-chain models in psychology have been concerned with transitions to hypothetical states. They are established by conjecture, and tests are designed to support or refute them. They are not observable states as are the "looking" and "switching" responses of the pigeons of this chapter. Instead of transitions being made among internal psychological states (storage, retrieval, CS–UCS associations), transitions are made to observations of stimuli. The subjects look back and forth and compare the stimuli from which a choice must be made. One of the innovations of this research was making these decision states (orienting toward the stimulus) observable and recordable. Many experimental settings do not naturally produce discrete, obvious "looking" behavior by the subjects. A rat on a Lashley jumping stand, a monkey in a WGTA, or a pigeon in a Skinner box typically need make only eye movements (cf. Schrier & Povar, 1979) or slight head turns in order to shift from observing one stimulus to another. The stimulus observations can occur so quickly that they go unnoticed and would be very difficult to deal with quantitatively. It is precisely this kind of hypothetical state, that is, assumptions about when and how often stimuli are observed, that is prevalent in many Markov choice process models (e.g., Atkinson, 1960; Atkinson, Bower & Crothers, 1965; Bower, 1959, 1962; Estes, 1960; Spence, 1960; Still, 1976). If the observing behaviors are themselves not directly observed, then they become hypothetical states, like the hypothetical learning stages in the stage models.

CONCLUDING REMARKS

The model of this article is based on objective responses of pigeons "looking" at the stimuli, switching between the comparison stimuli, and choosing one of them. Experimenters do not regularly record this "collateral" behavior, and instead rely exclusively upon the "choices" — key pecks. But it is this collateral behavior of looking (but not choosing/pecking) and switching that has allowed the decision strategy to be revealed. The key peck in only the final response in a chain of behavior involving a succession of choice points. The MTS Markov model is not a theory in the sense of hypothetical states and intervening variables. It is a model, a way of summarizing the data (looking responses, switches, and key pecks) and revealing their lawful relationships. Few behavioral processes have been shown to be Markovian. Still fewer have observable responses that fit a Markov process rule. Finally, the MTS Markov model makes no assumptions about the pigeon's cognitive processes, but the actual decision strategy, which is itself a cognitive process, falls out of the analysis.

ACKNOWLEDGMENTS

This research was partly supported by grants MH 42881 and MH 35202 to the author. The author is grateful for the careful assistance by Judith Cornish Brown and Jacquelyne Rivera in many phases of this research, and for the many good editorial suggestions and comments provided by the Editor Michael Davison on the manuscript. The realization that overall performance from the MTS Markov strategy was different from SDT came from some discussions of this MTS Markov model with Bruce A. Schneider. Reprint requests should be sent to Anthony A. Wright, Sensory Sciences Center, Suite 316 SHI, 6420 Lamar Fleming Ave., Houston, Texas, 77030.

REFERENCES

Atkinson, R. C. (1960). The use of models in experimental psychology. *Synthese, 12,* 162–171.
Atkinson, R. C., Bower, G. H., & Crothers, E. J. (1965). *An introduction to mathematical learning theory.* New York: Wiley.
Blough, D. S. (1959). Delayed matching in the pigeon. *Journal of the Experimental Analysis of Behavior, 2,* 151–160.
Bower, G. H. (1959). Choice point behavior. In R. R. Bush & W. K. Estes (Eds.), *Studies in mathematical learning theory.* Stanford, CA: Stanford University Press.
Bower, G. H. (1962). Response strengths and choice probability: A consideration of two combination rules. In E. Nagel, P. Suppes, & A. Taski (Eds.), *Logic, methodology and philosophy of science: Proceedings of the 1960 International Congress.* Stanford, CA: Stanford University Press.
Estes, W. K. (1960). A random walk model for choice behavior. In K. J. Arrow, S. Karlin, & P. Suppes (Eds.), *Mathematical methods in the social sciences.* Stanford CA: Stanford University Press.
Green, D. M., & Swets, J. A. (1966). *Signal detection theory and psychophysics.* New York: Wiley.

Hall, G. (1973). Overtraining and reversal learning in the rat: Effects of stimulus salience and response strategies. *Journal of Comparative and Physiological Psychology, 84,* 169–175.

Heyman, G. M. (1979). A Markov model description of changeover probabilities on concurrent variable-interval schedules. *Journal of the Experimental Analysis of Behavior, 31,* 41–51.

Jeffress, L. A. (1964). Stimulus-oriented approach to detection. *Journal of the Acoustical Society of America, 36,* 766–774.

Jeffress, L. A. (1967). Stimulus-oriented approach to detection re-examined. *Journal of the Acoustical Society of America, 41,* 480–488.

Newell, A., & Simon, H. A. (1972). *Human problem solving.* Englewood Cliffs, NJ: Prentice-Hall.

Pullen, M. R., & Turney, T. H. (1977). Response modes in simultaneous and successive visual discriminations. *Animal Learning and Behavior, 5,* 73–77.

Roberts, W. A., & Grant, D. S. (1978). Interaction of sample and comparison stimuli in delayed matching to sample with the pigeon. *Journal of Experimental Psychology: Animal Behavior Processes, 4,* 68–82.

Schrier, A. M., & Povar, M. L. (1979). Eye movements of stumptailed monkeys during discrimination learning: VTE revisited. *Animal Learning and Behavior, 7,* 239–245.

Siegel, S. (1969). Discrimination overtraining and shift behavior. In R. M. Gilbert & N. S. Sutherland (Eds.), *Animal discrimination learning.* London: Academic Press.

Spence, K. W. (1960). Conceptual models of spatial and nonspatial discrimination learning. In K. W. Spence (Ed.), *Behavior theory and learning.* Englewood Cliffs, NJ: Prentice-Hall.

Still, A. W. (1976). An evaluation of the use of Markov models to describe the behavior of rats at a choice point. *Animal Behaviour, 24,* 498–506.

Tolman, E. C. (1938). The determiners of behaviors at a choice point. *Psychological Review, 45,* 1–41.

Wright, A. A. (1972). Psychometric and psychophysical hue discrimination functions for the pigeon. *Vision Research, 12,* 1447–1464.

Wright, A. A. (1974). Psychometric and psychophysical theory within a framework of response bias. *Psychological Review, 81,* 332–347.

Wright, A. A. (1978). Construction of equal-hue discriminability scales for the pigeon. *Journal of the Experimental Analysis of Behavior, 29,* 261–266.

Wright, A. A. (1979). Color-vision psychophysics: A comparison of pigeon and human. In A. M. Granda & J. H. Maxwell (Eds.), *Neural mechanisms of behavior in the pigeon.* New York: Plenum Press, pp. 89–128.

Wright, A. A., & Cumming, W. W. (1971). Color-naming functions for the pigeon. *Journal of the Experimental Analysis of Behavior, 15,* 7–17.

Wright, A. A., & Sands, S. F. (1981). A model of detection and decision processes during matching to sample by pigeons: Performance with 88 different wavelengths in delayed and simultaneous matching tasks. *Journal of Experimental Psychology: Animal Behavior Processes, 7,* 191–216.

10 Psychophysics of Direct Remembering

K. Geoffrey White
University of Otago, New Zealand

The traditional problem of psychophysics is the problem of scaling—the quantification of relative stimulus effects on behavior. In the case of remembering, stimuli have their effect at a temporal distance. The problem is thus one of specifying how time modulates the stimulus effect. In the present chapter, I suggest that the action of temporally distant events is direct.

In a theory of *direct remembering,* the notion that the stimulus effect is direct follows J. J. Gibson's analysis of direct perception. Temporal distance may attenuate the stimulus effect in an analogous fashion to the attenuation of discriminability by spatial distance. In other words, the effect of the temporally distant event diminishes with increasing time in the same way that an event becomes difficult to distinguish with increasing spatial distance. This diminution function does not differentiate a time of perceiving from a time of remembering, in which case the rate of decrement must be constant. According to J. J. Gibson, "the traveling moment of present time is certainly not a razor's edge, as James observed, and no one can say when perception leaves off and memory begins (1966, p. 276)" (also see Gibson, 1979, p. 253; Turvey, 1974, 1977). Consequently the function relating forgetting to increasing time should fall off at a constant rate.

This "constant-rate" assumption of a theory of direct remembering is captured by supposing that the decrement in discriminability, Δ (log d_t), that occurs over a small interval of time Δ (t), is proportional to discriminability at the beginning of the interval, log d_t (Fig. 10.1).

The constant of proportionality is b (with units of t^{-1}). The decrement in discriminability is

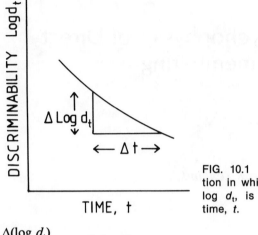

FIG. 10.1 A forgetting function in which discriminability, log d_t, is decremented over time, t.

$$\frac{\Delta(\log d_t)}{\Delta t} = -b.\log d_t. \tag{1}$$

Rearranging Equation 1 and integrating with respect to t gives

$$\int \frac{\Delta \log d_t}{\log d_t} = \int -b \, \Delta t$$

yielding

$$\text{Ln}(\log d_t) = -bt + c$$

The constant of integration c can be replaced by log d_0, discriminability at time $t = 0$ because when $t = 0$, log $d_t = $ log d_0. Exponentiating gives Equation 2, which expresses discriminability at time t as an exponential function of t.

$$\log d_t = \log d_0. \exp(-bt) \tag{2}$$

The parameters of the negative exponential function give measures of initial discriminability at time $t = 0$ (log d_0) and rate of decrement in discriminability with increasing time since stimulus presentation, b.

The exponential function is unique in that the rate of decrement is constant. Strong (albeit circumstantial) confirmation for the parallel between the effects of temporal and spatial distance is provided by Shepard's (1987) demonstration that for a wide range of perceptual dimensions, the falloff in ability to discriminate with increasing stimulus disparity follows an exponential law. It should be noted that the exponential function is not intended to describe some hypothetical process of trace decay (Simon, 1966), although the exponential accounts for as much data variance as other functions, such as a hyperbola (McCarthy & White, 1987). Exponential processes have been popular in previous accounts of indirect memory processes (Wickelgren, 1970). Instead, the present use of the exponential function follows from the treatment of remembering as direct, owing to its constant-rate-of-decrement property, and applies to the decrement in discriminability with increasing delay of choice, rather than to indirect decay processes (White, 1985; White & McKenzie, 1982).

The measure of discriminability employed here, log d_t, is Davison and Tustin's (1978) measure of stimulus discriminability, applied to signal-detection procedures where a delay separates the discriminative stimuli and a subsequent choice response (McCarthy & White, 1987). That is, log d_t measures stimulus discriminability at the time the discriminative behavior (remembering) is emitted (White, 1985). It has the advantage of being bias-free (Davison & Tustin, 1978; McCarthy & White, 1987). The measure is half the logarithm (base 10) of the product of ratios of correct to error responses following each sample stimulus (McCarthy & White, 1987). Equivalent discriminability measures could have been used, such as d' of signal-detection theory, or log d_s advanced by Alsop, Davison and by Davison and Jenkins (1985), but these are not explored here. If ratios of reinforcers for correct responses were varied, the discriminability measure may prove unstable, but under the present conditions it is assumed to be stable and is algebraically equivalent to the alternative measures.

The upper panel of Fig. 10.2 shows a set of negative exponential functions with the same rate of decrement, b, but with different values of initial discriminability, log d_0. The lower panel shows a set of functions with the same initial discriminability but with varying values of b. This figure illustrates the variation in one parameter without variations in the other, and how forgetting functions may be described in terms of two characteristics (White, 1985).

INDEPENDENCE OF INITIAL DISCRIMINABILITY AND RATE OF FORGETTING

In terms of the negative exponential function, the rate of decrement in discriminability, b, or more colloquially, the rate of forgetting, is *independent* of the initial discriminability of the stimuli to be remembered. This prediction is interesting because it appears counterintuitive, and is incon-

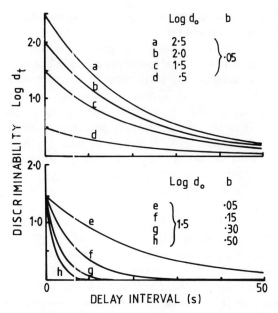

FIG. 10.2   Exponential functions for different levels of initial discriminability, log d_o, and the same rate of forgetting b (upper panel), and for different rates of forgetting and the same level of initial discriminability (lower panel).

sistent with theories of "indirect" remembering, according to which the memories of vivid events, or semantically encoded stimuli, are more resistant to forgetting. That is, with indirect memory, the rate of forgetting is assumed to depend on factors relating to initial encoding (Leibrich & White, 1983; Tulving, 1983). (Unfortunately, previous studies of human memory in which encoding factors have been manipulated have not included enough retention-interval values to allow an assessment of rate of forgetting.).

The rationale for this chapter is to explore conditions under which log d_0 and b vary independently. There may be instances where log d_0 and b appear to covary but such instances can often be attributed to floor effects (White & Bunnell-McKenzie, 1985). More informative instances are those where some experimental attempt is made to produce changes in log d_0 without corresponding changes in b. Several examples are described herein where different experimental conditions influenced one parameter but not the other.

VARIATIONS IN INITIAL DISCRIMINABILITY

In psychophysical studies, a choice or yes-no response is emitted in the presence of or very soon after the target stimulus or sample. Stimulus discriminability, measured by log d (Davison & Tustin, 1978) or by more traditional signal-detection measures (Green & Swets, 1974), is a function of physical stimulus disparity. The range over which discriminability measures can vary as a function of stimulus disparity is determined by procedural parameters. That is, parameters such as intertrial–interval duration and sample-key ratio requirement can set an upper limit on discriminability (White, 1985). For example, the disparity of stimuli associated with the choice response contributes to the discriminability measure (White, 1986) although the discrimination between choice stimuli is usually assumed to be asymptotic.

In delayed matching to sample, where the choice response follows sample-stimulus presentation after some delay, disparity of the sample-stimuli has a clear effect on matching accuracy. White (1985, Experiment 1) compared delayed matching-to-sample performance in pigeons for hard versus easy wavelength discriminations between sample stimuli. On each trial in White's procedure, five responses to a sample stimulus presented on the center key of a three-key chamber initiated a delay of .5, 2, 4, 8, or 20 s, with delay-interval duration varying within session. The dark delay interval terminated with presentation of comparison stimuli. Correct choices were reinforced with grain presentation and a 20-s intertrial interval separated trials. Samples were wavelength stimuli produced by Kodak Wratten filters with peak transmission at 538 nm and 576 nm in one condition, or at 501 nm and 606 nm in the other. In both conditions, wavelengths of comparison stimuli were 538 nm and 576 nm.

Fig. 10.3 shows values of log d_t as a function of delay for the two wavelength-disparity conditions, based on data summed for five birds from White (1985, Experiment 1). In this and other comparisons described here, statistically reliable differences in group data were ascertained by analysis of variance on parameter values for individual subjects. These group differences were additionally associated with corresponding differences for each of the five individual birds in the different conditions. VAC in Fig.

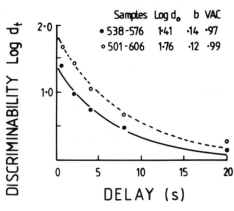

FIG. 10.3 Forgetting functions for discriminations between sample stimuli with wavelengths of 538 nm and 576 nm (filled circles) or with wavelengths of 501 nm and 606 nm (unfilled circles). Parameter values and variance accounted for (VAC) by the best-fitting exponential functions are shown (data from White, 1985).

Samples	Log d_0	b	VAC
• 538-576	1·41	·14	·97
○ 501-606	1·76	·12	·99

DISCRIMINABILITY Log d_t

DELAY (s)

10.1 and later figures gives the proportion of variance in the data accounted for by the exponential function fitted using a nonlinear least squares method. The data of interest are the parameter values given in Fig. 10.3 for the exponential functions best fitting the log d_t measures. Fig. 10.3 shows that whereas initial discriminability, log d_0, was higher for the discrimination between 501-nm and 606-nm samples than between 538-nm and 576-nm samples, there was no significant difference in rate of forgetting, b, for the two conditions. Thus, only the initial discriminability of the sample stimuli was influenced by their wavelength disparity.

A similar result was reported by White and McKenzie (1982, Experiment 2) for a symbolic delayed-matching-to-sample procedure for hard versus easy sample-stimulus discriminations and where the choice stimuli were simply left and right positions. Interestingly, the functions for the hard wavelength discriminations were similar to the functions for a complex discrimination between same versus different relations between successively presented hues (White & McKenzie, 1982, Experiment 1). The complex and simple discriminations differed in terms of the initial discriminability of the sample stimuli, rather than in the rate of forgetting.

These effects of stimulus disparity on initial discriminability are generally consistent with psychophysical studies using near-threshold stimuli. There are other conditions unrelated to stimulus disparity, however, that also determine initial discriminability. These conditions are interesting because their effects have often been interpreted in terms of memorial processes. The present analysis suggests, however, that they influence initial discriminability rather than rate of forgetting. Two examples follow:

The first example is the facilitatory effect of increasing the fixed-ratio (FR) requirement for sample-stimulus responding in delayed matching to sample. The increase in accuracy with longer fixed ratios has been construed as an effect analogous to that of repetition or rehearsal in human memory (Roberts, 1972). Fig. 10.4 shows the effect on log d_t of FR 5 and FR 1 requirements in delayed matching to sample using the procedure described (White, 1985, Experiment 2). With FR 5, initial discriminability (log d_0) was consistently higher than with FR 1, and there was no significant difference in rate of forgetting (b).

White (1985) reanalyzed data from some previous studies, using as an estimate of discriminability the log of the ratio of correct to error responses derived from the percentage of correct measures reported in the original papers (McCarthy & White, 1987). This estimate of discriminability is equal to log d_t when there is no response bias, a reasonable assumption for data averaged over subjects. Increasing the duration of the sample stimulus from 3 s to 12 s in a study by Nelson and Wasserman (1978) resulted in a corresponding increase in log d_0 with no obvious change in b. Similarly, increasing the frequency of repetitions of the sample stimulus in a study by

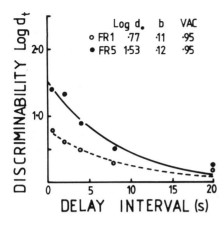

	Log d_o	b	VAC
○ FR1	·77	·11	·95
● FR5	1·53	·12	·95

DISCRIMINABILITY Log d_t

DELAY INTERVAL (s)

FIG. 10.4 Forgetting functions for conditions with ratio requirements of FR 1 or FR 5 for sample-key responding (data from White, 1985).

Grant (1981) gave an increase in log d_0, but no change in b (the reliability of these changes cannot be assessed). This set of examples shows that initial discriminability of sample stimuli is a function of procedural parameters in addition to physical stimulus disparity, and that the changes in log d_0 occur without corresponding changes in rate of forgetting.

The second example is provided by a recent study that compared the effects of different dose levels of scopolamine in delayed matching to sample with rats (Kirk, White, & McNaughton, 1988). Scopolamine is a central muscarinic antagonist that blocks cholinergic receptors and has an apparently amnestic effect in "memory" tasks such as the radial-arm maze (Beatty & Bierley, 1986), and delayed matching to sample (Dunnett, 1985). The amnestic effect of scopolamine is of interest because of its bearing on the cholinergic hypothesis for memory. Kirk et al. trained rats in a delayed matching-to-sample procedure in which sample stimuli were 400-Hz and 4,600-Hz tones. In each trial, a nose-poke response against a Plexiglas door of the central food magazine initiated a 1-s presentation of the sample stimulus, followed by a delay of 0.1, 1, 2, 4, 8, 16, or 32 s (varied within session). The first nose poke at the food-magazine door following termination of the delay interval resulted in insertion of left and right levers. Right-lever presses were reinforced following the 4,600-Hz tone, and left-lever presses were reinforced following the 400-Hz tone. The nose-poke requirement ensured that the rat was positioned centrally in the chamber at the end of the delay interval. Trials were separated by 10-s intertrial intervals.

Following extensive training in the delayed matching procedure, four of eight rats were injected with scopolamine hydrochloride and the other four rats received equivalent volume injections (ip) of 0.9% saline, over 10 sessions. Over the next 10 sessions, the first four rats received saline and the second four scopolamine. Drug administration for the first four rats was first in ascending order of dose level followed by descending order, with one dose level administered in a session. The dose levels were 0.005, 0.014, 0.042, 0.125, and 0.375 mg/kg, given in a volume of 1 ml/kg in a saline vehicle. Drug administration for the second four rats was first in a descending order, followed by an ascending order. Throughout drug and saline conditions, performance was maintained in the delayed matching-to-sample procedure.

Fig. 10.5 shows that log d_t measures, based on data summed over rats, increased systematically with increasing delay and with increasing level of scopolamine dose. There was a statistically reliable decrease in the initial discriminability parameter, log d_0, with increasing scopolamine dose, whereas the small changes in rate of forgetting, b, were not significant. These data provide further support for the independence of initial discriminability and rate of forgetting in that log d_0 was affected by scopolamine while b was not. The result is also of interest because it suggests that cholinergic functions may modulate processes other than memory processes, such as attention and discrimination processes.

VARIATION IN RATE OF FORGETTING

Instances where log d_0 remains constant and b changes tend to be less frequent than instances of changes in log d_0. Two clear examples are

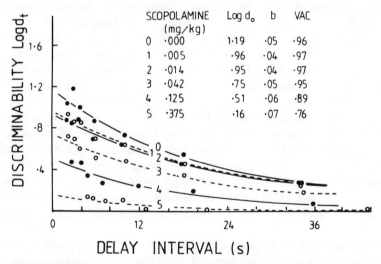

FIG. 10.5 Forgetting functions with different dose levels of scopolamine. Parameter values and variance accounted for are given for each exponential function best fitting the data (data from Kirk, White & McNaughton, 1988).

available from previous studies with pigeons. In the study reported by White (1985, Experiment 2), a house light was introduced into the delay interval with the effect of severely disrupting matching performance. In this experiment, and in White's reanalysis of data from studies where a house light was interpolated in a normally dark delay (Roberts & Grant, 1978) or the feeder was raised in a normally light delay (Jans & Catania, 1980), log d_0 did not change between conditions, whereas the effect of interpolating an interfering event in the delay was to produce a marked increase in the rate of forgetting, b.

Watson and Blampied (1989) administered several doses of chlorpromazine to pigeons trained in delayed matching to sample with six delays from 0 s to 16 s. Small changes in log d_0 were observed for the exponential fits to group data for the different dose-level conditions. In particular, b showed a clear increase, with values of 0.11, 0.16, 0.17, 0.22, 0.22 for dose levels of 0, 0.5, 2.5, 5.0, and 12.5 mg/kg chlorpromazine respectively. Watson and Blampied concluded that the decrease in log d_0 and the increase in b with increasing dose level were both reliable, although their data for individual birds indicate little effect on log d_0 but a consistent effect on b over the first four dose levels. The increase in b is of interest in view of the general learning impairment that is associated with the clinical use of chlorpromazine.

We have found a similar effect on both log d_0 and b of increasing dose levels of another clinically relevant drug, phenobarbital. With behavioral procedures similar to those that have been described (White, 1985) and drug administration procedures similar to those described by Kirk et al. (1988) and Watson and Blampied (1989), we showed a decrease in log d_0 and an increase in b with increasing doses of phenobarbital (Fig. 10.6). Both this result and that reported by Watson and Blampied (1989) for chlorpromazine do not provide strong evidence for the independence of log d_0 and b, because the changes in the parameter values tended to covary. Stronger evidence is provided by an instance where log d_0 does not change but b does. Further evidence for the empirical independence of log d_0 and b comes from our studies of proactive interference.

DISSOCIATION OF log d_0 AND b
IN PROACTIVE INTERFERENCE

Edhouse and White (1988a) identified two independent sources of proactive interference that have separate effects on initial discriminability and rate of forgetting. Intertrial-interval duration influences log d_0 whereas the correspondence of events between consecutive trials affects b. Intertrial correspondence, when the same sample and comparison stimuli are presented on

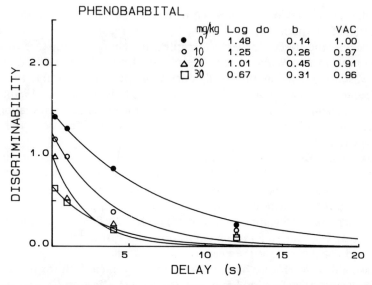

FIG. 10.6 Forgetting functions with different doses of phenobarbital. Data are summed over five pigeons and were obtained by the author and J. E. Watson.

consecutive trials, results in a lower rate of forgetting than when sample stimuli differ between consecutive trials. This result provides further support for the independence of log d_0 and b, in addition to its important implications for theories of memory.

In delayed matching to sample, shorter intertrial intervals result in impaired performance (Maki, Moe, & Bierley, 1977; Roberts & Kraemer, 1982). Further, matching accuracy is lower when the sample on the previous trial, and hence the correct choice on the previous trial, is the incorrect comparison stimulus on the current trial (Grant, 1975; Roberts, 1980). According to both trace strength theory (Roberts & Grant, 1976) and the temporal discrimination hypothesis (D'Amato, 1973), the effects of inter-trial-interval duration and intertrial correspondence are mediated by single mechanisms, trace competition and temporal confusion respectively. Inter-trial correspondence and intertrial-interval duration should therefore interact in their effects on performance. That is, single-process theories predict that the effect of intertrial correspondence should be modulated by the interval between consecutive trials.

White (1985) and Edhouse and White (1988a) fitted exponential functions to log d_t measures for different intertrial intervals and found that log d_0 increased with increasing intertrial interval durations. Values for b changed as well, as shown by the functions plotted in Fig. 10.7 from data reported by Edhouse and White (1988a). In Edhouse and White's procedure, both sample and comparison stimuli were green (538 nm) and yellow (576 nm)

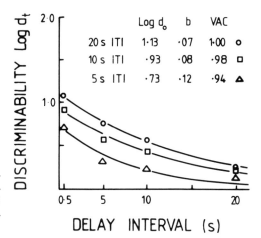

FIG. 10.7 Forgetting functions for conditions with different durations of intertrial interval (ITI) (data from Edhouse & White, 1988a).

wavelengths and delays of .5, 5, 10, and 20 were arranged within each session. The sequence of trials within sessions included consecutive trials where sample stimuli were the same (Sequences I, II) and trials where samples differed (Sequences III, IV). Because the relative left-right position of comparison stimuli on consecutive trials did not influence matching accuracy (Sequence I versus II and Sequence III versus IV), position was disregarded in the analysis. Intertrial intervals were 5, 10, or 20 s in different conditions.

When the intertrial-interval functions in Fig. 10.7 were broken down by type of sequence, or intertrial correspondence, a different pattern emerged as shown in Fig. 10.8 (Edhouse & White, 1988a). The effect of intertrial correspondence is shown as an effect on the rate of forgetting, with values of b for consecutive trials with same samples being about half that for consecutive trials with different samples. That is, the proactive interfering effect of the different sample on the previous trial is to double the rate of forgetting. The intertrial-interval effect is shown as a decrease in log d_0 with decreasing intertrial-interval duration. The independence of the parameters was verified by the absence of significant interactions between intertrial interval and sequence type for either parameter. Thus intertrial-interval duration affects log d_0 whereas intertrial correspondence affects b.

Edhouse and White (1988a, Experiment 2) experimentally separated the effects of intertrial-interval duration on log d_0 and intertrial correspondence on b, by interpolating a house light in the intertrial interval. The result was elimination of the intertrial-interval effect on log d_0, as shown in Fig. 10.9. But as Fig. 10.10 shows, the effect of intertrial correspondence on b persisted, with the rate of forgetting for Sequences III, IV where sample stimuli differed, being about twice that for Sequences I, II where sample stimuli were the same on consecutive trials. According to single-process theories, illuminating the intertrial interval should have disrupted a prior

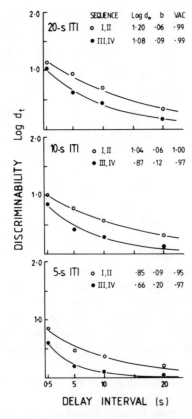

FIG. 10.8 Forgetting functions for 5, 10, and 20-s intertrial intervals, for trials where the sample was the same as the sample on the previous trial (Sequence I, II) and for trials where the sample differed from that on the previous trial (Sequence III, IV) (from Edhouse & White, 1988a).

trace or more clearly differentiated the intertrial interval from other temporal factors, and hence should have attenuated the intertrial correspondence effect. Interestingly, this effect on b persisted, and it was the effect on log d_0 that was eliminated.

These results are consistent with previous conclusions that there may be separate sources of proactive interference (Roberts, 1980; Roitblat, 1983; Roitblat & Scopatz, 1983). They also agree with White's (1985) reanalysis of previous studies of proactive interference in terms of the exponential function, where manipulations involving intertrial separation resulted in changes in log d_0, whereas the introduction of interfering prior-trial events produced changes in b. Together, these results constitute strong evidence against single-process theories of memory. Additionally, they reinforce the independence of log d_0 and b.

Wright, Urcuioli, and Sands (1986) have suggested that proactive interference from conflicting events on previous trials may build up as the events are repeated over a session. Accumulation of proactive interference was examined by Edhouse and White (1988b) using the same general procedure

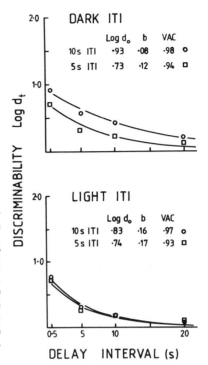

FIG. 10.9 Forgetting functions for conditions with 5-s and 10-s intertrial intervals. The functions in the upper panel are for dark intertrial intervals (same as data in Fig. 10.7). The functions in the lower panel are for otherwise identical conditions with house light interpolated in the intertrial interval (from Edhouse & White, 1988a).

as in the earlier study (Edhouse & White 1988a). In this experiment, delay functions for the different types of intertrial correspondence (Sequences I, II versus Sequences III, IV) were generated for successive quarters of each session. Fig. 10.11 shows the values of parameters for the exponential functions best fitting log d_t measures across delays of 0.5, 5, 10, and 20 s for trial sequences where samples differed (III, IV) or were the same (I, II) for successive quarters of the session. Measures were summed over 24 sessions for five birds and the group functions in Fig. 10.11 were verified by analysis of variance of parameter values for functions fitted to individual data.

Over successive quarters, the different types of sequence did not have a significant effect on log d_0, but did have a significant effect on b. There was an overall higher rate of forgetting on trials where samples differed across consecutive trials. Further, the effect of type of sequence on b changed over successive quarters, as shown by a significant interaction between the effects of sequence and quarter. There was no significant interaction between sequence type and session quarter for log d_0. The proactive interference effect that is manifest as a difference between rates of forgetting for corresponding and disagreeing trial sequences is therefore attenuated as a session progresses, and there is no evidence for an accumulation of proactive interference. Of particular interest to the inde-

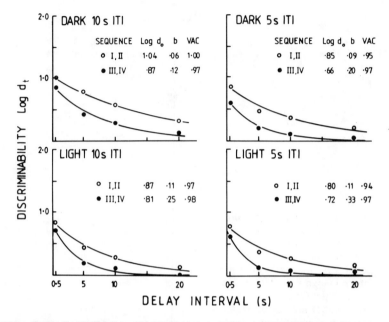

FIG. 10.10. Forgetting functions for 5-s and 10-s intertrial intervals which were dark or light, separated according to intertrial correspondence. In Sequences I and II samples were the same on consecutive trials and in Sequences III and IV samples differed on consecutive trials (from Edhouse & White, 1988a).

pendence of log d_0 and b, however, is the result that the changes in b over successive quarters of the session were unrelated to the changes in log d_0.

CONCLUSION

The evidence that has been presented favors the empirical independence of log d_0 and b. Several instances were described in which log d_0 shows systematic changes without corresponding changes in b. The conditions influencing log d_0 cover a wide range: the disparity, complexity, frequency, duration and repetition of sample stimuli; intertrial-interval duration; scopolamine dose; and ratio requirement for sample-key responding. The wide variety of conditions affecting log d_0 suggests that many of the effects reported for delayed matching-to-sample performance and interpreted in terms of memorial processes may be due to a change in initial discriminability.

Changes in b, particularly where log d_0 remains unchanged, appear to be associated with alteration of the conditions under which choice responses

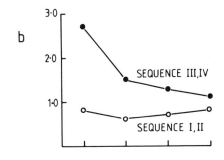

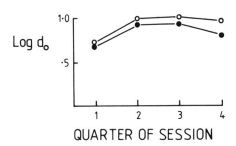

FIG. 10.11. Values of parameters, b and log d_0, for exponential functions fitted to discriminability measures for trials where the sample was the same (Sequence I, II) or different (Sequence III, IV) from that on the previous trial, over successive quarters of the session (data from Edhouse & White, 1988b).

are made to comparison stimuli. The analysis of proactive interference provides particularly strong evidence for the independence of log d_0 and b. Local and general forms of proactive interference, with their separate effects on b and log d_0, were identified. Further, elimination of the general effect on log d_0 as a result of interpolating house light in the intertrial interval, with the local effect on b remaining intact, offered experimental support for the independence of log d_0 and b. The independence of the two characteristics of forgetting functions, initial discriminability and rate of forgetting, is therefore well established.

What are the implications of these results for a psychophysics of remembering? They suggest that a psychophysics of remembering can be conducted in the same way as the psychophysics of discriminating differences between near-threshold and above-threshold stimuli. The present analysis involves a quantification of the effects of stimuli that does not differ in principle from traditional psychophysical analyses. Further, it contributes an additional component to the quantification of stimulus effect, namely, its decrement with increasing temporal distance to the time of remembering or the choice response. It may be that the decrement in stimulus effect over time is not best described by a negative exponential function. For example, the main purpose of the chapter by McCarthy and White (1987) was to compare the fits of exponential and hyperbolic functions with data from a range of studies of memory or delayed detection in human and nonhuman subjects. Across all the studies reviewed or reanalyzed the hyperbolic function accounted for as much data variance as the exponential function, and so it is difficult to decide between them on empirical grounds. In general, the functions fit the data extremely well, although the exponential function tends to underestimate log d_t values at long delays whereas the hyperbolic function underestimates log d_t values at short delays and overestimates log d_t values at long delays. An empirically useful program of future research would identify the general conditions favoring fits by one or other function (cf. White & Bunnell–McKenzie, 1985). However, there is a distinct theoretical advantage of the exponential decrement that follows from the treatment of *remembering as direct:* The psychophysical analysis that applies to the quantification of the effects of proximal stimuli is equally applicable to the quantification of the effects of stimuli at a temporal distance.

REFERENCES

Beatty, W. W., & Bierley, R. A. (1986). Scopolamine impairs encoding and retrieval of spatial working memory in rats. *Physiological Psychology, 14,* 82–86.

D'Amato, M. R. (1973). Delayed matching and short-term memory in monkeys. In G. H. Bower (Ed.), *The psychology of learning and motivation* (Vol. 7, pp. 227–269). New York: Academic Press.

Davison, M., & Jenkins, P. E. (1985). Stimulus discriminability, contingency discriminability, and schedule performance. *Animal Learning and Behavior, 13,* 77–84.

Davison, M. C., & Tustin, R. D. (1978). The relation between the generalized matching law and signal detection theory. *Journal of the Experimental Analysis of Behavior, 29,* 331–336.

Dunnett, S. B. (1985). Comparative effects of cholinergic drugs and lesions of nucleus basalis or fimbria-fornix on delayed matching in rats. *Psychopharmacology, 87,* 357–363.

Edhouse, W. V., & White, K. G. (1988a). Sources of proactive interference in animal memory. *Journal of Experimental Psychology: Animal Behavior Processes, 14,* 56–70.

Edhouse, W. V., & White, K. G. (1988b). Cumulative proactive interference in animal memory. *Animal Learning and Behavior, 16,* 461–467.

Gibson, J. J. (1966). *The senses considered as perceptual systems.* London: Allen & Unwin.

Gibson, J. J. (1979). *The ecological approach to visual perception.* Boston: Houghton Mifflin.

Grant, D. S. (1975). Proactive interference in pigeon short-term memory. *Journal of Experimental Psychology: Animal Behavior Processes, 1,* 207–220.

Green, D. M., & Swets, J. A. (1974). *Signal detection theory and psychophysics.* New York: Krieger.

Jans, J. E., & Catania, A. C. (1980). Short-term remembering of discriminative stimuli in pigeons. *Journal of the Experimental Analysis of Behavior, 34,* 177–183.

Kirk, R. C., White, K. G., & McNaughton, N. (1988). Low dose scopolamine affects discriminability but not rate of forgetting in delayed conditional discrimination. *Psychopharmacology, 96,* 541–546.

Leibrich, J., & White, K. G. (1983). Recognition memory for pictorial events. *Memory and Cognition, 11,* 121–128.

Maki, W. S., Moe, J. C., & Bierley, C. M. (1977). Short term memory for stimuli, responses, and reinforcers. *Journal of Experimental Psychology: Animal Behavior Processes, 3,* 156–177.

McCarthy, D., & White, K. G. (1987). Behavioral models of delayed detection and their application to the study of memory. In M. L. Commons, J. E. Mazur, J. A. Nevin, & H.

Rachlin (Eds.), *Quantitative analyses of behavior: Vol. 5. The effect of delay and of intervening events on reinforcement value.* Hillsdale, NJ: Lawrence Erlbaum Associates.

Nelson, K. R., & Wasserman, E. A. (1978). Temporal factors influencing the pigeon's successive matching-to-sample performance: Sample duration, intertrial interval, and retention interval. *Journal of the Experimental Analysis of Behavior, 30,* 153–162.

Roberts, W. A. (1972). Short-term memory in the pigeon: Effects of repetition and spacing. *Journal of Experimental Psychology, 94,* 74–83.

Roberts, W. A. (1980). Distribution of trials and intertrial retention in delayed matching to sample with pigeons. *Journal of Experimental Psychology: Animal Behavior Processes, 6,* 217–237.

Roberts, W. A., & Grant, D. S. (1976). Studies of short-term memory in the pigeon using the delayed matching to sample procedure. In D. L. Medin, W. A. Roberts, & R. T. Davis (Eds.), *Processes of animal memory* (pp. 79–112). Hillsdale, NJ: Lawrence Erlbaum Associates.

Roberts, W. A., & Grant, D. S. (1978). An analysis of light-induced retroactive inhibition in pigeon short-term memory. *Journal of Experimental Psychology: Animal Behavior Processes, 4,* 219–236.

Roberts, W. A., & Kraemer, P. J. (1982). Some observations of the effects of intertrial interval and delay on delayed matching to sample in pigeons. *Journal of Experimental Psychology: Animal Behavior Processes, 8,* 342–353.

Roitblat, H. L. (1983). Pigeon working memory: Models for delayed matching-to-sample performance. In M. L. Commons, R. J. Herrnstein, & A. R. Wagner (Eds.), *Quantitative analyses of behavior: Vol. 4. Discrimination processes* (pp. 161–181). Cambridge, MA: Ballinger.

Roitblat, H. L., & Scopatz, R. A. (1983). Sequential effects in pigeon delayed matching-to-sample performance. *Journal of Experimental Psychology: Animal Behavior Processes, 9,* 202–221.

Shepard, R. N. (1987). Toward a universal law of generalisation for psychological science. *Science, 237,* 1317–1323.

Simon, H. A. (1966). A note on Jost's law and exponential forgetting. *Psychometrika, 31,* 505–506.

Tulving, E. (1983). *Elements of episodic memory.* Oxford, England: Clarendon Press.

Turvey, M. T. (1974). Perspectives in vision: Conception or perception? In D. O. Duane & M. B. Rawson (Eds.), *Reading, perception and language.* Baltimore: York Press.

Turvey, M. T. (1977). Contrasting orientations to the theory of visual information processing. *Psychological Review, 84,* 67–88.

Watson, J. E., & Blampied, N. M. (1989). Quantification of the effects of chlorpromazine on performance under delayed matching to sample in pigeons. *Journal of the Experimental Analysis of Behavior, 51,* 317–328.

White, K. G. (1985). Characteristics of forgetting functions in delayed matching-to-sample. *Journal of the Experimental Analysis of Behavior, 44,* 15–34.

White, K. G. (1986). Conjoint control of performance on conditional discriminations by successive and simultaneous stimuli. *Journal of the Experimental Analysis of Behavior, 45,* 161–174.

White, K. G., & Bunnell-McKenzie, J. (1985). Potentiation of delayed matching with variable delays. *Animal Learning and Behavior, 13,* 397–402.

White, K. G., & McKenzie, J. (1982). Delayed stimulus control: Recall for single and relational stimuli. *Journal of the Experimental Analysis of Behavior, 38,* 305–312.

Wickelgren, W. A. (1970). Multitrace strength theory. In D. A. Norman (Ed.), *Model of human memory* (pp. 65–102). New York: Academic Press.

Wright, A. A., Urcuioli, P. J., & Sands, S. F. (1986). Proactive interference in animal memory. In D. F. Kendrick, M. E. Rilling, & M. R. Denny (Eds.), *Theories of animal memory.* Hillsdale, NJ: Lawrence Erlbaum Associates.

11 Behavioral Detection Theory: Some Implications for Applied Human Research

Dianne C. McCarthy
University of Auckland

Since its introduction some 25 years or so ago, signal-detection methodology has enjoyed wide application in many areas other than its psychophysical origins. For example, its impact has been felt in such diverse realms as vigilance situations, personality differences, memory, animal learning, clinical psychology, military target detection, weather forecasting, reaction times, subliminal perception, risk taking, medical decision making, and quality control in industry, to name but a few.

The practical advantages of the theoretical independence of its two measures—discriminability and response criterion—have been largely responsible for the popularity of signal-detection theory (SDT) over the years. But nowhere is the importance of its application more apparent than in the assessment of the detection performance of subjects suffering various organic insults (such as closed-head injuries, schizophrenia, and epilepsy). Clearly, some of these insults would be expected to affect only one of these measures; for example, damage to a sense organ would presumably change the discriminability measure but leave the response-criterion measure unchanged. SDT has been applied in these areas but since the necessary independence of the traditional SDT measures has been questioned (McCarthy & Davison, 1984), doubt can be cast on the meaning of the results obtained using these indexes in many applied human areas.

The signal-detection procedure necessarily involves choice between two responses "A" or "B," "Yes" or "No," "Respond" or "Don't respond," or other pairs of well-defined, mutually exclusive, alternatives (Fig. 11.1). Davison and his coworkers have shown how an empirically based quantitative formulation of choice provides a framework into which the effects of

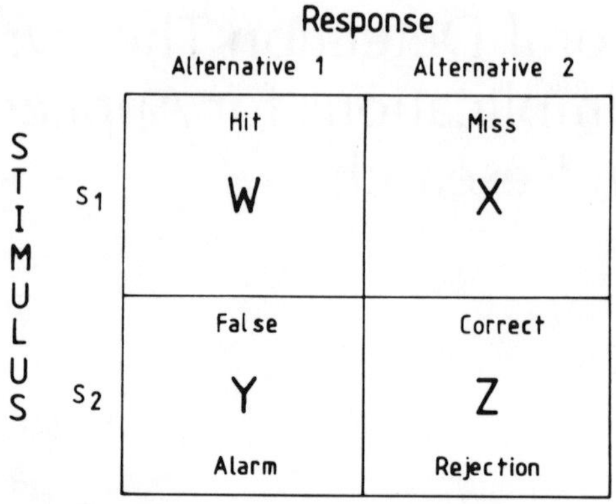

Response

Alternative 1   Alternative 2

Fig. 11.1 Matrix of events in a two-stimulus, two-response, signal-detection procedure with cells W, X, Y, and Z.

discriminative stimuli can be incorporated to generalize the choice formulation to detection experiments. This more recent approach has become known as behavioral detection theory, and it has been empirically shown (using laboratory research with pigeons) to provide reasonably independent measures of stimulus discriminability (or, a subject's ability to tell two stimulus conditions apart) and response bias (or, the tendency of a subject to emit one choice over another). In addition, this new approach makes contact with an extensive animal literature showing that a measure of the sensitivity of choice to its consequences is captured by the exponent of the power function relating behavior to its outcome. Such an index of behavioral sensitivity is not provided by the traditional detection-theory approach.

BEHAVIOR-DETECTION MODEL

The behavioral-detection model has its roots in research on concurrent schedules (Davison & McCarthy, 1988). Specifically, it treats the detection task displayed in Fig. 11.1 as two concurrently available reinforcement-extinction schedules: In the presence of one stimulus (S_1), behavior on Alternative 1 is reinforced while behavior on Alternative 2 is not. In the presence of another stimulus (S_2), behavior on Alternative 2 is reinforced while behavior on Alternative 1 is not. A large empirical literature attests to the fact that behavior on such concurrently available schedules may be adequately described by the generalized matching law (Baum, 1974). Translated to the detection situation (Davison & Tustin, 1978), this law states that the ratio of detection responses in the presence of each discriminative stimulus is a power function of the ratio of reinforcer frequencies obtained for correctly reporting the stimuli, and a function of the extent to which the two stimuli are discriminable. Thus, in the presence of S_1:

$$\log \left(\frac{B_w}{B_x}\right) = a \log \left(\frac{R_w}{R_z}\right) + \log c + \log d, \tag{1}$$

and, in the presence of S_2:

$$\log \left(\frac{B_y}{B_z}\right) = a \log \left(\frac{R_w}{R_z}\right) + \log c - \log d, \tag{2}$$

In these equations, the subscripts w, x, y, and z refer to the cells of the matrix in Fig. 11.1, and B and R denote behavior and obtained reinforcers, respectively. For example, B_w tallies the number of Alternative-1 responses in S_1, and R_z tallies the number of reinforcers obtained from Alternative 2 in S_2. The parameter a measures the sensitivity with which the behavior ratio changes when the obtained reinforcer-frequency ratio changes. If the power is 1.0, the behavior ratio matches the obtained reinforcer ratio (Herrnstein, 1970). Typically, a is about 0.8 in concurrent schedules (Baum, 1979), and lies in the range 0.4 to 0.8 in the detection paradigm (McCarthy & Davison, 1984). Thus, generally, behavior ratios undermatch reinforcer ratios. The parameter $\log c$ measures inherent bias, a constant preference toward responding on Alternative 1 or on Alternative 2, which remains invariant when stimulus differences or the reinforcer ratio are changed. The parameter $\log d$ is a measure of the discriminability of the stimuli. The better the subject can discriminate S_1 from S_2, the larger will be the ratio B_w/B_x, and the smaller will be the ratio B_y/B_z. Because the numerators in both equations are Alternative-1 responses, $\log d$ is positive in Equation 1 and negative in Equation 2.

Equations 1 and 2 can be combined to give independent measures of discriminability and response bias (McCarthy & Davison, 1980). A response-bias-free measure of discriminability is obtained by subtracting Equation 2 from Equation 1, leaving:

$$\log d = .5 \log \left(\frac{B_w \cdot B_z}{B_x \cdot B_y}\right). \tag{3}$$

Adding the two equations, and rearranging, gives:

$$.5 \log \left(\frac{B_w \cdot B_y}{B_x \cdot B_z}\right) = a \log \left(\frac{R_w}{R_z}\right) + \log c. \tag{4}$$

The measure on the left side of Equation 4 is called *response bias* (termed log *b* hereafter), and it has been shown to be independent of stimulus discriminability under a number of different experimental procedures (McCarthy & Davison, 1980, 1981, 1984; but see Alsop, this volume, for evidence of systematic interdependence). The expression on the right of Equation 4 specifies two sources of bias: One source is inherent bias (log *c*) as has been discussed. The other source is reinforcer bias, log (R_w/R_z), or here, the bias caused by changes in the obtained reinforcer-frequency ratio. Reinforcer bias can arise, for example, by scheduling different numbers of reinforcers for Alternative-1 and Alternative-2 responses. (Equally, reinforcer bias could arise by arranging different durations of reinforcement, different delays to reinforcement, etc.).

Variations in the frequency with which the stimuli are presented in a detection task can also be captured by the reinforcer-bias term. As McCarthy and Davison (1979, 1984) have shown, the bias produced by such a manipulation occurs because, in the typical detection procedure in which each correct detection is reinforced and obtained reinforcer ratios are uncontrolled, changes in the stimulus-presentation ratio (SPR) produce concomitant changes in the obtained reinforcer-frequency ratio. Thus, with reference to Fig. 11.1, if S_1 is presented on 80% of the trials, the subject would obtain approximately 80% of the total reinforcers from Alternative 1. It is these changes in reinforcer frequency that bias detection performance, and not changes in SPR per se.

Estimates of the *sensitivity* with which detection performance changes with biasing manipulations may be obtained from Equation 4. Specifically, assuming no inherent bias (log *c* = 0), a point estimate of *a*, for any given bias, may be computed by dividing the obtained bias (left-hand expression of Equation 4) by the arranged bias, that is, by the obtained reinforcer ratio or, alternately, by the obtained stimulus-presentation ratio (right-hand expression of Equation 4).

This chapter focuses on a selection of applied human research areas in which detection data are available for reanalysis within the behavioral framework. Generally, the aim is to explore ways in which laboratory-based detection work in the Experimental Analysis of Behavior could find human application. More specifically, the aim was to obtain estimates of *a*, the sensitivity of detection performance to its environmental consequences, and to investigate what use this measure might be in applied human research.

[In all analyses presented here, it was assumed that because reinforcer ratios were uncontrolled (McCarthy & Davison, 1984), the obtained reinforcer ratio covaried with SPR. Since the studies reviewed specify SPR but do not give obtained reinforcer ratios, log SPR was used in place of log R_w/R_z in Equation 4 to compute estimates of *a*.]

The impetus for this work was provided by a human concurrent-schedule analysis comparing a values between Korsakoff's patients and their matched controls (Oscar–Berman, Heyman, Bonner, & Ryder, 1980). This research showed that the behavior of Korsakoff patients, working on standard concurrent schedules, was less sensitive to changes in reinforcer frequency ($a = 0.03$) than was the behavior of their matched controls ($a = 0.38$). Despite the fact that the normal subjects in this study showed less than typical sensitivity values, these results suggest that the sensitivity parameter may indeed reveal interesting group differences in detection studies— differences that are not captured by the traditional discriminability and response-bias measures.

Clearly, my coverage will be limited by the availability of published data for reanalysis, but I shall look at behavioral sensitivity as a function of concussion, hypoxia, age, sleep deprivation, epilepsy, and blood-lead levels. It is important to note at the outset, however, that in all reanalyses presented here, sensitivity values were not of interest when the studies were carried out, and hence parametric estimates of a are not available. Rather, point estimates only are presented, and these were obtained using Equation 4, and assuming no inherent bias. Thus, *absolute* values of a are probably not very meaningful, but the relation between a values *within* a particular study (e.g., across different subject groups) certainly is meaningful. In addition, measures of discriminability were calculated using Equation 3, and these will be examined for group differences. Unfortunately, no statistical analyses are possible, due largely to the fact that (a) in many cases, individual-subject data were not available, and (b) when they were available, the occurrence of zeros in the error cells of the matrix in Fig. 11.1—the result of high discriminability—produced many infinite behavior ratios. Hence, any group differences evident here will be discussed qualitatively rather than quantitatively.

STUDIES: HEAD-INJURED

The first study presented here (McCarthy, 1977) compared the vigilance performance of 12 young, mildly concussed adults (17–27 years old) with that of their matched, nonhead-injured controls. [Note: Mild concussion is characterized by a posttraumatic amnesia (PTA) period of less than 1 hour, and is defined as the interval between injury and return of continuous memory. (Gronwall & Sampson, 1974)]. Control subjects were matched with concussed subjects for age, sex and occupation (provided they had no previous history of concussion).

The 30-minute auditory task consisted of a random series of digits (1 to 9) separated by two different interstimulus intervals (ISI) which constituted the stimuli to be discriminated. The shorter ISI was of 6-s duration while the longer, or "target," ISI was 9-s. The entire recording was composed of 56 target ISIs and 206 short ISIs (hence, the logarithm of the arranged stimulus-presentation ratio = -.57). The subjects were instructed to detect the target ISI, and to report their detection by repeating the digit immediately following the longer ISI. Verbal reinforcement followed each correct detection of the target ISI.

All concussed subjects were tested within 24 hr of injury (provided they were completely oriented in time and space and were fully out of PTA), and again 4 to 6 weeks later. The control subjects were likewise tested twice, in sessions approximately 4 to 6 weeks apart.

Fig. 11.2 shows point estimates of stimulus discriminability (log d), obtained using Equation 3, as a function of time on the task for the groups on both test (T) and retest (R) occasions. These data were averaged across all 12 subjects in each group. For the control subjects, high levels of discriminability were maintained across time on the task, and on both test occasions (mean overall log d = 1.50). Further, there appears to be no difference in discriminability between the two test occasions. By comparison, the concussed group was less able to detect the target ISI than was the control group when tested within 24 hr of injury (mean log d concussed on Test occasion = 0.89). When retested 4 to 6 weeks later, the discriminability of the concussion group had improved (mean log d = 1.24), but not to the level shown by the control group. This latter finding is consistent with McCarthy (1977), among others, who concluded that even a mild concussion may produce some "residual" deficit.

The performance of both groups was then compared with that of a group of elderly subjects who were exposed to the same auditory task on two test occasions spaced 4 to 6 weeks apart. The elderly group comprised residents of an old people's home, age between 70 and 80. Fig. 11.3 shows their data superimposed on those shown in Fig. 11.2 for the control and concussion groups. The striking finding was that the discriminability levels of young, mildly concussed adults tested within 24 hr of injury (mean log d = 0.89)

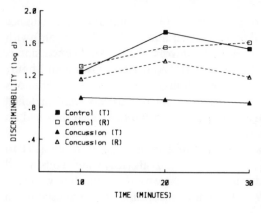

Fig. 11.2 Stimulus discriminability (log d) as a function of time on the vigilance task for both control and concussion groups on both test (T) and retest (R) occasions (from McCarthy, 1977).

were no different from those of the elderly group (mean log d = 0.81). Consistent with McCarthy's (1977) conclusion, then, these data suggest that, during the acute stages of head injury, the young, mildly concussed subjects are discriminating no better than the elderly subjects.

Interestingly, overall there appeared to be no decrement in discriminability over time on the task—contrary to the results of many vigilance-type studies. Cahoon (1970), for example, examined the vigilance performance of young male subjects on a 2-hr brightness discrimination task under hypoxia, and found a significant decrement in signal detectability as a function of task duration. However, the task used in McCarthy's (1977) study was relatively short compared with the usual vigilance tasks (i.e., 30 min as opposed to 2-hr or more). A shorter task was necessary here as it is not realistic to expect recently head-injured subjects to undergo a long test session. In addition, the task proved to be fairly easy, as shown by the generally high levels of discriminability. What is interesting, however, is that such an easy task still produced very clear group discriminability differences.

The *sensitivity* of each group's behavior to the arranged biaser, namely, the frequency with which the target ISI was presented, was measured using Equation 4; that is, dividing the obtained bias by the arranged bias (i.e., log SPR), and assuming no inherent bias. Fig. 11.4 shows point estimates of sensitivity (a) as a function of time on the task for the control and concussion groups on both test and retest occasions. Several findings are apparent: First, the behavioral sensitivity of the control group to the constant biaser was higher at retest than at test, and on both test and retest occasions, it increased as a function of task duration. Second, the behavioral sensitivity shown by the concussion group at test was generally lower than that shown by the control group, but it did increase from test to retest to be at a level similar to that of the control group, at least during the first 20 min on task at retest. However, during the last 10 min, the behavioral sensitivity of the concussed subjects decreased. Consistent with the conclusion drawn from Fig. 11.2, then, some "residual" deficit is still apparent even 4 to 6 weeks after sustaining a mild head injury.

Fig. 11.5 shows the sensitivity values for the elderly group superimposed on those shown in Fig 11.4 for the control and concussion groups. Consistent with the discriminability data shown in Fig. 11.3, the behavioral sensitivity of young, mildly concussed subjects within 24 hr of injury appears to be no different from that of the elderly, and further, low sensitivities are shown by both these groups (a = .40 and .33, respectively).

In a further study examining closed-head injuries (Ewing, McCarthy, Gronwall & Wrightson, 1980), 10 university students (mean age = 22.9 years) who had been concussed 1 to 3 years previously, and whose performance on tests of intellectual function had returned to normal, were

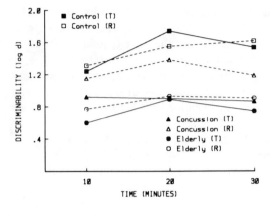

Fig. 11.3 Stimulus discriminability (log d) as a function of time on the vigilance task for control, concussion, and elderly groups on both test (T) and retest (R) occasions (from McCarthy, 1977).

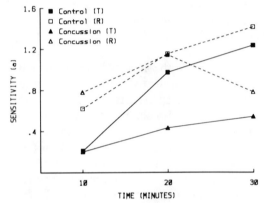

Fig. 11.4 Sensitivity (a) as a function of time on the vigilance task for both control and concussion groups on both test (T) and retest (R) occasions (from McCarthy, 1977).

exposed to mild hypoxia produced by a simulated altitude of 3,800 mm (12,500 ft) in an hypobaric chamber. The hypothesis was that such subjects would again show some of the changes seen in the acute stage of concussion when exposed to stress other than a further head injury. Such an effect would argue for a persisting effect of concussion (Gronwall & Wrightson, 1975). The control group comprised 10 university students who had not been concussed, each matched with one of the head-injury group for age, sex, and academic achievement (mean age = 21.9 years). Both groups received the same vigilance task as was used by McCarthy (1977).

The mean percentage P_AO_2 (alveolar oxygen level) values were calculated (Ewing et al., 1980) for each group at ground level and at altitude (using a Haldane–Priestley alveolar gas-sampling tube). There was no significant difference in percentage P_AO_2 between the two groups, either at ground level or at altitude. There was, however, a significant difference in percentage P_AO_2 between ground level and altitude for both groups. At ground level, mean percentage P_AO_2 for the concussion group was 14.55

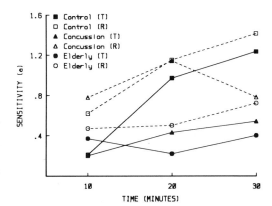

Fig. 11.5 Sensitivity (*a*) as a function of time on the vigilance task for control, concussion, and elderly groups on both test (T) and retest (R) occasions (from McCarthy, 1977).

and that for the control group was 15.60. At altitude, these values were 7.48 and 7.64, respectively.

Fig. 11.6 shows discriminability (log *d*) as a function of time on the task for both the hypoxic-concussion and the hypoxic-control group. Clearly, there was no consistent change in log *d* over time for either group. High levels of discriminability were maintained by both groups as task duration increased, but the hypoxic-concussion group's levels were slightly lower than those of the hypoxic-control group (Mean log *d* = 0.88 and 1.02, respectively).

Fig. 11.7 shows sensitivity (*a*) values as a function of time on the task for both groups. Clearly, sensitivity differences exist between hypoxic, head-injured subjects and their matched, hypoxic controls. While sensitivity values were similar for both groups after 10 min on the task, the sensitivity of the control subjects increased to 0.65 while that of the concussed group decreased to 0.16 over the remaining 20 min of the task.

A comparison of these sensitivity values (Fig. 11.7) with those shown in

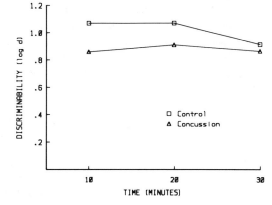

Fig. 11.6 Stimulus discriminability (log *d*) as a function of time on the vigilance task at altitude for both control and concussion groups (from Ewing, McCarthy, Gronwall, & Wrightson, 1980).

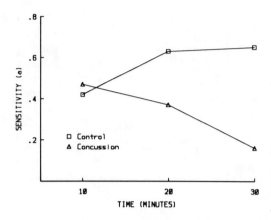

Fig. 11.7 Sensitivity (a) as a function of time on the vigilance task at altitude for both control and concussion groups (from Ewing, Mc-Carthy, Gronwall, & Wrightson, 1980).

Fig. 11.5 for the McCarthy (1977) study reveals some interesting points: First, the sensitivity levels of the concussed group at altitude (mean $a =$ 0.33) were very similar to those shown (in Fig. 11.5) by (a) concussed subjects during the acute stage of injury (mean $a = 0.39$), and (b) elderly subjects on test occasion (mean $a = 0.33$). Second, in neither study did the sensitivity levels of the concussed groups show the increase seen for the control groups as task duration increased. Third, the controls at altitude (i.e., hypoxic) were somewhat less sensitive than the controls at ground level (Ranges .42 to .65 and .41 to 1.32, respectively, across the 30-min task).

In summary, then, it would appear that for concussion, hypoxia, and aging, at least, behavioral sensitivity (a) is a variable that appears to change with various organic insults, and to provide fairly conclusive group differences (although, again, it should be noted that no statistical analyses were carried out).

Results such as those shown here could undoubtedly have important and far-reaching consequences for the treatment of and/or rehabilitation of such individuals. If sensitivity to environmental contingencies is a variable that frequently changes with organic insults, this result will force a reconsideration of some currently accepted and widely utilized therapeutic techniques (for example, those typically designed only to improve sensory deficits). Clearly, such rehabilitation programs should also be focusing on modifying in some way the sensitivity parameter. This is currently not done.

STUDIES: SLEEP DEPRIVATION

A quite different type of "organic insult," with resultant behavioral effects, is that produced by a lack of sleep. Recently, some very interesting articles on the effect of sleep deprivation on SDT measures have appeared in the literature. Here, I shall reanalyze, within the behavioral-detection frame-work, the data from two such studies.

The first was reported by Horne, Anderson, and Wilkinson (1983). Eight mentally and physically healthy young (21–26 years) graduate students underwent a vigilance task during both sleep-deprivation and nonsleep-deprivation (control) conditions. Auditory signals were presented at a rate of 30 per min for a total of 30 min. An average of 22.5 of these signals per min were of 0.5-s duration, and were designated "background" signals. Randomly interspersed between these were "target" signals of just percep-tibly shorter duration (0.45 s), presented at a rate averaging 7.5/min. The arranged biaser (logarithm of the stimulus-presentation ratio) was thus -0.6. Subjects were required to report the target signal by depressing a console key. They were given no feedback, but were encouraged to do their best.

Fig. 11.8 shows point estimates of discriminability (log d) as a function of clock time under both sleep-deprivation and control conditions. Under control conditions, discriminability remained high and constant (mean log d over 6 test occasions = 1.57). During sleep-deprivation conditions, however, log d decreased during night-time hours. But, during daytime hours, while it remained fairly constant, it was nevertheless lower than under control conditions, and appeared to decrease systematically as testing progressed.

Fig. 11.9 shows estimates of sensitivity (a) as a function of clock time. The controls on Day 1 clearly exhibited a bias that was more extreme than that arranged; hence, a was greater than unity (overmatching). On Day 2 the obtained bias was consistent with the arranged bias ($a = 1.0$, matching). Under sleep-deprivation conditions, however, response bias became in-creasingly more negative (i.e., a bias toward reporting no signal) as clock time increased. Hence, while a sensitivity of approximately 0.8 was obtained at the start of sleep deprivation, this sensitivity value gradually increased (signifying a relative decrease in the tendency to report signals)

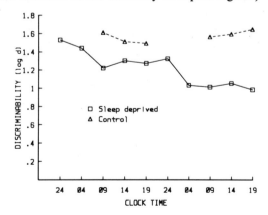

Fig. 11.8 Discriminability (log d) as a function of clock time under both control and sleep-deprivation conditions (from Horne, Anderson, & Wilkinson, 1983).

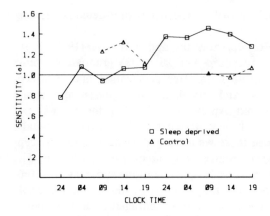

Fig. 11.9 Sensitivity (a) as a function of clock time under both control and sleep-deprivation conditions (from Horne, Anderson, & Wilkinson, 1983).

over the next 2 days so that there was reliable overmatching on Day 2. It is noted parenthetically here that a comparison of the data shown in Figs. 11.8 and 11.9 is suggestive of the systematic interdependence of a and log d reported by Alsop (this volume).

The second sleep-deprivation study was reported by Deaton, Tobias, and Wilkinson (1971). Here, 12 males (aged between 19 and 25) performed a vigilance task once after a night's sleep and once after a night without sleep. Each test lasted 30 min, during which time the subjects heard 0.5-s tones, well above threshold, at 2-s intervals against a background of moderate white noise. The task was to detect tones that were slightly shorter than the rest. These "signals" occurred at random intervals on average, one out of every four tones (stimulus-presentation probability = 0.25). Subjects reported these signals by pressing a console key. They were given knowledge of results (signals detected and false reports) following each test, but no trial-by-trial feedback.

Table 11.1 shows point estimates of discriminability, response bias, and sensitivity under both control (no sleep deprivation) and sleep-deprivation conditions. Consistent with the reanalysis of Horne et al. (1983) presented

TABLE 11.1
Point Estimates of Discriminability (log d), Response Bias (log b), and Sensitivity (a)[1]

	log d	log b	a
Control	0.81	− 0.51	1.06
Sleep-deprived	0.70	− 0.60	1.25
Control (I)	0.84	− 0.41	0.68
Control (II)	0.80	− 0.59	0.98

[1]Under control and sleep-deprived conditions, and for control subjects during the first (I) and second half (II) of a vigilance task (from Deaton, Tobias, and Wilkinson, 1971).

earlier, discriminability was lower and response bias slightly more extreme during sleep deprivation than under control conditions: Sensitivities were 1.06 and 1.25, respectively, for control and sleep deprivation. This difference was in a direction opposite to that seen after Night 1 in the Horne et al. study (mean $a = 1.22$ and 1.02, respectively, for control and sleep deprivation), but similar to that seen after Night 2 in the Horne et al. study (mean $a = 1.01$ and 1.37, respectively).

Table 11.1 also shows estimates of discriminability, response bias, and a for the first and second 15-min halves of the vigilance task under normal conditions only. There is clearly no change in discriminability (log d), but response bias is more extreme, and hence a is higher, in the second half of the test than during the first ($a = .68$ and .98, respectively, for I and II). Interestingly, Deaton et al. reported *no* criterion changes when criterion was measured using the typical likelihood-ratio index, β.

Thus, sleep deprivation, like concussion, hypoxia, and aging appears to have some effect on the behavioral-sensitivity parameter.

STUDIES : SUSTAINED ATTENTION

Perhaps one of the most widely used tasks in human applied research is the Continuous Performance Task (CPT). Originally, the CPT was designed as an index of sustained attention to assess children with brain damage (Rosvold, Mirsky, Samson, Bransome, & Beck, 1956). More recently, it has been used with young children to assess, for example, sustained attention in those at risk for schizophrenia (e.g., Rutschmann, Cornblatt, & Erlenmeyer–Kimling, 1977); specific learning disabilities (e.g., Beale, Matthew, Oliver, & Corballis, 1987; Swanson, 1981, 1983); effects of elevated blood-lead levels (e.g., Watson, 1983); and effects of phenytoin concentration in epileptic children (du Villier, 1984).

The task typically involves the presentation of a random series of visual or auditory stimuli at a fixed and rapid rate (about one every 1 to 1.5 s). Exposure times are brief, often in the 100 to 200 ms range. The child's task is to monitor these stimuli and respond whenever a predesignated target stimulus or sequence of stimuli appears. Thus, the CPT can be viewed as a signal-detection task in which the subject is required to decide, on the basis of the information he or she receives, whether or not the "target" appeared on any given trial.

For example, Watson (1983) assessed the effects of high (> 30 μg/100 ml) and low (< 15 μg/100 ml) blood-lead levels on the CPT performance of young children aged between 4 and 7. Here, the target stimulus (S_1) was the Letter X and a range of other letters of the alphabet made up the S_2 distribution. The subjects were required to button press whenever they detected an X on a computer screen, and to withhold button pressing whenever any other letter was presented. A total of 408 letters was presented in 10-min. The letters shown were: 34 each of T, Z, W, Y, S, M, O, Z, and A, 33 each of B and P, and 36 Xs (i.e., log SPR = -1.014). Stimulus presentation was random, and each letter was displayed for 0.5 s with an interval of 1.0 s between letters. For every lever press emitted given that an X had been presented ("Hit"), the word "correct" was flashed immediately onto the screen in the 1.0-s interval before the next letter appeared. There were no outcomes for false alarms, misses, and correct rejections.

Table 11.2 shows point estimates of discriminability, response bias, and sensitivity (*a*) to the arranged stimulus-presentation probability for the high and low lead-level groups. Clearly, there was no significant difference between the two groups on any of these measures. Despite the fact that no group differences emerged, the performance of both groups was moderately sensitive to its outcome (mean *a* = 0.63 and 0.64, respectively, for the high and low lead-level groups).

Du Villier (1984) used a version of the CPT (similar to that used by Watson, 1983) to investigate the effects of phenytoin concentration on the performance of two types of epileptic children and adolescents relative to the CPT performance of their matched controls. The subjects were aged between 5 and 16 and were matched for age, sex, IQ, and the socioeconomic status of their parents. The subjects were divided into a Generalized-Epilepsy Group (i.e., seizures characterized by EEG patterns that were bilateral, grossly synchronous, and symmetrical over both hemispheres), a Partial-Epilepsy Group (i.e., those suffering from partial seizures or seizures beginning locally and confined to part of a single hemisphere), and a nonepileptic Control Group.

The epileptic children were all on phenytoin maintenance therapy, and thus could be further divided according to their salivary concentrations of phenytoin: High salivary concentrations of phenytoin fell in the range of 5 or more μm/1; Low salivary concentrations of phenytoin fell in the range of 0 - 3 μm/1. Thus, those children with high salivary concentrations fell in the therapeutic range while those with low salivary concentrations fell in the subtherapeutic range.

TABLE 11.2
Point Estimates of Stimulus Discriminability (log *d*), Response Bias (log *b*),
and Sensitivity (*a*)[1]

	log d	(SD)	log b	(SD)	a	(SD)
High	1.18	(.49)	− 0.64	(.28)	0.63	(.28)
Low	1.19	(.46)	− 0.65	(.34)	0.64	(.33)

[1]Standard deviations (SD) are in parentheses, for 2 groups of children showing either high or low blood levels of lead (from Watson, 1983).

Like Watson's (1983) study, du Villier's (1984) task required the simple response of pressing a button whenever the target stimulus X appeared on a computer screen. All letters were displayed for 0.4 s with a 2.0 s interval between letters. Unlike Watson's study, however, du Villier used two versions of the CPT — one with the target letter X occurring in the ratio of 12:1 to other letters (log SPR = 1.08); the other with X occurring in the ratio of 1:12 to other letters (log SPR = -1.08).

Statistical analyses reported by du Villier (1984) showed no significant differences between the performance of the two epileptic groups and the control group. However, when the epileptic groups were further subdivided according to salivary concentrations of phenytoin, interesting behavioral-sensitivity differences emerged (these were not, of course, reported by du Villier).

Table 11.3 shows line estimates of sensitivity for each group. Interestingly, when *both* epileptic groups were receiving *therapeutic* doses of phenytoin, their sensitivity values (*a* = 0.4 and 0.5, respectively, for the partial- and generalized-epileptic groups) were similar to the behavioral sensitivity of the control group (*a* = 0.42). However, both partially and generalized epileptic subjects receiving *sub*therapeutic levels of phenytoin displayed *a* values not only lower than those of their respective epileptic groups, but also lower than their matched peers (*a* = .22 and .32, respectively, for partially and generalized epileptic children with low salivary concentrations of phenytoin). No differences between the groups were observed for the discriminability measure (log *d* = .94, .92, and 1.01, respectively, for the control, partially and generalized epilepsy groups).

CONCLUSIONS

The reanalyses presented here suggest that the sensitivity parameter afforded by behavioral-detection approaches may have wide use in applied

TABLE 11.3
Point Estimates of Sensitivity (a) for the Control Group and the Partial- and Generalized-epileptic Groups

Group		a
Control		0.42
Partial	High	0.40
	Low	0.22
Generalized	High	0.50
	Low	0.32

[1]The 2 epileptic groups were subdivided according to whether they were receiving therapeutic (High) or subtherapeutic (Low) doses of phenytoin (from du Villier, 1984).

human research as a measure of the behavioral effects of many types of organic insult. In particular, it has been shown qualitatively that sensitivity of behavior to its consequences is lowered by aging, concussion, hypoxia, and epilepsy. By contrast, sleep-deprived adults showed raised sensitivity values compared with their matched controls.

These conclusions must be accepted with caution, however, because the research sampled in this chapter suffers from (a) a lack of clearly defined outcomes for the behavior under study, and (b) no parametric variation of reinforcer frequency. Hence, as noted earlier, only point estimates of the behavioral-sensitivity measure could be calculated. If applied researchers were to become more rigorous in their specification and manipulation of reinforcer variables, *parametric* estimates of behavioral sensitivity could then be obtained. They have the potential to provide useful and powerful diagnostic tools in many clinical areas by providing measures of the sensitivity of behavior to its consequences independently of measures of the sensitivity of behavior to antecedent stimuli (i.e., discriminability). Clearly, this is an exciting new extension of laboratory-based animal research to the applied human domain.

ACKNOWLEDGMENTS

I am indebted to Michael Davison and Brent Alsop for their insightful commentary and unfailing support during the preparation of this chapter. In addition, I am very grateful to Philip Voss and Jacqui Barrett, who spent a large part of their summer vacation esconced in the library searching the literature for data suitable for reanalysis. Requests for reprints may be sent to Dianne C. McCarthy, Department of Psychology, University of Auckland, Private Bag, Auckland, New Zealand.

REFERENCES

Baum, W. M. (1974). On two types of deviation from the matching law: Bias and undermatching. *Journal of the Experimental Analysis of Behavior, 22,* 231–242.

Baum, W. M. (1979). Matching, undermatching, and overmatching in studies of choice. *Journal of the Experimental Analysis of Behavior, 32,* 269–281.

Beale, I.L., Matthew, P.J., Oliver, S., & Corballis, M.C. (1987). Performance of disabled and normal readers on the continuous performance test. *Journal of Abnormal Child Psychology, 15,* 229–238.

Cahoon, R.L. (1970). Vigilance performance under hypoxia. *Journal of Applied Psychology, 54,* 479–483.

Davison, M., & McCarthy, D. (1988). *The matching law: A research review.* Hillsdale, NJ: Lawrence Erlbaum Associates.

Davison, M.C., & Tustin, R.D. (1978). The relation between the generalized matching law and signal-detection theory. *Journal of the Experimental Analysis of Behavior, 29,* 331–336.

Deaton, M., Tobias, J.S., & Wilkinson, R.T. (1971). The effect of sleep deprivation on signal detection parameters. *Quarterly Journal of Experimental Psychology, 23,* 449–452.

du Villier, P. (1984). *Epilepsy and attention.* Unpublished master's thesis, Auckland University, New Zealand.

Ewing, R., McCarthy, D., Gronwall, D., & Wrightson, P. (1980). Persisting effects of minor head injury observable during hypoxic stress. *Journal of Clinical Neuropsychology, 2,* 147–155.

Gronwall, D., & Sampson, H. (1974). *The psychological effects of concussion.* Auckland, New Zealand: Oxford University Press.

Gronwall, D., & Wrightson, P. (1975). Cumulative effects of concussion. *Lancet, ii,* 995–997.

Herrnstein, R.J. (1970). On the law of effect. *Journal of the Experimental Analysis of Behavior, 13,* 243–266.

Horne, J.A., Anderson, N.R., & Wilkinson, R.T. (1983). Effects of sleep deprivation on signal detection measures of vigilance: Implications for sleep function. *Sleep, 6,* 347–358.

McCarthy, D. (1977). *Memory and vigilance after concussion.* Unpublished master's thesis, Auckland University, New Zealand.

McCarthy, D., & Davison, M. (1979). Signal probability, reinforcement, and signal detection. *Journal of the Experimental Analysis of Behavior, 32,* 373–386.

McCarthy, D., & Davison, M. (1980). Independence of sensitivity to relative reinforcement rate and discriminability in signal detection. *Journal of the Experimental Analysis of Behavior, 34,* 273–284.

McCarthy, D., & Davison, M. (1981). Matching and signal detection. In M.L. Commons & J.A. Nevin (Eds.), *Quantitative analyses of behavior, Vol. 1. Discriminative properties of reinforcement schedules* (pp. 393–417). Cambridge, MA: Ballinger.

McCarthy, D., & Davison, M. (1984). Isobias and alloiobias functions in animal psychophysics. *Journal of Experimental Psychology: Animal Behavior Processes, 10,* 390–409.

Oscar–Berman, M., Heyman, G.M., Bonner, R.T., & Ryder, J. (1980). Human neuropsychology: Some differences between Korsakoff and normal operant performance. *Psychological Research, 41,* 235–247.

Rosvold, A., Mirksy, A., Samson, I., Bransome, E., & Beck, L. (1956). A continuous performance test of brain damage. *Journal of Consulting Psychology, 20,* 243–350.

Rutschmann, J., Cornblatt, B., & Erlenmeyer–Kimling, L. (1977). Sustained attention in children at risk for schizophrenia. Report on a continuous performance test. *Archives of General Psychiatry, 34,* 571–575.

Swanson, H.L. (1981). Vigilance deficit in learning-disabled children: A signal detection analysis. *Journal of Child Psychology and Psychiatry, 22,* 393–399.

Swanson, H.L. (1983). A developmental study of vigilance in learning-disabled and nondisabled children. *Journal of Abnormal Child Psychology, 11,* 415–429.

Watson, S. (1983). *An investigation of impulsivity as a consequence of lead ingestion in children.* Unpublished research topic, Auckland University, New Zealand.

12 Signal-Detection Analysis of Illusions and Heuristics

John A. Nevin
University of New Hampshire

In the fall of 1959, Bill McGill introduced me to the theory of signal detection in a first-year graduate course at Columbia. I was hooked at once, and the hook is still holding firm. In my current version of McGill's course, I teach the classical theory, its fundamental challenge to the concept of threshold, and some of its elegant applications to vision and psychoacoustics, as well as recent behavioral versions of detection theory (e.g., Davison & Tustin, 1978). But what I really try to convey is something more general, which I will call here the signal-detection approach to quantitative behavior analysis. In its broadest terms, the signal-detection approach is concerned with the analysis of choice between discriminated operants—responses under the joint control of stimuli and consequences (Skinner, 1969; for a discussion in relation to signal detection, see Nevin, Jenkins, Whittaker, & Yarensky, 1982). The analysis involves separating the discriminative effects of the stimuli from the biasing effects of the consequences, each of which can be shown to be invariant with respect to variations in the other (see, e.g., Nevin, 1984). As such, it is a model of scientific analysis, and it has the further advantage of unifying two areas of behavioral research—stimulus control and reinforcement—that, although related, have long differed in their methods of analysis and styles of theory.

A coherent account of behavior that treats the effects of stimuli and reinforcers in common terms would be a major advance. Some steps in that direction appear in Vol. 1 of this series (McCarthy & Davison, 1981; Nevin, 1981); some more recent advances are explored by Davison and Jenkins (1985) and by Alsop and Davison (this volume). But that is not my topic here. Instead, this chapter will explore some promising extensions of the signal-detection approach to new domains in experimental psychology.

Initially, the signal-detection approach was applied to threshold problems in sensory psychology (Tanner & Swets, 1954). Traditional threshold studies presented signals of varying intensity on every trial, and the observer responded "Yes" (meaning that the signal was detected) or "No" (meaning that it was not detected) after each presentation. But since the signal occurred on every trial, a "Yes" response would always be correct, regardless of signal intensity. To deal with that problem, experimenters introduced occasional "catch trials" on which signals were absent, and treated false positives — saying "Yes" on catch trials — as guesses. The data could then be corrected for guessing. False negatives — saying "No" when the signal was actually present — were treated differently, as indicators that the signal was indeed below threshold. One of the principal contributions of signal-detection theory was to suggest that false positives and false negatives arose not from separate processes — guessing vs. true responses to subthreshold stimuli — but from a single decision process based on a continuum of sensory information with inherent variability, and a response criterion that could be influenced by nonsensory variables. Instead of trying to estimate a sensory threshold, signal-detection analyses attempt to separate stimulus variables that affect sensory information from nonsensory variables that affect the response criterion. To do this, both false positives and false negatives must be measured with equal accuracy.

The well-known Yes-No signal-detection paradigm assigns equal importance to all four possible responses: "Yes" given a signal or its absence, and "No" given a signal or its absence. These four outcomes are conveniently arrayed in the conventional 2 × 2 matrix exemplified in Fig. 12.1. Signal and nonsignal presentations are designated S_1 and S_2, and the two responses — "Yes" and "No" — are designated B_1 and B_2. The cells of the matrix are given their conventional names, and are designated w, x, y, and z for notational convenience. Plusses and minuses indicate the conventionally defined correct and incorrect responses, where correct responses are followed by feedback or payoffs, and errors are followed by different feedback, penalties, or no consequence. The paradigm generalizes naturally to cases with more complex stimuli that belong to one of two classes (e.g., presence vs. absence of a lesion in an x ray; Swensson, 1987). Within each class, there may be considerable variation in the stimuli from one trial to another, even in purely "sensory" experiments, because of random noise or quantum fluctuations (cf. McGill & Teich, this volume); but on each trial, the experimenter knows to which class the stimulus belongs, and therefore knows whether the response is "correct," as defined by the payoff matrix. Correctness does not, however, imply equal treatment. Payoffs and costs can be arranged differentially to produce explicit biases favoring one

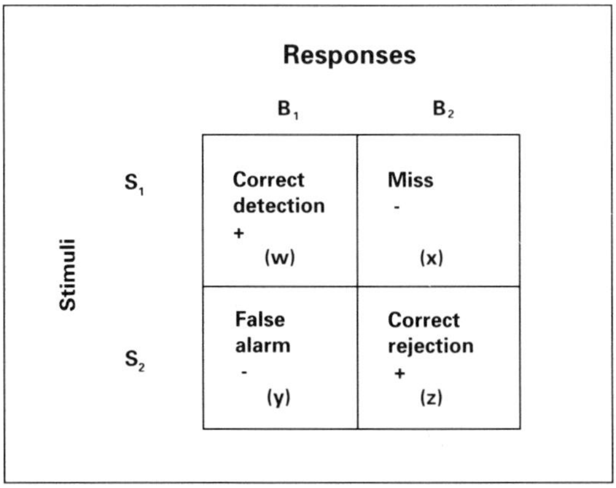

Responses

		B₁	B₂
Stimuli	S₁	Correct detection + (w)	Miss - (x)
	S₂	False alarm - (y)	Correct rejection + (z)

Fig. 12.1   The matrix of stimulus presentations and response alternatives in the Yes-No signal-detection paradigm, with standard nomenclature and present notation for each cell.

response or the other, and can be varied to trace out the well-known isosensitivity or ROC curve that has come to be a standard feature of detection analyses.

Given the empirical probabilities of correct detections and false reports, plus an appropriate model of the detection process, separate estimates of discrimination between the two stimulus classes and bias toward one or the other response are readily derived. Two principal sorts of models have been employed in detection analyses. By far the more common is given by the classical theory of signal detection (Green & Swets, 1966), which assumes (1) That the internal effects of stimuli from both classes vary from one presentation to another, and can be represented as Gaussian distributions on an "evidence" axis; and (2) That the subject's response on each trial depends on whether the stimulus produces evidence that falls above or below a response criterion. The model permits calculation of (a) a detectability or discrimination parameter, d', that is identified with the separation between the distributions; and (b) a bias parameter, beta, that is identified with criterion location. The account has been highly successful in many areas (e.g., Swets, 1973, 1986) and is used in several of this volume's contributions.

A second approach, known as behavioral detection theory (Davison & Tustin, 1978; McCarthy, 1981) bypasses the internal-process assumptions of the classical theory, and attempts instead to build its model inductively from an empirical, quantitative description of choice behavior: the matching law. (The development of this approach is reviewed in chapters by McCarthy and Davison and by Nevin in Vol. 1 of this series.) Its simplest version, which will suffice for present purposes, assumes strict matching of the ratios of the numbers of responses in the cells of the detection matrix to the ratio of reinforcers obtained for correct detections and correct rejections, R_w and R_z. The R_w/R_z ratio is multiplied or divided by a stimulus parameter d that characterizes the tendency to emit B_1 rather than B_2 on S_1 trials, and B_2 rather than B_1 on S_2 trials:

On S_1 trials,

$$B_w/B_x = d\ (R_w/R_z) \tag{1}$$

and on S_2 trials,

$$B_y/B_z = 1/d\ (R_w/R_z) \tag{2}$$

In effect, these expressions describe strict matching of choice ratios to reinforcement ratios, biased by the effects of the stimuli (Davison & Tustin, 1978).

Dividing these expressions leads to a measure of discrimination, D, that is independent of the consequences of responding:

$$D = (B_w/B_x)\ (B_z/B_y). \tag{3}$$

Multiplying these expressions leads to a measure of bias, B, that is independent of stimulus discrimination:

$$B = (B_w/B_x)\ (B_y/B_z) = (R_w/R_z). \tag{4}$$

D is the geometric mean of the ratios of correct to incorrect responses on S_1 and S_2 trials, and B is the geometric mean of the ratios of B_1 to B_2 responses on S_1 and S_2 trials, both having a certain face validity, in addition to their derivation from the matching law. Interestingly, these measures also follow from Luce's (1959, 1963) choice theory. Moreover, they have much the same properties as d' and beta of classical detection theory. Except at extreme response ratios, d' and log D are linearly related (Luce, 1963), and the isobias functions derived from signal-detection theory on the assumption that the subject maximizes overall payoff are much like the functions predicted by the behavioral approach based on matching to payoff ratios (Nevin, 1981). Thus, for the general signal-detection approach to behavior, it really does not matter whether the classical model of Green and Swets or the behavioral model of Davison and Tustin is used for the estimation of discrimination and bias parameters.

There is, however, an important difference in interpretation. In the classical theory, d' is determined by sensory variables—the properties of the stimuli themselves, and the observer's sensory system—whereas beta is determined by nonsensory variables such as payoffs or instructions. By contrast, the behavioral model treats both sensory and nonsensory variables as biasers. The stimuli determine *stimulus bias*, the extent to which S_1 and S_2 bias responding away from matching, and the payoffs or instructions determine *response bias*, the extent to which B_1 or B_2 occurs differentially without regard for the stimuli. The signal-detection approach permits the separation of biases controlled by the signals (discrimination) from biases controlled by other aspects of the experimental procedure.

The signal-detection approach has been applied successfully in many diverse areas of psychology (see, e.g., Swets, 1973, 1986). For example, Goldiamond (1958) used the signal-detection approach to criticize experiments that purported to demonstrate "subliminal perception," by noting that false negatives ("misses") should not be construed as indicating that stimuli were below a sensory threshold. More speculatively, Fuld and Nevin (1988) have used the detection paradigm to analyze why so few people work to prevent nuclear war. There are many other problems that would profit from a detection analysis. Consider, for example, Rosenhan's famous paper, "On being sane in insane places" (1973). In his first, and most notorious, experiment, Rosenhan succeeded in placing sane pseudopatients, including himself, in mental hospitals, where their sanity was apparently not detected by the psychiatrists and staff responsible for their treatment. Since sanity was viewed as the stimulus class to be detected, the uniform ocurrence of false negatives suggested that sanity was not detectable. In a second "catch-trial" experiment, he told members of the psychiatric staff at a teaching and research hospital that one or more pseudopatients would seek admission to the hospital, and asked for ratings of the likelihood that each new patient was in fact a pseudopatient. He obtained many high-confidence identifications of pseudopatients (false positives) even though none had appeared. He concluded: "It is clear that we cannot distinguish the sane from the insane in psychiatric hospitals" (p. 257).

However, this conclusion is not warranted. Both of Rosenhan's experiments involved only one sort of patient—pseudopatients in Experiment 1, and true patients in Experiment 2—and thus cannot separate the discrimination of sane and insane patients from biases induced by the psychiatrists' training histories, their expectations that sane pseudopatients would appear, and the overall effects of the hospital environment. Rosenhan commented on the likelihood of strong biases, but evidently did not see the need to separate their effects from the estimate of discriminability. Had he done so, he would not only have arrived at an unbiased measure of the discrimination of sanity in hospital patients, but might also have identified some sources of bias that could then be addressed by practical measures.

Rosenhan's report appeared in *Science*, which subsequently published a number of critical letters, and the *Journal of Abnormal Psychology* (Eron, 1975) ran a special series of articles commenting on and challenging his work. Although one or two commentators noted the bias toward Type II errors in medical diagnosis (that is, the tendency to diagnose a healthy person as sick) and one suggested asking whether 20 otherwise matched patients and pseudopatients could be distinguished, none suggested the appropriateness of a detection analysis.[1]

The situation studied by Rosenhan differs in many ways from the standard detection experiment. The basic detection paradigm makes explicit the relations between well-specified stimulus classes, choice responses, and their consequences, and research procedures typically expose individual subjects to hundreds of trials with each of the stimuli. By contrast, Rosenhan's "stimuli" (patients or pseudopatients) were not well specified; many people (the psychiatric staff) made one or a few judgments; and the consequences were uncertain, delayed, and poorly defined. This chapter will show that signal-detection analyses can also be applied to such situations.

Often, with adult human subjects, instructions alone suffice to define correct and incorrect responses and to maintain reliable performance in the usual detection experiment; thus, immediate, well-defined consequences are not required for effective application of a detection analysis. More interesting and challenging cases arise when the nature of the problem precludes specification of the correctness of a response, either by instructions or consequences, and the stimuli cannot be defined in the language of physics. Any psychologist interested in precise analyses of sensitivity to stimulus differences or reinforcement contingencies would instantly consign such situations to outer darkness; but in fact they are quite common in the study of perceptual, cognitive, and social processes. Signal-detection analyses, broadly conceived, can be applied to such problems to enhance the precision of measurement and interpretation in such situations. Two representative examples follow.

THE MULLER-LYER ILLUSION

Illusions, by definition, are judgments that deviate from the true, physically specified state of affairs. When the same erroneous judgments are made consistently by different individuals and are traceable to systematic features of the stimulus situations, they become available for scientific study. The much-studied Muller-Lyer illusion is a well-known example. Briefly, it involves the erroneous judgment that a line with outward arrowheads at its

---

[1]This treatment of Rosenhan's work was suggested to me by Elizabeth Fickett, and was presented at a symposium entitled "Signal Detection Analyses and Applications" at the meetings of the Association for Behavior Analysis, Columbus, Ohio, May, 1985.

ends is longer than a line of identical length but with inward arrowheads (this is the Brentano version of the illusion, illustrated as S_2 in Fig. 12.2). Many parametric studies have explored the relation between the apparent magnitude of this illusion and stimulus variables such as arrowhead angle and length (e.g., Dewar, 1967; Restle & Decker, 1977). All of them, to the best of my knowledge, have used the method of adjustment to assess the magnitude of the illusion. In this method, the subject adjusts the length of the right-hand, comparison half of the Muller–Lyer figure until it appears equal to the length of the left-hand, standard half. The measure of the illusion is the ratio of the comparison length to the standard length.

Several methodological features of this procedure, and of the measurement of illusions in general, deserve comment. First, no response consequences or feedback can be used. Presumably, if the subjects were told after each trial that the adjustment was wrong, or too long and by how much, he or she would learn to make shorter settings and perhaps eventually approximate the length of the standard line, regardless of the apparent inequality in length that would result. If our interest is in the subject's judgment of apparent length, rather than his or her ability to overcome the effects of the arrowheads and make a correct adjustment, consequences or feedback cannot be used; and thus, in principle, there is no such thing as a "correct" or "incorrect" response.

Second, only one sort of stimulus is presented, and therefore, separate

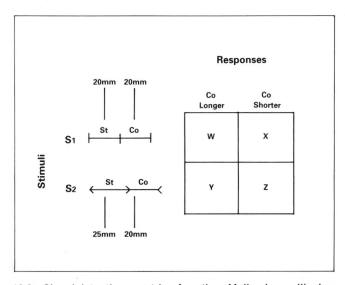

Fig. 12.2 Signal-detection matrix for the Muller–Lyer illusion, with examples of the stimulus alternatives with vertical (S_1) and angled (S_2) arrowheads. The right-hand comparison (Co) segment may be varied to give psychometric functions.

measures of line-length discrimination and bias toward saying "longer" when the lines are equal cannot be obtained. This issue is significant because interpretations of the illusion have invoked both discrimination and bias variables. Among the discrimination variables that have been proposed are optical blurring due to the limited spatial-frequency response of the eye, or scattering of light within the eye; lateral inhibition in retinal neurons; and lateral interactions among orientation-specific cells in visual cortex—all induced by the arrowheads, and all involving transformations of the stimulus that might alter line-length discrimination (Coren & Girgus, 1978). Some other explanations that presumably would not affect line-length discrimination involve various cognitive processes such as mistaken use of size-constancy mechanisms, and averaging or assimilation of linear extent (Coren & Girgus, 1978). Preparatory eye-movement patterns controlled by the arrowheads may also contribute to the illusion (Coren, 1986). Finally, Coren and Porac (1983) have shown that the illusion can be created or reversed by instructions designed to alter "attentional set." These cognitive, motor, or instructional processes could be construed as response biases, in that they operate independently of line length. It would be useful to obtain independent measures of discrimination and bias as a step toward selecting among these various interpretations. Accordingly, a signal-detection analysis is indicated despite the fact that correctness cannot be defined.

The following experiment was designed and conducted by Dr. Kenneth Fuld, Gerald Smith, and myself to separate the discrimination of differences in line length from the biasing effects of arrowheads in the Muller–Lyer illusion. As suggested by the foregoing discussion, it employed two sorts of trials: some with conventional angled arrowheads, and some with vertical lines. The subject saw each sort of presentation briefly, in irregular order, and was limited to the responses "longer" and "shorter" with reference to the comparison length. The stimuli are characterized and the resulting detection matrix is shown in Fig. 12.2.

Method

Subjects.   Twenty undergraduates at the University of New Hampshire served as a part of their introductory psychology course requirements.

Stimuli and Apparatus.   Stimuli were drawn in black ink on drafting paper and photographed, and were presented by a standard two-channel tachistoscope for 1 s after a ready signal. The left line segment was designated the standard, and the right segment the comparison. When the arrowheads were vertical (S_1 trials) the standard was always 20 mm long, with eight comparison lengths ranging from 14 to 26 mm, including 20 mm. When the arrowheads were angled (S_2 trials) the standard was always 25 mm long, with eight comparison lengths ranging from 13 to 25 mm. Thus, the standard was always greater than or equal to the comparison lengths. With these lengths, the comparisons tend to be judged longer or shorter than the standard about half the time, so that the two responses occurred with roughly equal frequency overall.

Procedure. Subjects were assigned randomly to one of five groups, designated by the arrowhead angle on S_2 trials: 15, 30, 45, 60, or 75 degrees from horizontal. After a few practice trials, each subject was shown 20 exposures of S_1 for each of the comparison lengths, and 20 exposures of S_2 for each of the comparison lengths, mixed in an irregular order. After each presentation, the subject was asked whether the comparison line was longer or shorter than the standard. The experiment was conducted in a single session, with a short break whenever the subject requested one. At the end of the session, the nature of the illusion was explained and the subject's data were analyzed on the spot to construct two psychometric functions, one for S_1 trials and the other for S_2 trials. The subject was shown how the discrimination of variations in line length could be estimated from the slope of each function, and how the magnitude of the illusion could be estimated from the horizontal displacement between them.

Results

To give an overall characterization of the findings, the data for S_2 trials were pooled for all subjects within an arrowhead-angle group, and the data for S_1 trials were pooled for all 20 subjects. The results are shown as psychometric functions in Fig. 12.3, plotted as ratios of "longer" to "shorter" responses on a logarithmic y-axis. Log response ratios have properties much like those of the z-score transformation that is often used to make ogival functions linear (Bush, 1963; Davison & Tustin, 1978). The figure shows that all functions are roughly linear, and that the S_2 functions are shifted increasingly leftward as arrowhead angle became narrower, at least up to 45 degrees. The slopes of all functions appear to be similar, indicating constant discrimination of variations in line length across all arrowhead angles, including vertical.

Table 12.1 presents slopes of lines fitted by the method of least squares for S_1 and S_2 trials separately for each group. There is no evidence of consistent slope differences between S_1 and S_2 trials, indicating that the angled arrowheads did not affect line-length discrimination. They did, however, affect bias, at least up to 45 degrees. The magnitude of the bias—the illusion—was estimated by the horizontal displacement of the fitted functions at $B_w/B_x = B_y/B_z = 1.0$ (at which point the lines are judged to be of equal length), and expressed as a ratio of the displacement to the standard length. These estimates are also shown in Table 12.1. These biases are entirely consistent in magnitude with the illusions reported by studies

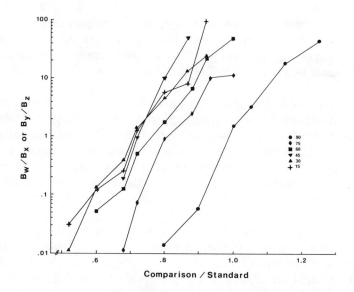

Fig. 12.3   Psychometric functions for the Muller–Lyer illusion, showing the ratio of "longer" to "shorter" responses on a logarithmic axis as functions of the ratio of the comparison to the standard line length. Each function presents the data for a different arrowhead angle, pooled across subjects.

TABLE 12.1
Slopes of the psychometric functions of Figure 3 and magnitude of the Muller–Lyer illusion

Group (arrowhead angle)	S_1 (vertical)	S_2 (angled)	Illusion
15 degrees	9.43	8.09	0.29
30 degrees	8.29	7.48	0.26
45 degrees	11.67	11.94	0.27
60 degrees	9.60	7.88	0.23
75 degrees	6.05	9.54	0.20

that used the method of adjustment to establish equal-appearing line lengths (e.g., Dewar, 1967; Restle & Decker, 1977). I conclude that the Muller–Lyer illusion is adequately characterized as a response bias effect that does not involve changes in line-length discrimination. The source of the bias remains a matter for speculation.

Discussion

The approach reported here was a blend of classical psychophysics using the method of constant stimuli, and a detection approach involving two classes of stimuli. A more direct detection approach might have chosen a pair of line-length ratios — say, 1.0 as S_1 and 0.9 as S_2 — to determine the probabilities of B_w and B_y for vertical and angled arrowheads with individual subjects. Presumably, the data would trace out an isosensitivity curve as the arrowhead angle was varied, indicating shifting biases with constant discrimination. Such a curve might have been constructed from the present data by cutting vertically through the psychometric functions at two line-length ratios. However, the choice of line lengths and the very high levels of discrimination in this experiment preclude a post hoc analysis of this sort. A future study should employ such a procedure to confirm the conclusion stated here.

THE "REPRESENTATIVENESS" HEURISTIC

Because of the confusability of the stimuli, a signal-detection experiment exemplifies the process of judgment under uncertainty. However, it is not entirely representative of such judgments in everyday life because it involves many repetitions of two trial types, typically with immediate consequences or feedback for correct responses and errors. In everyday life, however, people are often confronted with unique situations involving uncertainty, and must make decisions without the benefit of prior responses and their consequences. Kahneman and Tversky (1974) have suggested that, in nonrepeating situations of this sort, responses are determined by a few heuristic principles. Although these heuristics are generally useful guides through a world of uncertainty, they are often seriously in error. In effect, Kahneman and Tversky construe heuristics as sources of response bias, and state that biased responding based on heuristics reveals misconceptions of the nature of probability, or failures to discriminate prior probabilities correctly.

Kahneman and Tversky (1974) introduced their argument with the example of Steve, who is described as shy, withdrawn, meek, tidy, and concerned with order and detail (see Table 12.2 for their full verbatim description). After reading the description of Steve, subjects were asked to order the probabilities that Steve is a farmer, salesman, airline pilot, librarian, or physician. They overwhelmingly chose librarian as the likeliest, even though there are many more farmers than librarians in the population at large, and librarians are more likely to be women than men. This result is taken as evidence that people are strongly influenced by a stereotypical or "representative" description, and that they ignore (or do not understand) prior probabilities. However, as I have argued, control by biasing factors cannot be separated from control by discriminable prior events unless subjects are given two trial types that differ in some potentially discriminable dimension. With reference to judgments of occupation, then, it is necessary to provide subjects with at least two items that involve differences in their associated prior probabilities. The biasing aspects of the descriptions may then be varied in order to evaluate the separate contributions of knowledge-based discriminations and description-induced biases. The detection approach permits this separation even though the stimuli are deliberately ambiguous and there is no basis for identifying a response as correct.

To exemplify this approach to the analysis of heuristics, subjects were presented with the Kahneman–Tversky description (designated the "weak" description) of Steve, but for some the name "Steve" was replaced with "Sarah." A second description (designated "strong") was designed to bias responding away from the "librarian" choice, and also came in male and female versions. If the subjects correctly discriminated the relative frequencies of men and women in different occupations, this discrimination should be constant across the two biasing descriptions.

Method

Subjects. The experiment was conducted with an introductory psychology class of about 100 students at the University of New Hampshire. The students received credit toward course requirements for their participation.

Stimuli. Two descriptions of people were prepared in two versions each: one with a male name (Steve or John) and the other with a female name (Sarah or Jane). Immediately below each description was a seven-point rating scale, on which subjects could rate the likelihood that the person described was a farmer, salesman (or saleswoman), airline pilot, librarian, or physician (see Table 12.2). Each subject received both descriptions, with gender randomly allocated to each description.

Procedure. The experimenter (myself) informed the class that there was considerable interest in psychology in the processes whereby people make judgments under uncertainty, and that this experiment was intended to explore that process. Subjects were then given a sheet of paper bearing two descriptions as shown in Table 12.2. They were asked to read the descriptions and indicate their ratings of how likely each person was to work in each of the five listed occupations by circling one of the seven numbers. After all subjects had responded, the sheets were collected and a preliminary data analysis was performed while the experimenter explained the detection-theory approach to the problem. Subjects were then shown

TABLE 12.2
Items Used to Evaluate Gender-occupation Discrimination as Biased by
Stereotyped Description

Steve (or Sarah) is very shy and withdrawn, invariably helpful, but with little interest in people, or in the world of reality. A meek and tidy soul, he (or she) has a need for order and structure, and a passion for detail.

Please indicate how confident you are that Steve (or Sarah) is or is not:

	Confident that he (or she) *is*			Unsure	Confident that he (or she) *is not*		
Farmer	1	2	3	4	5	6	7
Salesman (or saleswoman)	1	2	3	4	5	6	7
Airline pilot	1	2	3	4	5	6	7
Librarian	1	2	3	4	5	6	7
Physician	1	2	3	4	5	6	7

John (or Jane) enjoys talking with people who seek him (or her) out, but he (or she) can keep his (or her) own counsel and does not mind working alone. A man (or woman) of quiet strength, he (or she) takes pleasure in dealing with problems that present new challenges.

Please indicate how confident you are that John (or Jane) is or is not:

	Confident that he (or she) *is*			Unsure	Confident that he (or she) *is not*		
Farmer	1	2	3	4	5	6	7
Salesman (or saleswoman)	1	2	3	4	5	6	7
Airline pilot	1	2	3	4	5	6	7
Librarian	1	2	3	4	5	6	7
Physician	1	2	3	4	5	6	7

some representative results, and their interpretation in relation to discrimination and bias was explained.

Results

The principal interest of the analysis is to determine whether subjects are sensitive to prior probabilities, and whether this sensitivity is constant across biasing conditions. The analysis concentrated on two occupations that are differentially associated with gender: librarian, a predominantly female occupation, and airline pilot, a predominantly male occupation. A 2×2 matrix was constructed with gender defining the stimulus classes S_1 and S_2, and with "librarian" or "pilot" as responses B_1 and B_2. A subject was scored as responding in a cell of the matrix if the rating was a 1 or a 2, indicating a high level of confidence. Responses were pooled for all subjects, each of whom actually made only four responses of interest: two occupation likelihood ratings on each of two descriptions.

The resulting numbers of responses are summarized in matrix form in Table 12.3, which also shows the values of gender discrimination (D) and bias (B) calculated for the two descriptions from Equations 3 and 4. First, note the strong bias in favor of saying "librarian" induced by the "weak" description, and the moderate bias away from saying "librarian" induced by the "strong" description. Clearly, the descriptions were successful in this regard. Second, note the rough constancy of gender discrimination across descriptions. This implies that subjects are in fact sensitive to the differential relative frequencies of men and women working as librarians or pilots, and this sensitivity is maintained despite the extreme "librarian" bias produced by the Kahneman–Tversky description of Steve. Whether the measured sensitivity is consistent with the actual statistics on men and women in these occupations is a separate question, and not relevant here. I conclude that the presumed use of the representativeness heuristic by these subjects does indeed result in strong biases, but it does not lead them into serious errors with respect to prior probabilities.

Because these data were gathered on rating scales, it is also possible to derive isosensitivity curves for the discrimination of gender–occupation associations. To do this, judgment frequencies were cumulated separately for librarian with female name, librarian with male name, pilot with male name, and pilot with female name. Cumulative response ratios were then calculated for each of these four cases by dividing the cumulative frequency at each rating by the total number of responses minus that cumulative frequency. Finally, the cumulative response ratio for librarian-with-female-name was plotted against the cumulative response ratio for librarian-with-male-name, and likewise for pilot-with-male-name and pilot-with-female-name, on logarithmic scales. The analysis is essentially identical to the rating-scale method for determining isosensitivity curves based on cumulative probabilities, where cumulative probabilities are converted into z-scores. Since the log ratio measure has properties much like the

TABLE 12.3
Detection matrices and results for judgments that males or females are librarians or airline pilots

		Weak description Responses		Strong description Responses	
		Librarian	Pilot	Librarian	Pilot
Stimuli	Female	41	2	11	12
	Male	27	6	6	24
		D = 2.1, B = 9.6		D = 1.9, B = 0.5	

z-score, comparable isosensitivity curves should be obtained. Fig. 12.4 shows that two reasonably linear isosensitivity curves were obtained by this method, each running roughly parallel to the major diagonal. This result suggests that the discrimination of gender–occupation associations is constant with respect to the subject's level of confidence, which is not under experimental control, as well as with respect to the experimentally induced biases analyzed herein.

All in all, these results are consistent with the notion that subjects distinguish the relative frequencies of men and women in two different occupations, despite their apparent error in stating with high confidence that a vaguely described male is a librarian. Kahneman and Tversky (1974) suggest that "if people evaluate probability by representativeness . . . prior probabilities will be ignored" (p. 1125). At least in the present case, that appears not to be true.

Discussion

There is one important respect in which the present demonstration is methodologically unusual, if not flawed. In the standard Yes-No signal-detection experiment, responses B_1 and B_2 are mutually exclusive and exhaustive. Here, however, it was possible for subjects to give high-likelihood estimates for both "librarian" and "pilot," or for neither. The

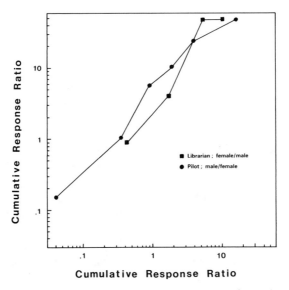

Fig. 12.4 Isosensitivity curves for discrimination of gender-occupation relations, based on rating scale data pooled across subjects.

frequency with which this occurred is unknown, because the data were pooled without regard to their source. Future applications of the detection approach to the role of heuristics in judgments of occupations or related problems should be constructed so that subjects make mutually exclusive choices on each item.

There is an element of arbitrariness in the foregoing analysis, in that it would have been equally possible to treat the descriptions as stimuli to be discriminated, and the gender of the person described as the source of bias. (This arbitrariness is evident in common usage, where sex discrimination and sex bias have the same meaning.) I chose to treat gender as the discrimination variable because there is information on the relative frequencies of males and females in various occupations, but the data treatment and the general conclusions would have been much the same if gender had been treated as a source of response bias. There is a lesson here: The discrimination and bias terms are interchangeable in a detection analysis that adopts a behavioral approach, and thus treats signals, stimulus contexts, payoffs, instructions, and indeed all aspects of the detection situation as sources of stimulus or response bias. Nevin (1981) suggested the interchangeability of stimulus and reinforcement terms in the analysis of detection performance, and Alsop and Davison (this volume) propose models of choice that give parallel treatment to stimulus and response terms in detection situations. These developments may lead us to a truly integrative and broadly applicable approach to the joint control of behavior by stimuli and consequences.

CONCLUSION

This chapter has demonstrated the applicability of signal-detection analyses to problems where the stimuli are not readily defined in physical terms (e.g., the occupation stereotype descriptions) and where responses cannot in principle be defined as correct or incorrect (as in both the illusion and gender-occupation problems). These applications were suggested by a behavioral model of signal detection in which the signals, as well as contextual factors and outcomes, are treated as determiners of stimulus or response bias.

The research described here was designed to be illustrative rather than definitive, to encourage application of the signal-detection approach to more problems outside its normal scope. In the language of this chapter, my purpose is to bias researchers toward the signal-detection approach when they choose a research strategy. If socially significant problems such as the discrimination of sane vs. insane patients are approached in this way, erroneous interpretations may be avoided and effective solutions can be promoted.

ACKNOWLEDGMENT

I am indebted to Dr. Kenneth Fuld for incisive comments on an earlier draft of this paper, and for many discussions of the relations between behavioral and sensory psychology.

REFERENCES

Bush, R. R. (1963). Estimation and evaluation. In R. D. Luce, R. R. Bush, & E. Galanter (Eds.), *Handbook of mathematical psychology* (Vol. 1, pp 429–469). New York: Wiley.

Coren, S. (1986). An efferent component in the visual perception of direction and extent. *Psychological Review, 93*, 391–410.

Coren, S., & Girgus, J. S. (1978). *Seeing is deceiving: The psychology of visual illusions.* Hillsdale, NJ: Lawrence Erlbaum Associates.

Coren, S., & Porac, C. (1983). The creation and reversal of the Muller-Lyer illusion through attentional manipulation. *Perception, 12,* 49–54.

Davison, M., & Jenkins, P. (1985). Stimulus discriminability, contingency discriminability, and schedule performance. *Animal Learning and Behavior, 13,* 77–84.

Davison, M., & Tustin, R. D. (1978) The relation between the generalized matching law and signal-detection theory. *Journal of the Experimental Analysis of Behavior, 29,* 331–336.

Dewar, R. E. (1967). Stimulus determinants of the Muller–Lyer illusion. *Perceptual and Motor Skills, 24,* 708–710.

Eron, L. D. (Ed.). (1975). *Journal of Abnormal Psychology, 84,* 433–474.

Fuld, K., & Nevin, J. A. (1988). Why doesn't everyone work to prevent nuclear war? A decision theory analysis. *Journal of Applied Social Psychology, 18,* 59–65.

Goldiamond, I. (1958). Indicators of perception. I. Subliminal perception, subception, unconscious perception: An analysis on terms of psychophysical indicator methodology. *Psychological Bulletin, 55,* 373–411.

Green, D. M., & Swets, J. A. (1966). *Signal detection theory and psychophysics.* New York: Wiley.

Kahneman, D., & Tversky, A. (1974). Judgment under uncertainty: Heuristics and biases. *Science, 185,* 1124–1131.

Luce, R. D. (1959). *Individual choice behavior.* New York: Wiley.

Luce, R. D. (1963). Detection and recognition. In R. D. Luce, R. R. Bush, & E. Galanter (Eds.), *Handbook of mathematical psychology* (Vol. 1, pp. 103–189). New York: Wiley.

McCarthy, D. (1981). Toward a unification of psychophysical and behavioural research. *New Zealand Psychologist, 10,* 2–14.

McCarthy, D., & Davison, M. (1981). Matching and signal detection. In M. L. Commons & J. A. Nevin (Eds.), *Quantitative analyses of behavior: Vol. 1. Discriminative properties of reinforcement schedules.* Cambridge, MA: Balllinger.

Nevin, J. A. (1981). Psychophysics and reinforcement schedules: An integration. In M. L. Commons & J. A. Nevin (Eds.), *Quantitative analyses of behavior: Vol. 1. Discriminative properties of reinforcement schedules.* Cambridge, MA: Balllinger.

Nevin, J. A. (1984). Quantitative analyses. *Journal of the Experimental Analysis of Behavior, 42,* 421–434.

Nevin, J. A., Jenkins, P., Whittaker, S., & Yarensky, P. (1982). Reinforcement contingencies and signal detection. *Journal of the Experimental Analysis of Behavior, 37,* 65–79.

Restle, F., & Decker, J. (1977). Size of the Muller–Lyer illusion as a function of its dimensions: Theory and data. *Perception and Psychophysics, 21,* 489–503.

Rosenhan, D. L. (1973). On being sane in insane places. *Science, 179,*, 250–258.

Skinner, B. F. (1969). *Contingencies of reinforcement: A theoretical analysis.* New York: Appleton–Century–Crofts.

Swensson, R. G. (1987). *ROC applications to chest-film interpretation.* Paper presented at the Harvard Symposium on Quantitative Analyses of Behavior, Cambridge, MA, June.

Swets, J. A. (1973). The relative operating characteristic in psychology. *Science, 182,* 990–1000.

Swets, J. A. (1986). Forms of empirical ROCs in discrimination and diagnostic tasks: Implications for theory and measurement of performance. *Psychological Bulletin, 99,* 181–198.

Tanner, W. P. Jr., & Swets, J. A. (1954). A decision-making theory of visual detection. *Psychological Review, 61,* 401–409.

Author Index

275

Subject Index

H

Head injuries, discrimination and, 243–245
Heuristics, 267
Hit, 170–172, 178, 179
Hue, 197
Hyperbolic model, 139–161
Hypothetical constructs, 216–218
Hypoxia, 243, 246–248, 251, 254

I

Ideal observers, 3, 4, 7
  Marill's, 4, 13, 15, 33
  maximum likelihood, 4
  minimum error, 3
Illusions, 262
Inattention, effects of, 127
Inattention, to stimuli, 132
Inherent bias, 60, 241, 241
Initial discriminability, 222–228, 233, 234
Insensitivity d, 148–161
Instructions, 262
Integration time, 2, 16, 17, 18, 20, 23, 34
Intensity discrimination, 2, 15, 18, 26–32
Interference, remembering and, 221,
  234–236
Intertrial interval, 225, 230–232, 234, 235
Intervening events, effects on memory,
  142–161
Isosensitivity curves, 271

J

Jumping stand, 217

K

K_o Bessell function, 30
Korsakoff syndrome, 243

L

Laser energy, 6, 7
Lashley jumping stand, 217
Learning, 206, 210, 211
Learning disabilities, 251
Light intensity, 44
Likelihood ratio, 212, 251
Line orientation, 41
Long-term memory, 130, 131
  noise and, 131
  presolution period and, 132

M

Maintained generalization, 59
Maintained numerosity discrimination,
  111–116, 118
Marill's equation, 4, 13, 33
Markov, 194, 202, 205, 206, 212, 214, 217
Matching, 39, 41, 42, 45, 46, 51–53, 241,
  249
Matching law, 45, 169–173, 180, 182–188
  generalized, 240
Matching-to-sample, 44, 79–81
  delayed, 199–200, 225
  discriminability, 203, 204
  pigeons, 191, 192, 210
  procedure, 225, 227
  stimulus, 203–206
Memory, 185, 186, 227, 235
  decision-making and, 121, 129, 130
  limitations, 121
  psychophysics and, 223, 234–236
Metathetic dimension, 83, 98, 99
Minkowski metric, 67, 68
Miss, 170–172, 178, 179
Mixture-negative discrimination, 105–107,
  109–111, 113, 114, 118
Moment generating function, 13, 19
Monkeys, 128
  edge effects and, 128
Monotonic stimuli, 126
Muller-Lyer illusion, 262–267
Multidimensional stimuli, 130
Multiple schedules, 52, 57

N

Negative binomial, 6, 19, 20
Negative time-order error, 84, 94
Network,
  amplifier, 9, 10, 21, 22, 26, 34
  birth-death-immigration, 9, 10, 22, 24,
    26, 31
  Poisson, 18–21
Neural counting, 5
Noise, 169, 171, 186
  additive, 144, 145
  background, 55
  band-stop (notched), 21, 28
  discrimination, 124
  effect on memory, 139–161
  frozen (nonstochastic), 10, 18, 21, 23
  intensity discrimination, 9, 28, 29